THE MERCHANT SCHOONERS

The photograph on the cover shows the launch of the three masted schooner *Rose* at the yard of R Cock and Sons at Appledore, North Devon, in 1905 — see Chapter 5 of this Volume. James Cock, master builder, stands by the stem of the vessel, wearing a beret. The woman nearest the stem is Rose Hobbs after whom the schooner was named.

THE
MERCHANT
SCHOONERS

*A portrait of a vanished industry, being a survey
in two volumes of the history of the small fore-
and-aft rigged sailing ships of England and Wales
in the years 1870-1940, with something of their
previous history and subsequent fate*

by

BASIL GREENHILL

VOLUME ONE

**National Maritime Museum
Modern Maritime Classics Reprint No. 1**

0 905555 10 4
ISSN 0140 9042
First published in 1951
by Percival Marshall & Co. Ltd.
New and Revised edition: 1968
by David & Charles (Publishers) Ltd.
Reprinted with small corrections and
new Author's note: 1978.
This edition © Basil Greenhill 1978

In Memory of Gillian

This reprint is authorised by David & Charles (Publishers) Ltd.

Produced in England by
Her Majesty's Stationery Office,
Reprographic Centre, Basildon
for the Trustees of the
National Maritime Museum

CONTENTS

LIST OF ILLUSTRATIONS

LIST OF PLATES

LIST OF DRAWINGS

AUTHOR'S NOTE

This is the second printing, with a few corrections of detail, of the revised second edition of a book first published more than 25 years ago. The book gives a portrait, not strictly a history, of the merchant schooners and their world. It is, if one may make so presumptuous a claim, in the tradition of Lubbock rather than Ralph Davis. It is a portrait of an industry and a way of life which had its roots very deep in the past and which brought the carpenter and blacksmith technology of wooden merchant sailing ships down far into the 20th century.

In the Author's Note to the first edition I thanked the numerous people who had made it possible to write *The Merchant Schooners* in the first place. The continued help and interest of the late H Oliver Hill, Gordon Harris, Captain William Lamey of the ketch *Hobah*, Captain W J Lewis Parker, United States Coastguard Retd., Grahame Farr, Michael Bouquet, and Alan Villiers, were invaluable in the preparation of the second edition. Ann Giffard typed the book in its revised form and made numerous suggestions. I found W L A Derby's great work *The Tall Ships Pass*, dealing with the last big square-rigged sailing ships, a source of much inspiration.

I want to thank Douglas Bennet for the detailed commentary which he prepared on the first edition of *The Merchant Schooners*, of all of which I took account in the revised second edition. I am most grateful to him also for his drawings, some of which appear in these volumes. Douglas Bennet had wide experience at sea in schooners in their last years.

I wish to stress one matter. Ways of doing things related to and on board small sailing ships and boats varied greatly from port to port. Even the terminology and the very pronunciation of the technical words used varied. In this book, the practices described are on the whole those of Appledore in North Devon, and the final authority throughout in such matters has been Captain W J Slade, the author of *Out of Appledore* who is the most experienced survivor of the last phase of the era of the merchant schooner in Britain alive at the time of this new printing. I have worked very closely with Captain Slade for many years and he has approved in detail the whole final text of this book as it is now published.

Since the second edition of this book was first published in 1968 there has been a great increase of interest in the subject of maritime industrial history and the schooners in particular. This has been reflected in a number of new publications, over and above those mentioned in Chapter 1 of this volume. These include many papers in academic journals and a number of books, among them Aled Eames two great volumes *Ships and Seamen of Anglesey* and *Porthmadog Ships*. Captain Hugh Shaw's journal (see page 20 of this volume) has been published under the title of *Schooner Captain*. Captain W J Slade himself has published a heavily illustrated study in detail of *Westcountry Coasting Ketches*. C H Ward Jackson has examined the history of the schooner of that name in his National Maritime Museum Monograph *The Last Voyage of the Schooner Isabella,* while Ian Merry's

The Westcotts and Their Times in the same series is a model history of a sailing fleet and the family which managed it. In a contribution to another National Maritime Museum publication I have described the history of the *Rigdin* (Volume II, page 128) in detail. There have been a number of port histories published.

At the last moment, or almost after it, some vessels have been saved in varying degrees of preservation. The ketch *Garlandstone* has been restored at Portmadoc in private hands and the schooner *Result* by the Ulster Folk Museum. The schooner *Kathleen & May* was restored by the Maritime Trust, the ketch *Shamrock*, built at Plymouth in 1899 and one of the very small ketches referred to on pages 150-155 of Volume II, by the National Trust and the National Maritime Museum. It is possible that the *Shamrock* may eventually in some degree fulfill the function of the "historian's ship" referred to on pages 206 to 208 of Volume II. At the same time the National Maritime Museum has mounted a very comprehensive display on the schooners in Gallery 13 of its East Wing and a regional display at its outpost on Cotehele Quay on the River Tamar in Cornwall.

The original draft of this book was prepared in the 1930s and 40s under the direct inspiration and with the help of men who had built, owned and sailed the schooners in their great days in the last century. These included Benjamin Tregaskes, the shipbuilder who was born in the 1850s, and Tom Stephens, born in 1862, who saw the rise and fall of his father's great fleet of Newfoundland trade schooners and who, in 1937, almost dictated the first draft of the chapter called "The Company of Little Ships" and thereby in fact began the writing of this book. There was William Ferris who watched the *Rhoda Mary* launched and who sailed to Newfoundland in the *Goonlaze*, and men who worked on the building of the *Waterwitch*, the *Hobah*, and the *Katie* and sailed in these vessels, and there were many more such men. The practical everyday working reality of the world of the schooners has gone with these men and their contemporaries and is now for ever lost, along with a whole way of life of that fundamentally important tool of western man, the wooden merchant sailing ship, and no amount of restorations and replicas and preserved vessels can ever remotely bring it back.

The subject has become academic, but its academic importance is now recognised and a great deal of documentation is now readily available at the National Maritime Museum and elsewhere which was once almost inaccessible. It is now very easy to check the oral traditions and recollections of the old men of the 1930s and from survey reports, registration documents, Articles of Agreement, and casualty reports, to confirm, for instance, that in her youth the ketch *Hobah* did indeed make the voyages to southern Europe and North Africa ascribed to her by oral tradition in the 1930s. It is possible easily to ascertain the name of the steamer that ran her down as she lay at anchor in Ryde Roads, windbound on her maiden voyage one hundred years ago — see page 149 of Volume 2. The steamer was the *Albert Edward* and she belonged to the Ryde Steam Packet Company and the casualty took place on the 12th of September 1879. The *Hobah* had a crew of five, just as my informant remembered, 68 years after he had pulled himself out of the fo'c'sle scuttle by his arms, and she was under the command of a certificated Master, William Cock, who was later to take her on her long voyages. The *Hobah* took eight months to raise and repair, going to sea again from Portsmouth on 10 May 1880.

Basil Greenhill
Boetheric
Cornwall   1977.

VOLUME ONE

'A FLEET of fore-and-afters at anchor has its own slender graciousness. The setting of their sails resembles more than anything else the unfolding of a bird's wings; the facility of their evolutions is a pleasure to the eye. They are birds of the sea, whose swimming is like flying, and resembles more a natural function than the handling of man-invented appliances. The fore-and-aft rig in its simplicity and the beauty of its aspect under every angle of vision is, I believe, unapproachable. A schooner, a yawl, or cutter in charge of a capable man seems to handle herself as if endowed with the power of reasoning and the gift of sweet execution. One laughs with sheer pleasure at a smart piece of manœuvring, as at a manifestation of a living creature's quick wit and graceful precision.'

Joseph Conrad, *The Mirror of the Sea*

CHAPTER ONE

A FRAGMENT OF INDUSTRIAL HISTORY

THE waterfronts of many coastal and riverside towns and villages in Britain show evidence of vanished trade. Artificial harbours designed to hold large vessels shelter small yachts and a few miscellaneous working boats. Great quays with traces of old rail tracks, sheds, warehouses and roads, have no apparent modern use. In some places there are old lock systems, with stone bollards deeply worn where thousands of ropes have griped them. Elsewhere, docks have silted up and reveal themselves only as slight depressions in a river bank, margined with massive masonry. In some places there is clear evidence of former shipbuilding activity, sometimes among fields at the side of a lonely creek or on an exposed shore. In others, long wharf systems lie rotting and abandoned, slowly engulfed by mud or overgrown with brambles, or fenced off and turned into bases for sailing clubs.

These are indeed the last traces of a vanished industry and a very old and great one. There was until the beginning of the twentieth century, and even in some cases for many years afterwards, a strong and vigorous commercial life in and around the small seaport towns of Britain. Only fifty years ago it was still almost impossible to approach a small harbour in the west or south of England without seeing as the first and most conspicuous feature the clustered masts of sailing vessels rising high above the waterside cottages (Plate 1). Villages and towns which have now turned their backs to the water, or become dependent on the tourist industry, or been over-run by urban sprawl were busy

13

maritime communities, their life centred on shipyards and filled harbour.

The small sailing ships and the industries required to support them, sail and spar making, ropewalks, repair grids below the tideline, shipchandlery and carpentry, gave the seaport towns their characteristic quality, for in those days the smells and the feeling of a small seaport were quite different from those of the inland market towns. There were seasoned baulks of timber cut at the sawpits to give forth a rich, sweet scent, which mingled with the pervasive rigger's tar at the quaysides, and salt, the salt wind that still blows around the empty quays today, tar from rigging and from the blackened wooden hulls, oil from the tanning of the brown sails, mud from a hundred harbours in the chain locker, all combining to make the smells of small seaport communities. And the sounds were those of the seaboard, the scream of straining blocks, the chanting of yard crews and seamen about their work, and the musical clinking of mallets on caulking irons at the building slips and on the grids while the tide was low (Plate 2).

A perfect example of maritime industrial decay is to be seen at Calstock in Cornwall. Here a busy shipyard was in operation until sixty years ago. The quays were lined with shipping loading granite and the products of the local mines. Upstream there were a succession of pits and quarries, a small dock system at Morwellham, and old quays still busy as far up river as the head of the tide water at Gunnislake. Every quay above and for miles below Calstock was regularly served by sailing barges and steamers. Today the trees are beginning to meet across the river below the docks where deep-sea ships used regularly to load cargoes. There are signs of vanished industry and former seaborne trade everywhere, but Calstock has turned its back upon the water and many of its people do not know that ships and maritime trade were once part of its life.

The prosperity and life of these vigorous maritime communities were based on ocean trade, for there was during much of the nineteenth century an increasing demand for small sailing ships to carry cargoes all over the world. When goods were made slowly and in small quantities, before the economies of large-scale production had become so apparent and the structure of industry assumed its modern form, both raw materials and finished products changed hands in much smaller parcels than they do today. Goods made slowly in many small factories and ordered by overseas buyers in small quantities, to be delivered, perhaps, at small ports serving an undeveloped hinterland, required small vessels to carry them. There was, in consequence, throughout this phase of the industrial revolution, a constant demand for relatively small ships to carry cargoes of every kind upon deep water. Later this demand persisted for many years alongside the demand from industries already developed, and those which by their very nature were of considerable scale, for large ships to carry large quantities of cargo from and to the big ports of the world.

This demand could be met and was met by the enterprise of the small ports. The small havens, in particular of the west of England, had for centuries built fishing boats and small merchant ships. In them was vested a tradition of skill in shipbuilding, ship management and seafaring, and above all they were communities which looked to the sea for their livelihood. As the demand for more small ocean-going vessels grew with the advance of the nineteenth century, it was therefore natural that these villages, which possessed in the total wealth of their inhabitants just sufficient capital to finance the construction and management of this very type of vessel, should set out to fulfil that demand. They did so slowly, as was the way in those times when the spread of information and the growth of capital were slow. When they met with success, so their enterprises became bolder and larger, not usually in terms of the size of the vessels employed, but rather of their number and quality, and the nature of the voyages undertaken. The greatest days of these small ships were in the fifties, sixties and early seventies of the nineteenth century, when thousands of small barques, brigs, brigantines and sloops, and increasingly as time went on of schooners and ketches, were built in the small havens and sailed with cargo all over the world.

Thereafter, the process of economic development growing apace, the demand for small ships slowly grew less. By the end of the century, although still considerable, the opportunities for small sailing ships of all kinds were much smaller than they had been. But there were still some trades which, because the industries that gave rise to them were not susceptible to centralization and development, continued to employ small ships on deep water. Small steamships of the size required by these trades, about 100 or so feet in length and with a draught of ten feet or less, are not an economical proposition in ocean trade. Nor was the steam auxiliary for vessels of that size a proposition either, and there were, of course, no motorships. So it was that small sailing ships continued to prosper on deep water for years after the decay of the last large wind-propelled vessels had set in. Schooners were still being built for ocean trade long after big sailing ships had ceased to be built in any numbers for owners in this country.

And throughout this period the home trade, which had been the main business of many of the small ports concerned before the expansion of the nineteenth century, continued to develop and to absorb a proportion of their enterprise. The home trade is the business of carrying cargoes about the narrow seas, the seas that lie between the Elbe and Brest, and a large part of it is made up of the trade about the coasts of these islands themselves, from port to port of the United Kingdom, the coasting trade. In this business many thousands of small sailing ships were always employed, adding to the host that filled the harbours of Britain. In the home trade, many small deep-sea vessels found employment from time to time when suitable cargoes were not offering in the long-distance trades.

Small sailing ships were still built after the turn of the century, and the ships that were launched then were considered by some contemporary shipowners and seamen to be the finest of them all. This new building was by no means sufficient to keep pace with the total annual losses among small vessels, though the numbers of ships employed in the remaining specialized deep-water trades did not decrease rapidly until about 1914. When, after 1918,

1. Schooners and ketches in Padstow about 1900

2. Captain Stanley Rogers (with long-handled brush) and others repairing the ketch *Acacia* at Appledore in 1902. The vessel is being caulked (the middle man of the group of three is using a caulking mallet and iron) and tarred. Mr Thomas Lock, seated, is rolling oakum for the caulkers

3. The ketch *Ade*, built at Barn-staple as the schooner *Annie Christian*, and the three-masted schooner *Haldon*, built at Plymouth as a ketch

4. A painting by Simon de Vlieger, who lived from 1600 to 1653, showing a Dutch two-mast boat

these deep-water trades ceased for a number of reasons to offer profitable employment, there were, nevertheless, great numbers of small merchant sailing ships still remaining. They were sufficiently numerous even to keep a few of the building yards in business on maintenance and repair work, and certainly sufficient to maintain much of the old character of many of the towns to which they belonged.

These ships went into the home trade and, at first, in the post-war boom there was employment for many of them. But this state of affairs did not last for long and very rapidly their numbers were reduced by laying up, sale overseas and unreplaced loss. Even so, they long outlived the large merchant sailing ships, and in 1929 when the last of these continuously to have flown the red ensign was lost, the small sailing ship was still fairly commonly to be met with. Not until the second world war did they finally cease to be a factor in the business of the home trade. Indeed, in somewhat altered form a score or so survived in employment for some years longer. Almost incredibly, the last commercial voyages of the last fully rigged three-masted wooden schooner and the last wooden ketch were not made until 1960. These historic vessels were the *Kathleen & May* of Bideford (Plate 22 and Plate 48 of Volume 2) and the *Irene* of Bridgwater (Plate 21).

The history of British merchant shipping even for much of the nineteenth century is still relatively sparsely recorded. A good deal has been written, both in Europe and in North America, about the history of the big square-rigged sailing ship in its last phases in the late nineteenth and early twentieth centuries, and about the great American and Canadian four- and five-masted schooners of the same period. The later sailing ship era in some special trades has also been very adequately treated. Whaling, the North Atlantic cod fishery, the British fishing industry in the last days of sail, the sailing barges of south-eastern Britain, Scandinavian schooners, all have their several historians. But the small British sailing ships, which in the last days of sail were mostly schooners and ketches, have been the subject only of

B

scattered references and of two autobiographical books, the first Lord Runciman's *Collier Brigs and their Sailors* and W. J. Slade's *Out of Appledore*. Fortunately, both are books written by men who knew the particular ships with which they dealt at first hand as a means of earning a livelihood and both are very fine records. There is also Captain Robinson's account of his experiences in sail, which are recorded in an appendix to Volume 2 of this history. In addition, there is an unpublished autobiography written by Hugh Shaw, master and owner of the three-masted schooner *Camborne*, in the manuscript collection of the National Maritime Museum at Greenwich, and this also is a most valuable document.

This dearth of printed information arises from a number of causes. The inhabitants of small seaboard towns and villages, the sort of men who financed these ships and built and managed and sailed them, were not given to putting their thoughts and experiences on record. Some of the best of the builders could neither read nor write, many of the masters were not qualified in the modern sense, and those that could make shift to pass a Board of Trade examination were not literary men, nor did their busy lives, even on their longest voyages, give much opportunity for the development of a contemplative faculty. As for the owners, I have frequently been surprised in the course of collecting information for this book that the authors of some of the records which remain could ever have been capable of conducting the extensive and prosperous businesses that they did. In their own vernacular, they were more handy with the marlinspike than the pen.

Superficially, too, the small brigs and sloops and later the schooners and ketches did not possess the attraction of the larger sailing ships. Their beauty was not less, but it was of a more subtle and less awe-inspiring kind. They were the miniatures to a sea panorama in oils. They did not much visit the large ports where the mass of mankind might see them, and when they did they were so dwarfed by their large sisters that the landsmen might never distinguish them at all. After the middle of the nineteenth century their voyages rarely excited public comment. Though in total they were of considerable importance, individually they contributed very little to the economic system. They were noted and remembered in the small ports where they were important. But elsewhere they were of little interest to those who did not come in contact with them by way of business.

Thus the factors which have worked against the compilation of any general history of the later small sailing ships were the dearth of readily available written sources, the inability of most of the people in whose memories the unwritten history remained to express themselves on paper, and the fact that by the time the absence of other sailing ships at sea brought the existence of the remaining small vessels to the public notice, the majority of the people concerned were either dead or at a very advanced age. Moreover, the subject itself is vast and very complicated. There were many thousands of schooners in the last thirty years of the nineteenth century and the first score of this, perhaps ten times as many as there were of the great iron and steel barques of the same period.

The only way in which the merchant schooners will be dealt with adequately will be in port histories. As Professor Ralph Davis says in the second appendix to his book, *The Rise of the English Shipping Industry*—'The next advance in the history of the merchant marine may well come from the writing of substantial histories of the ports; there are none now in print.' Since Professor Davis' book was published in 1962, papers on different aspects of the history of some ports have been published. Mr Richard Pearse has produced his admirable brief *The Ports and Harbours of Cornwall* and Ann Giffard and I have sought to record Bideford's North Atlantic trade in the fifty years after Waterloo in *Westcountrymen in Prince Edward's Isle*, but the statement quoted above still remains generally true. It is the port and trade and industrial histories which will in due course do justice to the neglected theme of merchant shipping in British history and, in so doing, will cover the era of the merchant schooners. There are meanwhile a number of older books no longer in print which deal partly with the theme of local schooners, notably the late Henry Hughes' *Immortal Sails* about Portmadoc, D. W. Morgan's *Brief Glory* on the history of Aberdovey and Grahame Farr's *Somerset Harbours*.

This book attempts to survey only one aspect of one period of the history of the small merchant sailing ships of England and Wales. The period is that between 1870 and 1940, the era of the merchant schooner, and the history to be examined is that of the fore-and-aft rigged vessels alone. These two volumes do no more than to sketch in the rough outlines, and attempt, by the selection of certain aspects of the subject, to give an impression of the life of the small coastal communities. Schooner building in the early years of this century at Appledore, although a comparatively sophisticated affair, still retained the methods and traditions the small yards had built up in hundreds of years. The design of the schooners is examined, and also the way in which they were managed. There is an account of the life of the shipmaster and seaman and a brief study of the great Newfoundland trade. The story of John Stephens' fleet, although it was an unusually large one, has many typical aspects; the barquentine *Waterwitch*, never a deep-water trading vessel, experienced in her career many aspects of the home trade. The life story of the ketch *Hobah* runs as a thread through the two volumes. At the same time, there is attempted a very brief survey of the maritime history of some of the coastal districts of England and Wales in this period, in so far as they were concerned with the building and management of small merchant sailing vessels.

In the course of writing, vessels of very many types other than schooners have been mentioned. Barquentines and brigantines I have treated as if they were schooners. To treat the brigantine thus is convenient but against any historical sense, since she developed from the fully square-rigged brig, but the barquentine can rightly be said to belong here, because she grew from the three-masted schooner in American waters and takes the place of the square-topsail schooner in later American sailing ship history. Not only these ships, but brigs and barques have been dealt with in due proportion, and, of course, the history of the ketches and the later sloops is an essential part of the history of the merchant schooners, of which they were the smaller sisters. Many hundreds of them sailed with the schooners both in the home trade and on deep water. The larger ketches were inter-changeable with schooners. Preference in rig was a matter of trades and local tradition. Two ships of the same size might be respectively a ketch and a three-masted schooner and changes were made in both directions (Plate 3).

As far as small commercial sailing ships were concerned the period after 1870 was the era of the merchant schooner. The efficient economical vessel, almost always with square topsails on her foremast, and the ketch, had at last largely replaced the brigs and sloops and small barques which were traditional. The schooner had gradually been increasing in numbers since the end of the eighteenth century. In some ports it had been common for seventy years or more, in others for only forty. But after 1870, for as long as sailing ships lasted as a tool of commerce, the schooner predominated and was the representative small mer-chant ship of Britain. The next chapter explains how this came about.

CHAPTER TWO

THE RISE AND FALL OF THE BRITISH MERCHANT SCHOONER

HOW THE SCHOONER BEGAN

PROFESSOR E. P. MORRIS of Yale in *The Fore and Aft Rig in America* showed that the schooner, as she was known in Britain and North America in the nineteenth century, was the result of development from two entirely different sources into two main types of sailing ship bearing the same name, closely resembling one another in general form and, in later years influencing one another, yet still revealing their different ancestry. These two types were the topsail schooner, the vessel setting square-sails from yards on her foretopmast, and so overwhelmingly preponderant in British waters that it was referred to simply as the schooner without the technical qualification, and the fore-and-aft schooner, without any square canvas and often in its smaller versions without even a foretopmast, which was so dominant in North America that there, in its turn, it was thought of simply as the natural form of schooner.

As far as it is possible to tell among the profusion of sail combinations which existed in the seventeenth century, when people thought of sails and rigging very differently from the way the late nineteenth-century seamen did, the schooner with square topsails was the end product of the evolution of one form of square-rigged ship. In the course of the eighteenth century the brigantine of the period, the vessel with the square-rigged foremast, a fore-and-aft sail on the main and a staysail in between, acquired a gaff sail on the foremast. By 1765 vessels so rigged, like the famous

24

Baltick of which a coloured sketch exists in the Peabody Museum of Salem, were already being called schooners. In time, the staysail was abandoned and the gaff sail replaced the square foresail as the main working canvas on the foremast, and so the topsail schooner as she was known in the late nineteenth century was born. By the end of the eighteenth century, she and the schooner with square topsails on both masts (which had evolved from the kind of eighteenth-century brigantine which had square topsails on her main topmast) had become very common in North America.

But at the same time a sail plan which was to have descendants in common with the topsail schooner was existing alongside it. Very early in the seventeenth century and most probably in the sixteenth, some Dutch vessels were equipped with a two-masted fore-and-aft rig with the foremast the shorter and stepped in the eyes of the vessel and the mainmast about amidships (Plate 4). Mr Michael Robinson late of the National Maritime Museum has drawn my attention to the earliest illustration of one of these which I have yet seen, an engraving published by C. J. Visscher after a painting or drawing attributed to Jan Porcellis who died in 1632. This illustrates such a developed vessel as to suggest that the form was already old, well-established and widespread. To such a ship it is only necessary to add a headsail to make a vessel fulfilling the minimum requirements for a schooner. L. G. Carr Laughton pointed out what appears to be a clear representation of such a vessel as early as 1628 in a line-engraving by D. van Bremden representing Piet Hein's capture of the Plate Fleet off Havana in that year. Vessels which fulfil the simple definition of the schooner may therefore have been in use by the end of the sixteenth century. They were common in the second half of the seventeenth century in both Britain and Holland. Early in the eighteenth century there is positive evidence of their existence in Colonial America. A characteristic of the two-masted fore-and-aft rigged vessel in the seventeenth and eighteenth centuries was the uneven rake of the masts, the main sloping aft more steeply than the fore.

Two survivors of these small schooners have come down to us today. At Castletown in the Isle of Man, a twenty-six foot schooner the *Peggy*, built in 1791 as a working boat has by accident been preserved intact and is today the centre of the nautical branch of the Manx Museum. Travelling round the Gaspé Peninsula at the mouth of the St Lawrence in Canada some years ago, I came across a fleet of working fishing schooners which resembled late eighteenth-century North American schooners in almost every respect. It is now generally accepted that they are survivors of the eighteenth-century type.

The technology of the seventeenth and eighteenth centuries limited the size of the fore-and-aft rigged vessel. Neither the rope, nor the iron fittings, nor the simple mechanical aids such as blocks, were good enough to stay a tall single part mast, or to set and control a big gaff sail, even if it had been possible to make a well-setting sail with the fabrics and techniques available. This was perhaps one of the reasons for the uneven rake of masts which was retained in Swansea pilot schooners until the late nineteenth century. With crude gear it was easier to set a big soft-bellied sail of loosely woven fabric from a steeply raking mast than from a vertical one, so the mainmast with the large sail raked more steeply than the fore. These technical limitations held the fore-and-aft sail in a state of delicate balance. Although unhandy in big seas and on long runs to leeward, it was cheaper, handier, and more efficient to windward than the square sail, all qualities which commended it to ship-owners and seamen engaged in trades where conditions were such that the sail's weaknesses were not brought out. But as soon as the small fore-and-aft schooner reached a certain size, the necessary additional canvas had to be square, because square sails were a much easier problem to a relatively primitive technology than fore-and-aft. For the same reason it was only the smaller class of brigantines which could evolve a schooner branch in the family.

As Professor Morris has put it, '—the fore-and-aft rig was carried over from boats to larger and larger vessels, until a size was reached, varying with the period, on which square sails were superior; there the encroachment came to an end.' A study of the readily available material among Admiralty drafts would suggest that the critical size was about seventy feet overall in the second half of the eighteenth century, though most schooners were smaller, and that it grew fairly rapidly in the early years of the nineteenth century.

There is as yet too little evidence available to generalise about the extent to which schooners were involved in British trade in the eighteenth century. This is one of the many questions which await the writing of an authoritative general history of the fore-and-aft rig. But the schooner's widespread adoption as a rig for cargo-carrying vessels up to the size limit imposed by the current technology probably came later in Britain than in the American colonies and subsequently in the United States, British North America and the West Indies. Indeed one United States authority (Howard I. Chapelle of the United States National Museum in *The History of American Sailing Ships*) has stated that '—by the time of the Revolution the schooner was in such general use as to be the most numerous of all classes of carrier'. Certainly in the illustrations to Des Barres' *Atlantic Neptune* of the 1760s schooners outnumber all the other vessels depicted on the coasts of Maine and Nova Scotia. The development and widespread adoption of the schooner by the United States and British North America was fostered by the Revolution, the Napoleonic Wars and the War of 1812. Schooners had the twin advantages of requiring less capital investment than the square-rigged ships, and this was very important to a young economy and was perhaps the largest factor in the schooner's general adoption in North America, and of being better performers to windward and therefore able to out-distance square-rigged pursuers often much larger. Thus during the long unsettled period schooners were able to carry the bulk of the cargoes in American bottoms and, again according to Chapelle, in August 1814, it was estimated that nine-tenths of the foreign trade of the United States was carried on in schooners of the specialised type known as Baltimore Clippers.

Several recent studies have cast some light on the prevalence of the schooner among British merchant shipping in the late eighteenth and early nineteenth centuries. In Grahame Farr's analytical study of the Chepstow ship registrations between 1786 and 1882 published as *Chepstow Ships*, no schooners appear among the eighty-six vessels registered between 1786 and 1800. They are mostly sloops, brigantines and brigs. Vessels up to fifty feet in length or so are sloops, the larger ones are square-rigged. There may, of course, have been vessels among the brigantines which would in later years have been classified as schooners, and some of the sloops were converted into schooners and brigantines many years later, but the first time the description schooner appears is in 1806 and it is then applied to a little vessel about the size of the Manx Museum's *Peggy* and built in the same year, 1791. Chepstow was a thriving shipbuilding centre and numerous brigs, brigantines, snows and full-rigged ships were launched into the river Wye, many of them large ships for their period. Between 1784 and 1814, over 160 ships were built but the first schooner of any size was the *Lord Hill*, seventy-two tons, of 1814. Not until the 1820s were schooners built regularly each year. D. W. Morgan's study of the shipping of the river Dovey, published in *Brief Glory* tells the same story. Between 1828 and 1850, seventeen sloops were built and thirteen schooners. Before 1828, the sloop had been overwhelmingly more numerous. In the ten years after 1850, twenty-three schooners were built and four sloops. Similarly Dr Dennis Chapman's study of ships built at Portdinllaen between 1776 and 1875 shows the first schooner built in 1839. Of thirty-four ships built after 1840 all but two were schooners.

An analysis prepared by Grahame Farr as part of the research project which led to the writing of *Westcountrymen in Prince Edward's Isle* lists the vessels owned by prominent Bideford shipowners between 1786 and the middle of the nineteenth century. The 139 ships listed as owned by the Burnard family from 1786 to 1849 were engaged in every kind of commerce not only inside the Bristol Channel and in general home trade, but also in

the Mediterranean and the North American trade. Four of them
were registered at Bideford Custom House as schooners. The
Chappell family, whose history as Bideford shipowners went back
to the seventeenth century, were recorded as owning or sharing
thirty-six ships between 1787 and 1844. Two of them were
schooners. The Ellis family were part-owners of nineteen ships
between 1786 and 1838 but there were no schooners among
them. The researches into the structure of Bideford's trade over
the same years, which formed part of the same project, showed
that the port's coasting trade, at least until the 1830s, was carried
on in sloops, brigs and brigantines. Some of the sloops were converted into brigantines and there were probably many polaccas
among them. The North American trade was carried on in brigs,
barques and full-rigged ships. Relatively few schooners were reported before the 1830s.

After the beginning of the 1830s, however, the schooner begins
to appear more frequently and between 1830 and 1845 one Bideford shipowner, Thomas Burnard Chanter, held shares or total
ownership of some seventeen schooners among the sixty or so
vessels in which he had interest. The How family, over roughly
the same period, owned shares in six schooners out of twenty-
seven vessels. Richard Heard and his sons owned six schooners
among twenty-nine vessels. There is a very significant difference
between these Bideford shipowners and the others mentioned
above. Bideford's North American trade had almost totally died
away after the American Revolution, but after Waterloo it began
slowly to revive. Chanter was the first merchant to operate in
the North American trade on a large scale for three-quarters of a
century and he had considerable business interests in that continent. The Hows and the Heards followed his example. Many
of the schooners he and they owned were built in British North
America. Many Bideford men became familiar with the North
American coasts. Some settled there and others spent years working in shipyards in Prince Edward Island before returning to
Devon. They became familiar with a British North American
coasting trade which, the records of shipping movements show be-

yond all doubt, was carried on very largely in schooners the size of Bideford's brigantines and sloops. It is legitimate to surmise from the evidence so far available that this was one of the factors which led to the wide adoption of the schooner at Bideford in the mid-nineteenth century.

If this is so, then it might be expected that the schooner would have been adopted earlier in British ports which had a continuous connection with North America through the years when Bideford's Atlantic trade was broken off. It so happens that another study of a type comparable with Grahame Farr's supports this speculation. While Bideford's North American trade was dying in 1742, ships sailing from St John's, Newfoundland, for the Port of Dartmouth (which includes Brixham and Salcombe) carried the bulk of all the dried and salted codfish imported into England. And many more Dartmouth ships must have joined in the vast carrying trade from Newfoundland to the Mediterranean, which, in 1742, totalled over 120,000 hundredweight units as against 22,500 units imported into Britain. Though the business declined markedly after 1775, Dartmouth and its creeks maintained their interest in the North Atlantic trade continuously until far into the nineteenth century. John Horsley of the Brixham Museum has analised the Custom House records of Dartmouth, particularly so far as they are relevant to the creek of Brixham. He has found the schooner far more prevalent than it was at the same period in North Devon. Over fifty schooners were registered as owned in Brixham before 1815. Of 346 merchant ships owned in Brixham between 1824 and 1863, no less than 289 were two-masted schooners.

This evidence suggests that the schooner rig was much more slowly adopted in Britain than in North America and that it did not become generally popular as an alternative to the traditional rigs, sloops (Plate 5), brigantines, brigs (Plate 6) and snows until the 1830s. This statement, of course, is a very general one. The extent of the local variations is demonstrated by the fact that the brig illustrated in Plate 6, the *Pelican*, was built at Hastings in 1838 as one of a small group of schooners launched there around that time and was subsequently altered to become a brig. The evidence suggests that the American example may have been followed as a result of direct contact with North America, and the habit of rigging vessels as schooners may have spread slowly outwards from ports where the seamen and ship-builders were familiar at first hand with North American practice. The trades which were the main concern of some ports were more suited to schooners than some others and I shall show that at Dartmouth this was particularly so and that the established pattern of business, as well as continuous contact with North America, favoured the early adoption of the schooner at that port.

Plates 7 and 8 show what appears to be a typical West Country merchant schooner of the 1840s, when the type was first being widely adopted in Britain. In essentials, the British two-masted schooner did not change much from this form for as long as it was used. She is the *Hope* of Bideford, 101 tons, built at Appledore by Thomas Waters in 1849 and she was employed in the Mediterranean trade, as the painting at Plate 7 indicates, and in the Quebec lumber trade. Although better canvas and cordage were now available, the rake of the mainmast still shows the influence of eighteenth-century technology and the single topsail that of her square-rigged ancestry. The *Hope* was still working in the twentieth century and the photograph at Plate 8, showing her in her last years, confirms the accuracy of the painting as to hull shape and mast rake. But, as might be expected, the cut of the sails has much changed.

If the *Hope* is a typical British schooner of the mid-nineteenth century and was not to appear incongruous in the last years of the sailing ship, she would already at the time of her building have been something of an anachronism in North America. Here in the first half of the nineteenth century the two kinds of schooner, the grown-up fore-and-aft rigged boat like a Gaspé schooner and the brigantine turned into a vessel carrying the greater part of her canvas fore and aft, merged into the schooner of brigantine size without square sails. Improved ropes and tackles made possible the big gaff and boom sail with a well-setting gaff topsail above it. The schooner without square sails became the characteristic small American and Canadian merchant sailing ship. The schooner with square sails in the eighteenth-century style became her British and, generally speaking, her European equivalent. Why the North American schooner took this extra step in evolution before the extinction of the small merchant sailing vessel and the European schooner did not is not easily explained. Social factors played some part, and perhaps, too, the American schooner's environment and trades called for greater windward ability than was required in Europe.

The general appearance of the North American equivalent of the *Hope* is represented by the *Alice S. Wentworth* (Plate 9). She was built at South Norwalk, Connecticut, in 1868 for the New England coastal trade and at the time of writing she is still afloat. In her youth, she and her thousands of sisters set a gaff topsail on the main topmast, long since removed when this photograph was taken. But the typical small schooner had no fore topmast and in America when the *Wentworth* was built square canvas was already a thing of the distant past. Like hundreds of her American contemporaries, but only one or two British schooners, she had a centreboard.

From the *Hope*, only one further type of British schooner was developed. This was the efficient, small, three-masted schooner with several square sails on her foremast. But in the dynamic and expanding economy of North America the schooner still had a very long way to go. While vessels like the *Alice S. Wentworth* continued to be built far into the present century—indeed for the specialized cruising trade on the New England coast they are still being built without engines in the 1960s and handsome modern versions of them like the *Westward* of Oyster Bay are being built as yachts—the development of the schooner in Canada and the United States was pushed, under the impetus of commercial opportunity seen and grasped, along three different but parallel lines. The three-masted schooner without square sails was developed into an efficient, handy, economical and usually extremely handsome type of vessel three or four times as big as her British equivalent and regularly engaged in trans-ocean as well as long-range coastal trades.

Beyond three masts, conditions in the long-range coastal trade made it profitable to develop the four-master and the five- and six-master. Although designed as bulk carriers for certain special trades, many of these ships were taken up in the general tonnage market and, over the years, many hundreds of trans-ocean passages were made in direct and successful competition with contemporary square-rigged ships. Plate 10 shows a typical if rather ugly four-master, the *Agnes Manning*, 988 tons, built at Camden, New Jersey, in 1892. She spent some time during the first world war laid up at Appledore near Bideford after suffering damage at the end of a trans-Atlantic passage. These enormous schooners were the final example of the potentialities of the gaff and boom sail, given a sufficiently advanced industrial economy. Costing far less then the equivalent square-rigged ship to build and maintain, they were made technically possible by using steam winches to hoist the sails, sometimes steam steering engines, and lazy jacks to control the sails when they were taken in. Finally, in the 1890s the American and Canadian fishing schooner, which in the mid-nineteenth century had been little different in general appearance from its cargo-carrying contemporaries, was developed with the aid of new design techniques into the finest fore-and-aft rigged commercial sailing ship there has ever been. These last fishing schooners were quite different from cargo ships.

THE FRUIT TRADE

The schooner was gradually adopted in Britain as a rig for small, general purpose, merchant sailing ships in the years about the middle of the century, but shipowners in some ports had already been operating schooners for seventy-five years or more. It has been shown that one of these ports was Dartmouth, and one of its constituent harbour towns, Brixham, was deeply involved in a trade for which schooners were particularly suitable, as they were for the trading conditions which faced the infant

United States in the same period. This was the soft fruit trade from the Azores and the Mediterranean. Dartmouth had long been heavily engaged in the trade with Newfoundland and, in the eighteenth century, this turned from a fishing business to a carrying trade in which fish caught by Newfoundland settlers was picked up by British vessels and taken to the Mediterranean. From the Mediterranean, the West Country vessels returned to Britain and, over the years, they began to bring soft fruit cargoes home with them. From these passages the fruit-carrying business developed as a trade in its own right and gave a considerable fillip to the general adoption of the schooner in Britain.

Why were small schooners employed in the fruit trade? They had to be small vessels for a number of reasons. The ports into which they sailed were small, and if they had carried more than a hundred tons or so the weight of their cargo would have been self ruinous. The time spent in loading by the methods then used would have been such that the first cargo taken on board would have been rotting before the schooners were many days out. Finally, to employ many small vessels in so highly speculative a trade was to spread the risk of loss. One small vessel slow on passage meant a fraction of the disaster that would have occurred if the cargoes of half a dozen schooners had been packed into one larger vessel, similarly delayed. For these reasons the schooners employed in the orange trade (and this was the most important of the fruit trades and lasted the longest) were rarely able to carry more than 150 tons.

They were schooners because of all commercial sailing vessels at all times their trade was most literally dependent upon speed. Without continuous speed in all weathers under all conditions of wind and sea, their cargoes became valueless beneath the feet of their large crews. Since their voyages were out of the zones of constant wind, they had to be able to cope with every point of sailing as nearly as possible equally well. For such requirements, the topsail schooner is best suited. With their yards forward (and, with royal, topgallant, deep topsail, huge flying square sail, and topmast and lower studding-sails, some of these small fruit schooners

5. The sloop *Emerald*, built at Plymouth in 1835, with a Mount's Bay fishing lugger

6. The brig *Pelican*, a regular local trader, moored bow and stern off Hastings beach in the 1860s. When the tide ebbed her coal cargo was discharged into carts

7. A painting by Nicola Fonda of the schooner *Hope* of Bideford, built at Appledore in 1849, entering Naples in 1854

8. The *Hope* in her old age

carried an immense area of square canvas) they could sail off the wind as well as any square-rigged ship of their size or perhaps much larger, and yet they could give that square-rigged ship a point or more in sailing on the wind. Moreover, they lost no time in the restricted waters at either end of their passages.

From time to time in the mid-nineteenth century the *Illustrated London News* published engravings of fruit schooners and generally these were accompanied by a brief account of the trade as it was conducted at that time. From these notes it is apparent that Southampton was another centre of the business; that in the forties between 200 and 300 vessels ran to the fruit ports giving employment to some 3,000 seamen, for the fruit schooners carried big crews by later standards. The fruit was gathered when just about to turn from green to yellow, each orange being wrapped separately, and packed in chests of 1,000 each, boxes of 400 and small boxes of 300. The pay of a seaman on the St Michael's passage in the middle of the century (when the Crimean War resulted in a shortage of seamen) was £4 a month, and it seems that the fastest passages from St Michael's to London were between six and seven days.

By far the most important part of the business, and the most significant in its influence on vessel development, was the orange and lemon trade from the Azores and the western Mediterranean to London. By 1854, sixty million oranges were imported for the London market alone, and some fifteen million lemons. In that year there were 240 schooners in the business; of these seventy supplied the local demands of London. At any time between December and May, schooners from the Azores and Lisbon could be seen unloading their cargoes in London river, for the season was a short one and oranges were a winter luxury. Besides these specialized cargoes mixed loads of grapes, oranges, lemons and currants were sometimes picked up at Mediterranean ports. There were other fruit trades. The West Indies pineapple trade began about 1842 and rapidly increased so that by 1854 200,000 pineapples were brought yearly into London in schooners. There was a trade in melons, which came from both Spain and Portugal,

c

there was a currant trade from the Greek Islands, which, since the cargo was less perishable, employed larger and slower vessels.

But the greatest trade was always that with the Azores for oranges. By the middle of the century, many British families in the trade had settled in the Islands, where the fruit grew in terraced gardens. Because of their light cargoes, the fruit schooners were heavily ballasted and as some were not very much bigger than the largest modern ocean-racing yachts and were sailed with the same determination to reach their destinations as quickly as possible, life on board was frequently a prolonged experience of violent motion and imposed great strains on masters and crews.

Mr Benjamin Tregaskes of Par, probably the last man alive who had to do with the business in the years of its greatness, told me many years ago of the orange trade :

> Only small vessels were used, not even over 200 tons, because of the weight of the cargo on top spoiling the cargo underneath if the cargoes were too big. They were extremely careful with the cargo, opening hatches in the daytime when the weather was good to give it all the ventilation they could. They had an inspection hatch into the hold and the mate had to carry out an inspection daily. If any of the cargo went rotten, it went overboard or else it would affect the rest. If the cargo was brought home with no rotten fruit, the master might receive a bonus from the merchant of as much as £50. Only oranges were carried, as I remember the trade. Bristol was a delivery centre for distribution in the West and the Midlands. The schooners came from Devonshire—Dartmouth, Brixham and Salcombe—and only came into Fowey and Falmouth for orders. Only classed vessels were taken up by the merchants.

Merchants would risk cargoes only in vessels classed by Lloyd's; when a vessel fell out of class she went out of the fruit business and off deep water into the home trade. The great fruit-schooner ports throughout the history of the trade were those of the South Hams of Devon, and to a less extent eastwards to Rye. Cornish vessels carried occasional fruit cargoes in the later days of the business, but the trade was a highly specialised one and centred on ports further up Channel. As vessels fell out of the trade, so they were sold westwards down the coast, and the old fruit ports lost their former importance and did not play so great a part in the later history of the small, deep-sea sailing ships. Since they were classified vessels, it is instructive to examine the Register Books of the fifties and to see how many small schooners there were with Dartmouth as their port of survey and St Michael's as their 'destined voyage'.

THE PACKET TRADE

There was another trade to which the schooner was particularly suited. At the beginning of the nineteenth century, road transport between London and the Scots towns was slow, intensely uncomfortable, difficult and dangerous. The sea route was the natural one and there had developed from early carrier smacks, which brought salmon and other fish down to London, a fine type of purely passenger-carrying sloop, of seventy to eighty feet in length, heavily rigged and providing a fast, reliable and relatively comfortable service. They took on average five days for the journey from London to Leith; often, of course, they spent more than a week at sea, often less; the record passage is said to have been forty-two hours. They provided two large cabins, one for passengers of each sex, were heavily manned, well maintained and regulated, and they seem to have provided a very good service by the standards of their times. A model of one of these sloops is to be found in the Science Museum, another is in the Glasgow Museum, and there are others in the possession of shipping companies.

During the first half of the nineteenth century, the London to the Forth packet trade offered obvious opportunities to early steam vessels, and, by the 1830s, the sloops were in competition with them. There were, of course, not only fast passenger sloops in the business but also fast cargo vessels and many slower ships carrying goods in bulk. In 1840, there were no less than 250 sailing ships built in Aberdeen alone employed in trade between that port and London. Although the mails were already carried by rail and road, there was still a lucrative trade to compete for and from this competition there evolved, whether consciously or incidentally to the contemporary laws of tonnage measurement is not clear at this distance of time, a local type of very fast schooner.

The first of these was launched by Alexander Hall and Company at Aberdeen in 1839. In the *Scottish Maid*, as she was called, and in her immediate successors, the stem was raked far more than in any previous vessel and, indeed, than in those that followed them. This raking, curved stem with the planking carried out to it throughout its length, combined with hollow entrance lines, a much older invention, formed what was called the 'Aberdeen bow' and, although this design became rapidly less extreme in later vessels, its introduction altered the general appearance of ships in a manner historically uncommon, since it was both sudden and complete.

The lines of the *Scottish Maid* were published in the *Mariners' Mirror*, the Journal of the Society for Nautical Research, in April 1943. They show a British schooner of the period designed with the Aberdeen bow. She has moderate dead rise, her point of maximum beam is well aft, and her length-beam ratio is quite high. She has no great drag. Within five years of the launch of the *Scottish Maid*, a schooner of similar type had been built for owners in Dartmouth and her appearance must have had its influence on local shipbuilding. In the next fifteen years many fine ships of this type were launched by both English and Scottish builders for the fruit trade. Their length-beam ratio tended to rise, so that in some of the fast fruiterers it was more than five to one, and the bow became less extreme; although the rabbett was still raked, the slope of the stem became far less marked.

Schooners were in use at this time on other packet routes, that is, wherever they had to sail against time under all conditions of wind and sea, and they had been so used for some time. The Waterford-Bristol trade had employed schooners since early in the century. At Aberdeen, Hall built clipper schooners for several packet firms and schooners were used on scheduled routes down

Channel from London river. These packet ships had to carry a reasonable weight of cargo. The fruit trade, and in particular, the orange trade, was a seasonal one, and for parts of the year the schooners engaged in it had to find other cargoes; they had in fact to combine a reasonable economic capacity with their speed. It was particularly important that they should be able to lie aground in drying harbours. The premium, therefore, in all the trades in which British schooners were employed, was on a practical working vessel with no great clipper pretensions.

MIRACLE IN PRINCE EDWARD ISLAND

Prince Edward Island lies in the Gulf of St Lawrence separated from the shores of New Brunswick and Nova Scotia by the narrow Strait of Northumberland. It is today the smallest of the provinces of Canada, in area about seven-eights of the county of Devon in England. From 1765 until 1873 it was a British colony. Even in the eighteenth century it had a small shipbuilding industry but it was not until after the battle of Waterloo, and as a result of the duties imposed on Baltic timber some years before, that the colony's maritime trade began to develop. Merchants from the west of England, some of them already established in the colony, and others such as the Pope family, Thomas Billings and James Peake from Plymouth, William Way and William Curtis from Brixham, Lemuel and Artemas Cambridge of Bristol, Thomas Burnard, Thomas Burnard Chanter, William Grigg, William Heard, John How, James Yeo, George Hooper and others from Bideford and William Richards of Swansea, set up lumbering and shipbuilding, store-keeping and farming businesses in the island. The business of building ships to be sailed to Britain and sold there developed steadily for fifty years from 1815 to 1865. An extensive North Atlantic trade between the west of England and the island grew up which employed among other vessels, a large number of schooners. In 1817 thirty-four ships were built in Prince Edward Island, all schooners. Ten were sold to Newfoundland, seven to England, nearly all at this date to

Liverpool. Four years later, out of twenty-five new ships, twenty-two of them schooners, nine were sold to England. By the middle of the century an economic miracle had taken place, a great shipbuilding industry had developed on the beaches between the island's forests and the sea. Exports of ships were worth between fifty and sixty thousand pounds a year and were paying for more than half the colony's imports. From 1830 to 1865, the number of ships launched steadily rose until it reached well over one hundred each year. A great deal of the colony's labour force was absorbed by the industry; the settlers' farms and other businesses were neglected. At times, the island probably built more ships for owners in the United Kingdom than any other place outside metropolitan Britain. Out of at least 350 ships built between 1833 and 1893 by one group of financiers, James Yeo and his descendants, at least 250 were sold to British owners soon after their launch. British shipping records of the third quarter of the last century are rich in references to Prince Edward Island-built ships. Many of these were large square-rigged ships, others were brigs, but a great many, especially at the later period, were brigantines and schooners.

For use in the North American coasting trade the islanders built simple fore-and-aft schooners rigged in the North American style. For sale in Britain, they built more heavily-rigged schooners with square topsails and these vessels played their part in the gradual adoption of schooners by British shipowners. A good example is the *Troubadour* (Plate 11), built in 1867 at Mount Stewart, up river from Charlottetown, the island's capital and only harbour with a Custom House. She was sold in 1868 through the agency of John Cannon and John Black of Liverpool for 'not less than £700' to Thomas Daunt of Cork. When the photograph was taken, she belonged to John Downes, master mariner, of Portishead, Somerset.

In the middle 1800s and before, the island shipwrights built polacca brigantines. These were sold in the south-west of England where this survival of the eighteenth century remained in fashion as a rig for ships between forty and eighty feet long on deep water as well as in the home trade until well into the third quarter of the century. As far as is known these Prince Edward Island brigantines are the only example of pole-masted square-rigged ships built in North America.

THE SCHOONER IN THE FIFTIES AND SIXTIES

An examination of *Lloyd's Register* of the year 1851 shows that there were already a very large number of schooners hailing from ports in the United Kingdom. The great majority are shown simply as coasters, although a number are running in the Baltic trade. In comparison with square-rigged craft, the number on deep water is still small and the voyages of many of them are given as to the Mediterranean and the Azores, but some were sailing to the West Indies, South America and a few to Newfoundland.

A study of the *Mercantile Navy List* when rigs first began to be recorded in it at the beginning of the 1870s, shows that by the third quarter of the century the schooner was very well established among the sloops and brigs which traditionally had comprised the bulk of Britain's fleets of small merchant sailing ships. Examination of *Clayton's Annual Register* for the year 1865 gives some interesting information about the distribution of small ships of various rigs about the British Isles. On the west coast the schooner predominates, in the south she gives way to small square-rigged ships, in the south-east the barge outnumbers all the rest, north of the Thames the schooner is more numerous, but north of the Humber the brig is still much the commonest of small ships.

This Register gives some measure of the change which took place in the economy and industry of the coasts of the United Kingdom during the period covered by this history. In 1865, 296 small sailing ships and 4 steamers were registered at Aberystwyth, 190 sailing ships at Beaumaris, there were 94 small sailing ships among the numerous vessels owned in Bristol, Bridgwater had nearly 100, Bideford had 90 ships, Barnstaple only 44, Bridport and Lyme Regis 30 between them, Chepstow 18, Dartmouth 250. Exeter and Falmouth had 100 vessels each, Faversham (including Whitstable) nearly 200, Goole 400 and Penzance about 60. In the Scilly Isles 36 sailing ships, including barques of over 500 tons, were owned. It was on the north-east coast, at the coal loading ports, that the numbers were greatest. Sunderland still had over 700 ships of which the great majority were brigs, and the twin Shields, 850. Forgotten ports had large fleets. Truro had 60 ships. Wells-next-the-Sea 100, Woodbridge 37 and Caernarvon (which includes Portmadoc) 400.

A certain number of these ships were already registered as ketch-rigged. The modern fore-and-aft rigged ketch certainly existed very early in the nineteenth, if not in the eightenth century, for engravings of about 1830 show her in fully developed form without square topsails, but the rig did not become common until the second half of the nineteenth century. Then, in the 1870s, it suddenly became very popular. Many masters considered it to be the most economical and handy of all rigs for small merchant sailing ships and there was consequently a tendency for larger and larger ships to be rigged as ketches (Plate 12). The extra size of the mainsail was compensated for, within certain limits, by economy and the added handiness of the ship, and was made possible by the widespread adoption of roller reefing gear. This tendency was never fulfilled in Britain, where small sailing ships ceased to be built before it could properly develop, but in Denmark in the middle of this century heavily-rigged ketches, larger than the ordinary British three-masted schooner, were being built for deep-sea trade, and schooners had almost ceased to be constructed. Here the cycle of inter-continental influence was completed, for the purely fore-and-aft ketch began to be used in America only at the end of the history of commercial sails.

The merchant ketch came from two or three sources which influenced one another. The old square-rigged ketch was the first by the natural process of technical evolution to turn into a fore-and-aft rigged vessel like a modern ketch. Then fishing cutters grew larger and needed a little lug-rigged mizzen, so that they became what West Country seamen used to call 'dandies'; then, as they grew bigger, the mizzen became a gaff sail. Finally, the old trading cutters of the east coast, the billyboys and hoys with their square topsails, also acquired a mizzen as they grew larger. The form of the rigging of merchant ketches varied around the coast with the origin of the rig in each particular district. The billyboys of the Humber kept the square topsails of the old cutters. The barge ketches, which developed in the late nineteenth century in the waters where billyboys were common, adopted the old rigging. On the south coast, where ketches had been in use for longer, square topsails were much less common, and on the west coast where, by the end of the century, the ketch had become a deep-water trader, square sails were rarer still.

After the middle of the century the sailing vessels in the fruit trade came into competition with steamers. The currant trade was the first to decline, in the early 1850s, and although there were many technical difficulties and much prejudice to overcome, steam vessels gradually took over the rest of the business. The construction in the early 60s at Ponta Delgada in the Azores of an artificial harbour where steamers could be loaded quickly made great inroads into the fruit schooners' principal trade. It is difficult to tell just how rapidly it contracted, but probably by 1865 it was very much reduced. Certainly by 1870 schooners had ceased to be employed regularly in the business, although some from Devon and Cornwall were still carrying occasional orange cargoes. John Stephens of Fowey (see Chapter 4 of Volume 2), who in the later 60s was conducting a ship-broking business in south Cornwall, fixed occasional fruit cargoes in his early career but the vessels which he himself managed very rarely carried fruit, and he began to manage ships in 1870, or just before. By the beginning of the 70s, some of the best known of the surviving schooners of the south Devon fruit ports, vessels designed by their builders to carry fruit for much of their time, were already regular traders to the Newfoundland saltfish ports (see next chapter).

As the 1860s advanced, therefore, the fruit trade became

steadily more and more an *ad hoc* business as far as sailing vessels were concerned and the regular fruit carriers had to look more and more for other cargoes. The crucial decade in the replacement of the small square-rigged ships by schooners was 1870 to 1880; after the latter date the schooners had established themselves as economical and efficient vessels for all trades at home and on deep water that offered small cargoes. They were much less expensive to build than square-rigged ships, and very few brigs and small, three-masted square-rigged vessels were built afterwards. The economic tide was finally moving against the sailing vessel.

THE THREE-MASTED SCHOONER

Another change took place at the same period. The three-masted schooner had come into existence in the eighteenth century. For example, a ship named the *Jenny*, which was built in Newfoundland and owned in Bristol, was described in registration documents as a three-masted schooner when she visited the west coast of North America in 1792. In 1814 the Cambridges of Prince Edward Island built the three-masted schooner *Dispatch*, subsequently registered in Bristol. At least one three-masted schooner, the *Munster Lass*, was in the Atlantic trade at the beginning of the 1830s, and at the same period several towns in Maine were building three-masters. In 1854, William Heard of Bideford launched the three-masted schooner *Choice* at Charlottetown, Prince Edward Island, and she was sailed across the Atlantic and sold to British owners. Four years later, according to Captain John Parker's *Sails of the Maritimes*, the first three-master was built in Nova Scotia.

But despite these early developments there were technical, economic, social, and even superstitious, reasons why the three-masted schooner did not become common until after the American Civil War. After the war, it rapidly became popular in North America and big three-masters from the United States made many overseas voyages in the 1870s. From Prince Edward Island, big three-masted schooners came into British ownership in the early 70s and were used in the exacting copper-ore trade from Chile around Cape Horn to the Bristol Channel.

In the early 70s, the three-master came into general use in the home trade and in the deep-sea trades in which the schooners found employment. They begin to appear regularly in the Dartmouth registrations at this period and at what was to become the great North Atlantic trade town of Portmadoc they appear in the same years. Here the pioneer ship was the *Frau Minna Petersen* (Plate 14) which, on one of her voyages, sailed up the Danube to ports in Roumania. The merchant schooner became a bigger vessel by British standards, and better able to compete with brigs and small barques in deep-sea trade. The rig was more economical on gear than that of the two-masted schooner and easier to work. Not surprisingly, a number of the bigger two-masters were converted into three-masters. The drawings in this history include a diagrammatic representation of how this was done in the *Rhoda Mary*, held by many seamen to have been one of the fastest schooners ever built in Britain. (Fig. 11, Vol. 2.)

THE ERA OF THE MERCHANT SCHOONER

From 1870 until the first world war, then, was the era of the merchant schooner. Although in the latter part of that period the advancing economic system had rendered the small ship obsolescent on deep water, there were still very many of them at the turn of the century.

Schooners continued in the North Atlantic trade until the end of the first world war. A few persisted afterwards. Almost unbelievably, the last of them, the *Lady St Johns*, was still sailing the North Atlantic from a Devon port until 1930. Thus the sea life of the eighteenth century persisted far into the twentieth. But after the turn of the century the schooner was more and more a vessel of the home trade, and after the first world war almost entirely so. The schooners decayed as their trades decayed. Auxiliary oil engines, introduced before the first world war and widely adopted after it, became almost universal in the 1930s, but the last sailing schooners without engines persisted into the second world war. The story of the slow decline of the schooner is told in detail in Chapter 6, Volume 2, of this history.

As to the sort of trades in which the schooners sailed at the beginning of their great period, what they cost to build, what their sails cost, the freights they made, the way they were owned and what they cost to run, what their crews were paid and what profits they made, all this is told in Appendix I of this volume. The life story of the schooner *Thetis* of Fowey is told in the terms of her own account book, covering the four years of her short life. She carried varied cargoes and made only one voyage with fruit. This document contains much information about the working of small ships in the contemporary ocean trade.

CHAPTER THREE

THE NEWFOUNDLAND TRADE

S O far as the voyages made by the *Thetis* are concerned, her
account book, which covers the period 1873-7 would
probably have presented a very different picture a few years
later.

The cod fishery of the north-western Atlantic has been the
subject of one of the greatest industrial histories ever written,
the late Professor Harold Innis' *The Cod Fisheries—The History
of an International Economy*, published by the University of
Toronto Press. The cod of the shallow seas off Newfoundland and
Nova Scotia, in Massachusetts Bay and in the Gulf of St
Lawrence, drew Europeans from the end of the fifteenth century.
The late Dr J. A. Williamson suggested in *The Cabot Voyages
and Bristol Discovery* that fleets from Bristol were going to Newfoundland perhaps as early as the 1480s. These misty, often
stormy waters were the first of the successive frontiers which have
played such a fundamental part in North American history. Salt
fish was an important item in European diet, possessing certain
qualities which made it very valuable as a preserved food in a
technically primitive society. It was an important provision for
ships sailing on long voyages to tropical waters during the early
periods of European commercial expansion, while as provender
for armies on the march it was easily transportable and durable.
Because it can be caught, prepared and transported with relatively little capital investment, it has remained a staple of Europe
and later of North America, the West Indies and Africa, for
more than five centuries. For much of this time the cod fishery
has constituted an important economic and political factor in the
history of the nations engaged in it.

Despite the pioneering efforts from Bristol, British merchants were slow to exploit the cod fishery. But by 1625 Barnstaple, which then included Appledore, was sending ships by the score to the fishery. During the seventeenth century, the river Taw silted up and Barnstaple gave place as a port to Bideford. In 1700, thirty Bideford ships sailed from Newfoundland, thirteen of them for Portugal and the Mediterranean, as against twelve ships from Barnstaple and sixteen from Dartmouth. Only London, with forty-five ships, had more vessels than Bideford in the Newfoundland trade.

Gradually, in the seventeenth and eighteenth centuries, to the accompaniment of great political disputes over the permanent settlement of Newfoundland, the business turned from one of sending ships from Britain to catch fish and bring it back to one of sending ships to buy fish from settlers on the Newfoundland coast and carry it to Spain, Portugal, the Mediterranean, and in smaller quantities to Britain. Small British trading vessels regularly carried dried and salted cod across the North Atlantic throughout the nineteenth century. In the last thirty years of the century and until the first world war, the Newfoundland fish export trade enjoyed a boom period. Easier communications following the development of the railways and a growing population in Europe meant expanding markets. At the same time the general standard of living was still very low and very cheap staple foods, even though lacking in variety, could still command a large market. So, throughout the era during which the merchant schooner was predominant among small British merchant sailing ships, the Newfoundland salt fish carrying trade provided regular employment for many hundreds of vessels.

By its very essence this was a small ship trade. The cod was caught either from boats based on the small harbours and quays of the Newfoundland and Labrador coasts, or from dories mothered by schooners which lay out on distant banks for weeks on end, or nearer to the shores of Newfoundland for a shorter period. As soon as possible after it was caught the fish was beheaded, boned and cleaned, and then washed and salted. The salt took a lot of the water out of the flesh of the fish and after it had been in salt for some time it had to be thoroughly washed again, and then dried off in wind and sun to reduce the water content to the degree necessary for the fish to be preserved. The entire process was subject to disaster if the fish was mishandled at any stage and the quality of the finished product varied with the care taken in drying.

Fish caught on the inshore fishery were dried by the fishermen and their families in the small settlements to which they belonged; the fish drying stages, called 'flakes', are still the most conspicuous feature of every creekside settlement in Newfoundland (Plate 15). The fish caught on the Labrador, where the weather was not suitable for drying, was salted and then either taken in salt bulk to the Newfoundland settlements, from which the men fishing seasonally on the Labrador came, or direct to Europe. The banks schooners also took back their fish salted on board in salt bulk and it was treated on land in the rather larger settlements from which these vessels sailed.

Apart from the fact that it is now supervised and subsidised and that the ships and boats now have engines, the industry continues on much the same lines but on a greatly reduced scale. The results of all these processes of fishing were the same; large quantities of the finished product lay awaiting collection at all the obscure and inaccessible settlements of the shattered coat of Newfoundland, while bulk salted cargoes were gathered in the ports of the Labrador, both countries deficient in land transport. The collection of these cargoes was, both physically and economically, a small vessel trade and because of the nature of the seas to be traversed between Newfoundland and Europe and of the winds that blow over them, it was a trade peculiarly suited to topsail schooners; brigs were employed in it, but they were not happy on the long beats against the westerlies, nor in the guts of the Newfoundland creeks.

When the finished product was ready for shipping it was bought by the great Newfoundland merchants, such firms as Munn and Company of Harbour Grace, C. T. Bowring of St

John's and Liverpool, Job Brothers of Liverpool and Baine and Johnston of Glasgow. These merchants instructed brokers in Bristol and Liverpool who chartered two separate types of ship, the large vessel of up to 1,000 tons for the southern trade and the small West Country schooners and schooners from Portmadoc and Scotland for the European trade. These charters were made through established channels, whose development was, of course, one of the factors controlling the form taken by the trade in the years of its expansion in the 70s. Once bought, assembled and shipped, the fish cargoes were then re-sold by the merchants to buyers in Europe and South America, often while the schooner was at sea, so that she received orders at Pernambuco or Gibraltar telling her where she was to discharge.

The ships took salt or wine or general cargoes over to Newfoundland, depending upon where they began their journey. At the fish ports the cargoes had to be loaded with care, those for the hot South American ports being packed in drums, while the Mediterranean ones were carried in bulk. Basil Lubbock in *The Last of the Windjammers* describes the method of dunnaging. 'First of all "longering" or "longhirst" (lengths of small trees) was laid on the floors; then spruce brushwood to the depth of six inches in the bottom and nine inches in the bilges. Lastly ranes or rinds (strips of bark) came next to the fish to preserve it from dampness.' While loading, the schooner, whose visit might be the event of the year for the settlement at an obscure outport, was often dressed (Plate 16) and the crew were generously entertained in the village. The cargo was reckoned in hundredweights, 'quintals' as they are called by trade custom.

To carry these bulk cargoes, the schooners had to be in the very best condition and, as in the fruit business twenty years earlier, the merchants took up only highly classed vessels for the job. The trade was one of the most exacting there has ever been and very many of the schooners made only one passage in a season. Some put in two voyages, and a very few, notably some of John Stephens' vessels from Fowey, were continuously employed in the business at all seasons and did not regularly take

9. The American schooner *Alice S. Wentworth*

10. The American four-masted schooner *Agnes Manning*

11. The schooner *Troubadour*, built in Prince Edward Island in 1867

12. The *Alpha*, built near Truro in 1871, a typical West Country trading ketch

up the home trade, or other deep-water charters, in between Newfoundland voyages.

Portmadoc ships began to sail regularly in the Newfoundland trade in 1879. The 'jack barquentines', as they were locally called, *Venodocian* and *C. E. Spooner*, and the three-masted schooner *Frau Minna Petersen*, built with a view to employment in the phosphate trade from the West Indies, all in fact went almost at once into the Newfoundland trade and stayed in that business. These ships were large enough to take cargoes for South America and, too large for direct loading at the small Labrador ports, they took their fish on board at St John's. In 1879 thirty-four smaller schooners loaded in the creeks of Labrador. Two of these came from Portmadoc, the schooner *Finlaggen* came from Campbeltown and the rest were nearly all from the west of England. They loaded at havens like Punch Bowl, White Bear Island, Tub Harbour, Tunavick, Fishing Ships Harbour and Snug Harbour for Genoa, Lisbon, Valencia, Gibraltar, Leghorn, Queenstown, Zante, Plymouth, Exeter, Poole and Naples.

The west of England ships were sailing to Newfoundland in large numbers ten years earlier, and in 1870 over fifty loaded in Newfoundland and Labrador. A decade earlier many of them had been regularly carrying soft fruit. There was the whole Vittery fleet from Brixham including the *Susan Vittery* (Plate 13), the *Fruit Girl*, later owned by Bowring Brothers, and the *First Fruits* of Bridport, four ships from Bideford and five from Dartmouth. Fowey, like Portmadoc, was later in the trade but in 1870 the *Silver Stream* and two other Fowey schooners were already in the fleet.

In the records of charters, many of them from the late Mr Robert S. Munn of Harbour Grace, assembled by the late Mr Emrys Hughes of Portmadoc, the names of the same schooners appear again and again. The *Lizzie R. Wilce*, the little 'flat' *Snowflake* of Runcorn (Plate 19), the *Finlaggen*, the *Guiding Star* and the *Venodocian* traded into Harbour Grace right through the late 70s and early 80s. The *Venodocian* loaded in

D

Harbour Grace almost every year from 1882 until 1908, when she was sold away from Portmadoc, and the famous *Blodwen*, the first of the later Portmadoc schooners, probably did not miss a single season in Newfoundland throughout her life of twenty-five years. The *Cadwalader Jones* was in the Newfoundland trade for thirty-eight years. She was a small, handy ship and worked every port of Labrador. Robert Cock's brigantine the *Elizabeth Maclea* from Appledore, the *Antoinette* from Plymouth (Plate 16), the *Maude*, also one of Cock's ships, the *A. M. Fox* built in Appledore (Plate 40), and all the later Portmadoc-built schooners appear year after year.

The ketch *Progress* (Plate 45) sailed to Newfoundland for nineteen years, making four crossings each year. It is said that during this time she never lost a member of her crew and only once suffered serious damage—when she was hove-to for thirty days. On another occasion she is said to have made passing contact with an iceberg, and on yet another to have sailed from Newfoundland to the English coast in fourteen days.

An even more noteworthy ketch was the *Rosie*, launched by Robert Cock at Appledore in 1885 as a schooner, copper-fastened and sheathed. She began her life in the Atlantic trade under her builder's management. In 1894 she went ashore on the Labrador coast and the wreck was bought by Captain G. E. Dedwith, a very experienced schooner master of Portmadoc. For eighteen years she sailed twice each year across the North Atlantic. In 1912 the ship was sold to the Hudson's Bay Company and refitted as an auxiliary ketch. She then traded up the Labrador coast for many years and was not again sold until the 20s, when she was put to work in home waters. In 1945, I saw her hull still lying on the tideline of a creek off Milford Haven.

The schooner *William Pritchard* (Plate 18) was owned in Portmadoc from 1903 to 1916 and during that period she crossed the Atlantic twenty-eight times. The name of the little schooner *Isabella*, belonging to John Stephens of Fowey, also appears consistently in voyage records for year after year. There follows a summarised account of her work for the ten years from 1894.

1894 Left Par in July for Newfoundland, where she arrived on 9 August. Left Newfoundland on 10 September for Oporto; thence proceeded to Rouen. Returned to Par in November.

1895 In British waters.

1896 Left Par in March for Cadiz; thence proceeded to Newfoundland and back to Oporto. Made two further round trips from Oporto to Newfoundland. Returned to UK for the winter.

1897 Left Newport on 8 May for Oporto, thence to Carthagena; left Carthagena on 15 December for Bristol, calling at Gibraltar.

1898 At Bristol in January. Left Newport on 21 May for Newfoundland, then made two trips between Newfoundland and Figueira.

1899 Arrived at Mevagissey from Figueira on 13 March. Left Fowey on 10 May for Newfoundland where she arrived on 7 June. Made two further trips between Newfoundland and Oporto, then proceeded to Par where she arrived on 30 November.

1900 Left Par on 24 April for Figueira, where she arrived on 30 April. Made three trips between Portuguese ports and Newfoundland and returned to Par on 16 December.

1901 Arrived at Cadiz on 4 May. Made three trips between Portuguese ports and Newfoundland.

1902 Returned to Fowey early in January. Arrived Cadiz on 17 April. Made two trips between Portuguese ports and Newfoundland and returned to Fowey on 10 November.

1903 Arrived Cadiz on 18 April. Made three trips between Portuguese ports and Newfoundland.

1904 Returned to Portugal from Newfoundland early in February, and arrived back at Fowey on 21 March. Proceeded to Newfoundland, thence to Oporto where she arrived on 28 July. Proceeded again to Newfoundland, thence to Carthagena, where she arrived on 29 October. Arrived Bristol 31 December.

The fastest crossing made by a Portmadoc vessel was ten days from Newfoundland to Oporto by the Kingsbridge-built *Cariad*. The fastest passage of all was perhaps that of the brigantine *Belle*, owned by the Munn family, which, it was claimed by J. S. Munn, sailed from Harbour Grace on a Wednesday in

1855 and arrived in Lisbon the following Wednesday. The performances of later ships were more consistent. Most of the later Portmadoc schooners sailed from the Newfoundland coast to Gibraltar in less than fourteen days at one time or another.

All the fast passages were from west to east, the same ships sometimes taking months to cross in the opposite direction. So mercilessly persistent are the autumn westerlies that many schooners setting out on a coastwise passage from Newfoundland to Labrador found themselves in European waters. This happened more than once in the period between the world wars. In 1934 one small schooner laden with cargo and passengers, including women, and bound from port to port in Newfoundland, was next reported some weeks later, all well, in Tobermory Bay. In 1890 the schooner *Rescue* entered Swansea fifty-five days out from Sydney, Nova Scotia, with a cargo of coal intended for Harbour Grace.

As far as the small British schooners were concerned, the trade was at its greatest between 1890 and 1910. In those years it employed large numbers of vessels and almost every deep-sea schooner of the later period carried fish at one time or another. The majority made at least one North Atlantic passage in each season, although of course they carried very many other cargoes as well. Under the stimulus of this exacting trade the British merchant schooner developed to its best in the vessels designed and built specifically for the Western Ocean trade at Portmadoc between 1891—when the first of them, the *Blodwen*, was launched—and 1913, when the last ship left the ways there. These ships, usually called the 'Western Ocean Yachts' by contemporary seamen, were the product of a conscious attempt by Portmadoc shipowners and builders to design and produce an ideal small merchant sailing ship to trade continuously under all conditions on deep water. The *Blodwen* justified their ideas by sailing from Indian Tickle, Labrador, to Patras in Greece in twenty-two days.

They were lovely ships. The grace of their hulls and the balance of their tall spars gave them a beauty, both under way and lying

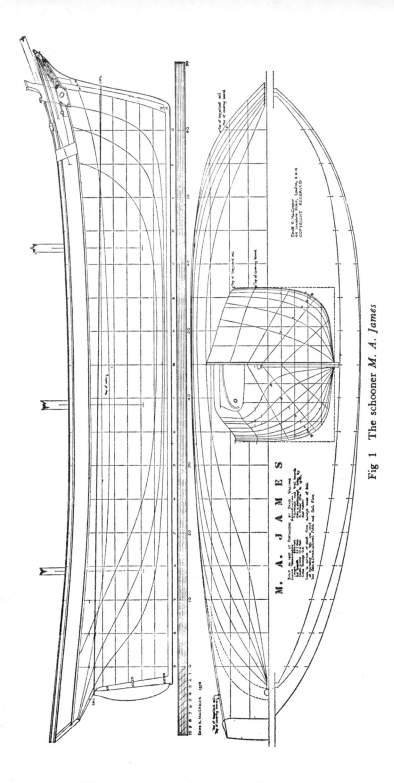

Fig 1   The schooner *M. A. James*

to an anchor, not exceeded in all the history of sailing vessels. They soon became famous and shipbuilders elsewhere on the coast, notably at Appledore, launched vessels of similar type. The *Katie* (Plate 39) whose building will be described in Chapter 5 was one of these. A list of these later Portmadoc schooners appears at Appendix 1 to Volume 2.

These ships were three-masted schooners with double topsails and a standing topgallant sail on the fore (Plate 18). They were very similar in appearance, dimensions, rigging plan and quality, being very heavily rigged with tall topmasts, very square yards, long heavy crosstrees, long bowsprit and sometimes a fitted jib-boom. Each vessel had a sloping transom at the end of her counter and their stem timbers were notably heavy and thick. Including vessels of this type built under Portmadoc influence at other ports, there were only about fifty of them in all.

None had very long lives and the last to survive was the *M. A. James* (Plate 17) which was still afloat as a hulk in the Torridge river in 1948. The lines reproduced in this book (Figs 1, 2, and 3) were drawn from measurements taken on the vessel as she lay on the hard at that time. They show a highly developed and very beautiful schooner, notable for her fine run and the way in which relatively shallow draught has been combined with easy curves, and capacity with a sharp, well balanced hull. Although smaller than some of the Western Ocean Yachts, the *M. A. James* was larger than the *Blodwen* and her form may be taken as typical of these last and most successful British small, ocean-going, merchant sailing ships.

The Newfoundland trade to the Mediterranean declined after the first decade of the present century so far as schooners from the United Kingdom were concerned. The United Kingdom trade itself had ended at an earlier date, the last cargoes for Liverpool being carried in the schooners *C. E. Spooner* and *Antoinette* in 1908. Bristol had a last cargo just before the first world war. Until 1910 schooners were being launched at the rate of two and three a year both at Portmadoc and at Appledore, and other ports were also building on a small scale. But

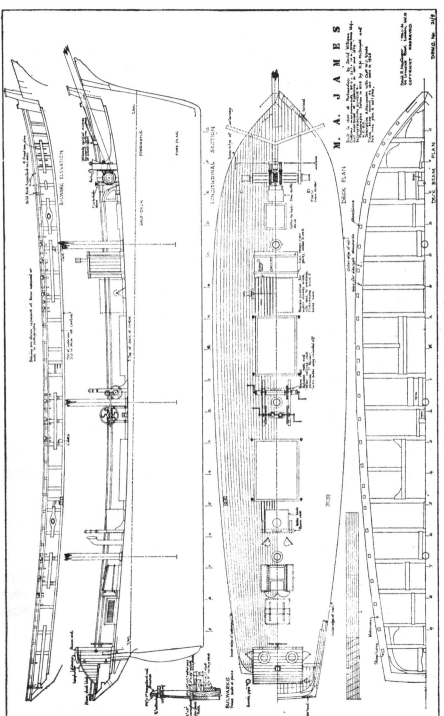

Fig 2 The schooner *M. A. James*

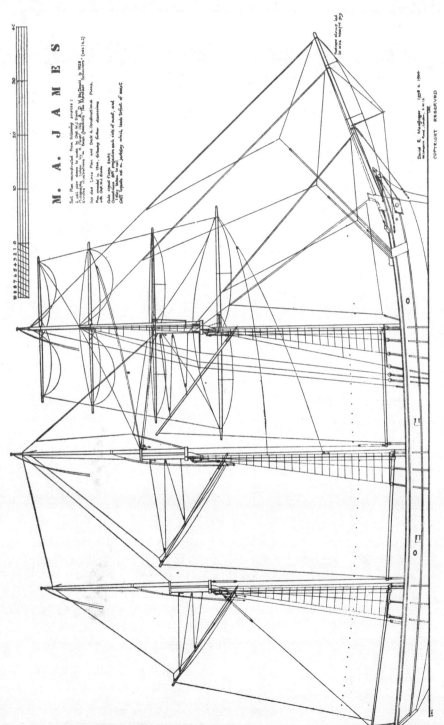

M. A. JAMES

Sail Plan reconstructed from following sources:
A sail plan drawn to scale, by Capt. W.J. Slade
(Formerly Master of the 'M.A. James') in 1958
Various illustrations in "The Merchant Schooners" (vols 1 & 2)

Not also Lines Plan and Deck & Construction Plans.
Plan amended in 1964, following further discussions
with Capt. W.J. Slade.

Code signal (Capt. W.J. Slade) R.H.P.C.
Construction: gaff proportion each side of mast, and
7-Way Tables, to rail.
Gaff topsails set on jackstay which leads behind of mast

David R. MacGregor 1958 & 1964
Westminster School London S.W.12.

Fig 3   The schooner *M. A. James*

after 1910 very few small sailing vessels were built. The last schooner was launched at Appledore in 1912, and even she had been laid down some time before. Portmadoc ceased a year later, and the last schooner of all was built at Arklow in 1921. The reasons for the contraction of the home trade will be discussed in the last chapter of Volume 2 in this history; the general deep-sea trades had, of course, been giving fewer and fewer opportunities to small vessels for many years as the scale of industry, and with it the size of cargoes, increased. Indeed by the first world war the deep-sea schooners were largely engaged in the Western Ocean and associated trades. Many of them were lost during the first world war, including ten ships of John Stephens' fleet alone and at least that number of the later Portmadoc schooners. After the war, although the trade continued to exist, its prospects were not sufficient to attract fresh capital into building new schooners in this country. Moreover, it would not have been possible to support a Newfoundland trade in isolation. In its years of prosperity the business was complementary to the home trade and was the peak of the pyramid of enterprise of the coastal districts. It depended upon the existence of a virile and enterprising seafaring and shipowning community in the small ports of England and Wales, a community which it could not in the end support alone.

The very last British schooner in the Newfoundland trade was the *Lady St Johns*, which, as mentioned in the previous chapter, continued to sail the North Atlantic until the middle of 1930. As many schooners crossed in each of these later years as in the days of the Western Ocean Yachts, but they were ships owned in Nova Scotia, in Newfoundland itself and in Denmark. In the middle of 1928 there were over forty such ships on their way across the Atlantic together. In 1939, I watched a small Danish two-masted schooner set out from Bristol to load salt cod at Black Tickle, Labrador. It was not until the end of the second world war that the work of small schooners in the North Atlantic came to an end, and, indeed, occasional fixtures of modern Danish and Portuguese schooners were still being made in 1950.

As the years went by, the passages of schooners in the Atlantic trade became faster and more regular. The later Canadian and Danish schooners, bigger ships than their United Kingdom predecessors, consistently sailed wonderfully well. The Canadian schooners—sharp-hulled vessels, rigged without standing square sails—were almost all built of softwoods in Nova Scotia in the first seven years after the first world war. The *Nellie T. Walters*, 175 tons gross, crossed the Atlantic twice each year from 1922 to 1927 and only once took more than thirty days in either direction. The *General Wood* made four successive westward passages in thirty-one days and less. An examination of successive voyages of four or five ships, the *General Trenchard*, the *Emily H. Patten*, the *Enid E. Legge*, the *Ria* and the *Joan McKay* in the middle 1920s shows that the longest passage, east and west, was forty-three days, the average easterly passage twenty-five days and the average westerly twenty-nine. These were all comparatively large ships, but small schooners of the size of the British ships did almost as well. The *Bastian*, a pretty ship of about 100 tons gross, which sailed until the second world war, made over five years eastward passages of an average length of twenty-four days. A little schooner called the *Dauntless* of seventy-eight tons made a twenty-nine day eastward passage as late as 1925.

The Danish schooners did no worse in the trade. They were smaller than the Canadian ships and could be compared with the later Portmadoc and Appledore schooners in size, but they were of the fuller and more powerful Danish hull form. Their design advantages are shown not only by their performance in relation to size but by their small losses, and from this point of view they were indeed the most successful of all the Atlantic schooners. The *Energi* made an eighteen day westward passage in 1922 and in 1925 was only thirty-one days from Marstal to St John's. The *Haabet* sailed from Burgeo to Oporto in twenty-three days in 1925. The *N. E. Schmidt* in 1926 sailed from Iceland to St John's in thirteen days. The average eastward passage for Danish schooners in 1928 was seventeen days, for the westward passage twenty-five. Many of these Danish schooners were still afloat and on deep water in 1950, including the little *Start* which, in 1926, made an eastward passage of eighteen days.

The *Lady St Johns*, the last of the remarkable series of fine-hulled schooners which W. Date launched at Kingsbridge in Devon in the 1890s, and the last of the United Kingdom based schooners, deserves some record of her later passages. Between 1924 and 1926 she made five easterly passages of average twenty-nine days including one from St John's to Oporto of only fourteen days. In 1927 she was twenty-seven days westward and in 1928 her three eastward passages averaged eighteen and a half days. She was lost without trace shortly after her sale to French owners in 1930. The *Lady St Johns* was the last British sailing vessel in a sailing vessel trade which had continued uninterrupted for four and a half centuries.

The high standard of the passages of these later ships derived from several causes. Their cargo was light and bulky and when fully laden they still had good freeboard. They had the low, simple, sail plan of the schooner and suffered little in gales that crippled larger more heavily square-rigged ships. They were fast to windward, and the later Canadian and the Danish schooners were of very good hull design. Their crews had a kind of parochial team spirit. They came from the same small seaport on the west coast of England, or in Nova Scotia, or in the southern islands of Denmark. They were of necessity good seamen, all concerned with the financial success of their voyages. They were small-ship seamen born and bred, each potentially a schooner master and owner, much better material than the big sailing ships of the later period could employ. Their masters were shareholders in the ships in which they sailed. It is not surprising that the later sailing records in this historic trade are so good.

CHAPTER FOUR

THE SHAPE OF THE SCHOONERS

FOR lack of such detailed evidence as would be provided by long series of half models or drafts of identified vessels, it is even more difficult to write with any degree of certainty about the history of the shapes of the hulls of British schooners than it is about other classes of merchant ships. But the hulls of schooners built after 1850 and which were sailing in the present century provide a good deal of evidence, as do the memories of those who were intimately concerned with them as a means of livelihood. On the basis of this evidence some general statements can be made, at least about the schooners of south-western and western Britain.

On the evidence of some of the best examples, the *Rhoda Mary* (Plate 31 and Fig 9, Volume 2), the *Katie Cluett*, the *Sunshine*, the *Ocean Swell*, the *Alpha* (Plate 12) and *Ulelia*, vessels built by different builders in different parts of the county, Cornish schooners tended to have certain similar characteristics. They were flat sheered. They carried such flat floors as they had well forward and they were very wide across the shoulders, that is across the fore-rigging where the beam was at its greatest. They tapered aft, with small bottoms and few flat floors. Thus they were described by seamen as having a 'gurnet's head and a mackerel's tail'. They were usually very deep and required a lot of ballast. They were fast and beautifully shaped and, because of their wide shoulders and flat floors forward, they would mount a sea very easily and thus were good sea boats apart from a tendency to slam their long counters down on to the water. They seemed to be designed for speed and sailing qualities even at the cost of earning power. They were fine ships to carry small cargoes for high freights on deep water and perhaps the hull form grew from the requirements of the Mediterranean trade, for they were a relatively poor economic proposition in the home trade. The drawings of the *Rhoda Mary* in Volume 2 of this history show a particularly fine example of the Cornish type.

Brixham vessels, also influenced by deep-water tradition, did not have the broad shoulders of the Cornish schooners. The *Susan Vittery* (Plate 13), which will be referred to many times in these volumes, carried her maximum beam further aft and did not have her flat floors far forward like the Cornish ships. Brixham vessels' bows were sharp, as opposed to the full bows of the Cornish schooners, but they were not hollow. Douglas Bennet wrote of the *Susan Vittery* in which he served as a seaman during her last years on the coast :

> She was low and stumpy in her rig compared with the tall top-gallant yard fishboxes, but she still needed about forty tons of ballast to sail with, she took water aboard through her hawse pipes while her lee scuppers were still dry, and no amount of enthusiastic application of hot pokers could keep it from the bunks below, you could stand on the ceiling of the hold under the main hatch only, elsewhere you could stand with one foot on top of the keelson and one on the ceiling, she must have been a regular submarine on the Newfoundland run, and she could still have given a very good account of herself had not her skipper's advancing years and the same with regard to her gear prevented her from being shoved very hard.

Fig 4 shows another type of South Devon-built schooner, a vessel designed at the yard of William Date of Kingsbridge. Vessels built at this yard, many of them for the Newfoundland trade, were differently shaped again. The *Lady St Johns* was built at Kingsbridge, as were the ketch *Progress*, and the schooners *My Lady, Little Wonder, Little Mystery* and *Little Gem*. These schooners were narrow and straight-sided and inclined to be thick in the run. They could not carry their canvas in heavy weather and were in consequence slower than the Cornish-built schooners. They were hard to steer because they dragged the water along with them, but they could carry more cargo than the Cornish ships.

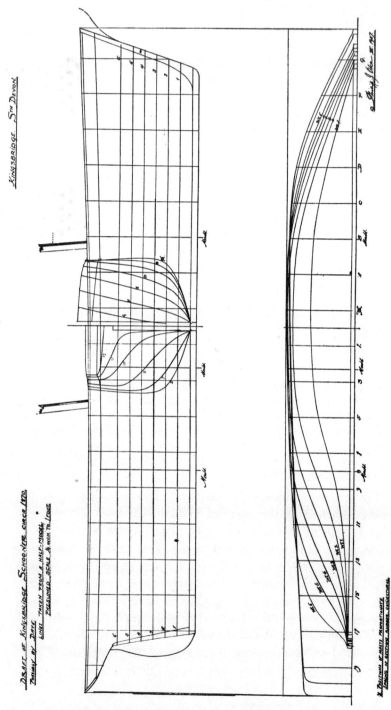

KINGSBRIDGE. S^TH DEVON

DRAFT OF KINGSBRIDGE SCHOONER circa 1870
TAKEN BY DATE TAKEN FROM A HALF-MODEL
LINES TAKEN FROM A HALF-MODEL
FORESHIP SCALE ¼ INCH TO 1 FOOT

Fig 4   Lines of a schooner built at Kingsbridge *circa* 1870

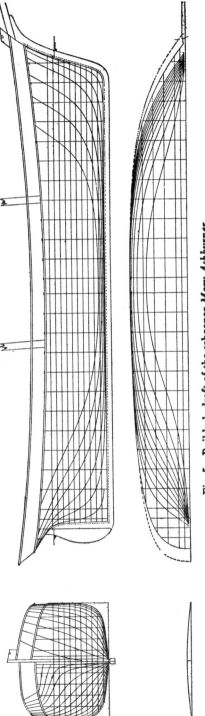

Fig 5 Builder's draft of the schooner *Mary Ashburner*

Of North Devon-built ships, Westacott of Barnstaple in the 1870s and 80s tended to build hollow-bowed vessels. The *Heather Bell*, the *Annie Christian* and the *Emma Louise* were sharp in the entrance, the first fine in the run, the other two fuller. The schooners built by the Cock family at Appledore a few years later, and the vessels launched before and after the *Katie*, whose construction will be described in detail in the next chapter, carried their flat floors far forward, but not so far as the Cornish ships had done thirty years before. They had more flats than the Cornish ships, and they carried more cargo and were shallower and better able to take the ground. The later Portmadoc schooners, which the Appledore vessels somewhat resembled, were a class to themselves. They had big shoulders, were high in the floors in the bow and in the stern, but had long flat sections amidships which gave them cargo-carrying ability. They had more sheer than the Cornish ships had had. From the billboard forward they rose suddenly to the massive knightheads, which gave them a high bow for going over a sea. The lines of the *M. A. James* in Fig 1 show this shape very well.

Despite the differences between them, all these vessels of the southern part of western Britain, from the *Rhoda Mary* built in Cornwall in 1868 to the *Gestiana* built at Portmadoc in 1913, were similar in being relatively deep and of complex shape with a limited number of flat floors. They were designed for deep water, or at least in a tradition influenced by ocean sailing. Shallow-draught sailing vessels were built, but not in any great numbers. But on the Dee and north to the Clyde a very different general type of vessel developed, though again by no means to the exclusion of other types. She was shallower than the schooners of the south-west and had many more flat floors. In her more developed forms, the *Kathleen & May* and the *Mary Ashburner* (Fig 5) she had an elliptical counter, but the great majority had a pointed stern with none of the vessel carried beyond the stern-post or at the most a tiny turned-up counter which was little more than an extension of the bulwarks (Fig 6, Plate 19).

This type of schooner may have developed from the river

13.   The three-masted schooner *Susan Vittery*, later named *Brooklands*, built at Brixham in 1859

14.   *Frau Minna Petersen*, later named *Jane Banks*, the pioneer three-masted schooner of Portmadoc

15. Fish drying on flakes on the shores of a small Newfoundland harbour

16. The *Antoinette*, built at Plymouth in 1905 and the *Ruby*, a local schooner, hauled out at Harbour Grace

barges of the Mersey and the Weaver through sea-going sloops into schooners as the demand for more and larger vessels developed in the second half of the nineteenth century. The characteristic stern can be seen in the big Lake Windermere boat believed to have been built at Workington in the late eighteenth century and preserved at Bowness by Mr George Pattinson. There were many variations on the basic pattern, but these schooners of the north-west coast of England tended to a form which had great advantages in the home trade. The hull form had practically no drag and, consequently, the vessel could be laid on the ground anywhere without much list. On average, they drew 9 ft 6 in forward and 10 ft or so aft. For example, the *Millom Castle*, built at Ulverston in 1871, drew 10 ft 6 in aft and 9 ft 6 in forward. The Plymouth-built ketch *Haldon*, by way of contrast, drew 9 ft forward and 11 ft aft. The *Millom Castle* could be laid alongside a jetty and there was hardly any necessity to watch the fenders. West Country vessels with a deep heel took the ground aft as the tide ebbed and the bow tended to move off while it was still afloat, thus putting all the weight on the after fenders, perhaps damaging the bulwarks and tending to twist and strain the vessel. This behaviour was a product of the sharp hull, 'high in the floors', as the Appledore expression was. North Country schooners tended to be of shallow draught, and their full-bodied hulls enabled most of them to sail without ballast, a very great advantage indeed. They were also very handy under sail, both light and loaded. For example, the *Millom Castle* once beat up through the shutes in the river Severn without ballast and with three rolls in her mainsail and never once missed stays. They were good sea boats. There was no weight abaft of the sternpost, and no counter to slam down on the sea. They were cheap to build and economical to maintain and they were immensely strong, a quality which followed partly from the building traditions of the Lancashire and Cumberland coasts and partly from their relatively simple shape. The *Millom Castle*, for instance, is still in existence, though she is nearly one hundred years old.

E

The North Country schooners were slower than the West Country ships and they tended, because of their flat bottoms, to throw the bilge water into the hold. But they were not always slow, nor were they confined to the home trade. The *Snowflake* of Runcorn (Plate 19) a vessel of North Country type, spent years in the Newfoundland trade, and so did the *Gleaner*, which is credited with a passage of thirteen days from Harbour Grace to Bristol.

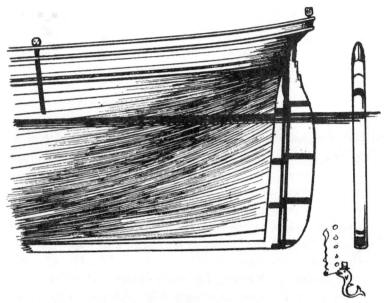

Fig 6   Stern and rudder of a schooner built at Barrow

The North Country schooners were seen at their best in the ships built at Barrow, especially those launched by the Ashburner family, and at Ulverston. In Appledore, these ships were dubbed 'Barrow flats'. The pointed stern of a Barrow flat was one of the most distinctive of British schooner sterns, but you could often tell a schooner's birthplace by her hind end for there were well-marked shapes of stern in many of the shipbuilding districts of Britain. The Cornish stern was a very steeply sloping transom, growing from the vessel's after timbers. This shows in the drafts of the *Rhoda Mary* and the *Hobah* later in these volumes. Portmadoc vessels had a transom nearer to the vertical on a short counter as did some Devon-built ships (Plate 20). Schooners built on the east coast of Scotland showed Scandinavian influence in their heavy flat transoms (Fig 7). Some

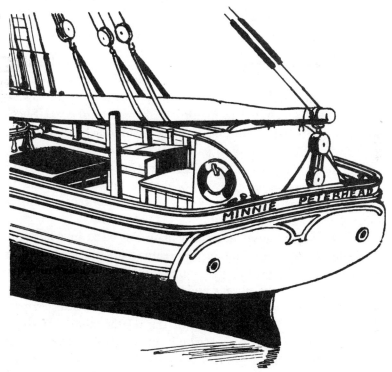

Fig 7   Stern of a schooner built on the east coast of Scotland

schooners built at Appledore, and some ketches built at Falmouth and at Bridgwater, had long elliptical counter-sterns of great beauty (Plate 21). Schooners built at Connah's Quay also had a very handsome elliptical counter (Plate 22). Ketches built at Castle Pill had the Milford stern, a miniature cruiser stern. Some very small ketches had cocked-up miniature counters, which had the appearance of the hind feathers of a goose and were in consequence known in Appledore as 'guze arsed'. Prince Edward Island-built schooners were noted for their curved raking stems, flaring bows and big square transom counters making them broad in the stern. They were handsome, powerful ships and they tended to be sharper than their British-built contemporaries, with more rise of floor and at the same time more beam.

THE SPEED OF THE SCHOONERS

It is very difficult to compare the performance of small sailing ships, and all such comparisons are doubtful. The qualities required of ships in different trades were so dissimilar that to speak of one as being better than another is almost meaningless. Sheer speed under ideal conditions was never of much importance. Speed was only important in particular trades at particular times, and standards of speed varied greatly with the capacity and economy of operation expected of a ship. Speed in relation to her direct competitors was, however, very often an economic asset much prized in a ship.

In large ships, speed depended upon the trade in which the ship was sailing, upon luck of the weather, upon her trim, upon the state of her gear, upon the quality of the crew and perhaps most of all upon the master and mates. The final and the only constant factors were her hull form and sail plan. Selected passages therefore give no measure of the relative ability of ships, even if ability is held to rest simply in speed of sailing. If this is true of large sailing ships it is doubly true of small ones. To make the most of them required more skill in the master. The small crews suffered much more from the defects of the one man who, literally, did not pull his weight. They were much more likely to be held up by bad weather than bigger ships. The condition of their gear—particularly on deep water—was even more important. As might be expected, therefore, the variations in performance, not only of different small sailing ships but of the same ship at different times, are even more marked than those of larger ships.

The passages of small craft were not watched with the care given to large ships. Lloyd's records are not so complete for the schooners as they are for the barques and full-rigged ships of the same period. There is, therefore, a lack of data upon which to base close comparison. As far as ships in the home trade are concerned, all arguments based on particular passage times are valueless, because tides played such an important part in passage making that the duration of a particular voyage could be doubled by a difference of an hour or two in sailing.

Conclusions about a small sailing ship's qualities must, therefore, be based on a review of her performance over a number of years in various trades with different masters and crews. In the absence of details of passages, a new method of comparing the abilities of ships has to be used. Acting therefore rather like a public opinion poll interrogator, I made a survey which was concerned with the speed of the schooners. I asked everybody I met who had been connected with the schooners and ketches, which ships they recollected as being the fastest over a period of years. This process of interrogation was carried on for about fifteen years, though interrupted by the second world war. The survey gained its value from the fact that the answers given were quite independent of one another and therefore gave a fairly reliable indication of the performance of the ships concerned on different parts of the coast at different times.

As far as schooners in the home trade were concerned, the result of this survey was surprisingly simple. Almost all the people questioned replied that the *Rhoda Mary* and the *Katie Cluett* were the two fastest schooners, considering their performance and reputation over a period of years, that they could remember. Close behind this redoubtable pair in the estimation of nearly all these old gentlemen came the schooners *Trevellas*, *Perseverance* and, if performance off the wind alone is considered, the *Result*. The first three of these fast schooners were built in Cornwall, the *Perseverance* in Lancashire and the *Result* in Northern Ireland to designs by a Barrow shipbuilder.

The results of this survey for ocean-going schooners were such as might be expected. The deep-water trading ships began and ended their voyages far from home and the duration of their passages was known only to those closely connected with them. The condition of the ship's gear and the quality of her command and management were the most important factors in passage making. Deep-water ships were therefore remembered not as individuals, but as groups and fleets, the members of which showed the same standards in these respects. Within the memory of men living in the 30s and 40s, the early Fowey schooners of the generation of the *Thetis*, John Stephens' schooners, and the 'Western Ocean Yachts' were always spoken of as the finest of deep-water ships. The names of few ocean-going schooners seem to have stuck in the minds of their contemporaries. John Stephens' *Isabella* is an exception and she was widely remembered.

DRAUGHT

As the small sailing ship had to compete harder for her cargoes she had to become shallower. She had to be able to enter the small harbours of Labrador, and to use the tidal havens of the United Kingdom as often and for as long as possible. The general tendency throughout the era of the merchant schooner was towards the building everywhere of shallower draught vessels. In some trades, shallow draught had always been required. The harbours of the east coast of England between the Humber and the Thames are shallow and to carry the trade to them special vessels were evolved, some of which (like the schooners *Zebrina* and *Friendship*) are described in E. J. March's book *Spritsail Barges of Thames and Medway*. The 'Smeed Barges', shallow-draught ships of several hundred tons, were barquentine- and schooner-rigged. A fleet of big, shallow, hard-bilged ships was built at Emsworth in Hampshire, including the ketch *Annie Florence* and the brigantine *Thorney Island*. There was even a flat-bottomed barque—the *Enterprise*—built by J. T. Crampton at Portsmouth for the coal trade.

Most of these ships had all the disadvantages of hard bilges not associated with V-bottom construction and it was not until later that shallow-draught round-bilged construction of the modern type came into fashion. Some of them had leeboards, though none to my knowledge had centreplates, and only one round-bilged ship of this type with a centreplate seems to have been launched. She was the *Fortuna* of Faversham, built by Fosters of Emsworth, a firm of advanced ideas who were later to bring the sailing fishing ship to its highest point of development in England.

On the North American coast, centreboard merchant sailing ships of all sizes were very common and most successful. Accounts of the *Fortuna* vary, but it seems likely she was a profitable vessel. It is not easy to see why the centreboarder was not developed in Britain. Conservatism and the hold of the traditional lee-board alone do not seem sufficient reasons. Schooner owners and masters with whom I have discussed the matter raise various objections of lack of strength, leaks around the case, difficulty of repairing the board, of painting inside the case, and so forth, none of which proved any hindrance to its development in the United States and Canada where it was used in thousands of schooners from vessels much smaller than the *Alice S. Wentworth* to five-masters. The real reason for the absence of the centre-board in English ships was, I think, that small ships trading in home waters must take the ground frequently, whereas American ships seldom had to. The centreboard case often jams, twists and strains in ships subject to regular grounding, especially with cargo, and this made the device uneconomic and even unsafe.

MASTERS' QUALIFICATIONS

The requirements specified by the various British Merchant Shipping Acts as to the qualifications necessary in the masters of ships of different sorts and sizes had an important effect on the development of the merchant schooners.

At the end of the nineteenth century, the Masters' Certificates issued by the Board of Trade were of three types :

(a) Ordinary Master—entitling the holder to go to sea as the

master of any vessel, steam or sailing, square-rigged or fore and aft.

(b) Master, fore and aft—entitling the holder to act as master of a fore-and-aft-rigged vessel, but not to act as a master in any case in which a certificate for a square-rigged vessel was required. Square-rigged vessels were listed as full-rigged ships, barques, brigs, barquentines and steamships carrying square sails.

(c) Master, steamship—entitling the holder to go to sea as the master of a foreign-going steamship only.

These certificates remained in use until 1 January, 1931, when the present system of certificates with their endorsements came into being.

Under the old system, the only way to get the first type of certificate was to have had wide experience of square-rigged ships. In the schooner ports by the end of the nineteenth century, such experience was becoming rare because the small square-rigged ship had been dropping out of use for more than twenty years. In consequence, the shipmasters of these ports mostly had the second kind of qualification—the fore and aft certaificate. Masters for schooners were not normally recruited from outside the district around a ship's home port, and the ships were very often built for a particular master. The schooner rig, therefore, tended to be self-perpetuating, in that once it had become popular it could not be replaced by an official square rig without employing strangers to help in the process.

This was certainly the reason for the development of the staysail schooners (the *Venodocian*, and the *C. E. Spooner*) at Portmadoc a decade before the topgallant schooners were introduced. It was one of the factors in the widespread use of the topgallant schooner at the last stage of the merchant schooner's development. This rig was the most efficient and economical developed for small ocean-going ships, but it is doubtful if it would have become so common so rapidly and have so completely replaced the barquentine in the waters around Britain if the Merchant Shipping Acts had not greatly helped it.

CHAPTER FIVE

THE BUILDING OF THE SCHOONERS

THE MOULD LOFT

AT Appledore in North Devon in the year 1903 a wooden three-masted schooner was being built by the Cock brothers in the Bell Inn yard. She was designed to be of some 120 tons gross register tonnage and was being built for Mr William Griffiths, master mariner, born at Llanbedr, near Harlech, and later to settle in Appledore for his home, and for Mr Robert Pritchard, shipowner, of Portmadoc, Caernarvonshire. These two intended that the schooner, which was going to be called *Katie*, should be employed in the Atlantic trade.

Once the building of a merchant schooner had been called for, the *Katie* was first conceived as a ship in the mind of James Cock, manager of the yard, who fulfilled also the function of 'moulder', as he was called in Appledore. Elsewhere the term 'loftsman' was used. He was the designer of the ships that were built there and it was his responsibility to ensure that, as the vessel grew on the slipway, she developed into a full-sized replica of the design that had been agreed upon for her. The loftsman was a responsible and respected member of the maritime community and it is said that in some parts of the east coast of England the two-foot folding rule showing from his breast pocket, which was his trade badge, gave him priority in the barber's shop and at the bar of the shipyard arms.

At the conception of the *Katie*, Mr Griffiths specified in broad terms the sort of vessel he wanted, speaking of her in terms of carrying power, or draught and length, of rig and of the sort of business he meant to do with her. James Cock thereupon began to make of this vessel a half model, a small image of one side of the proposed schooner, cut from stem to sternpost through from deck to keel. This half model was nearly always the first stage in the building of a merchant schooner and, when finished, it was shown to the future owner and modified in accordance with his ideas of what a schooner should be. Perhaps a fraction of an inch would be taken off here, she might be made a little fuller in the bilges, a little shallower astern. If the future owner had complete confidence in the moulder, or if the moulder was able to convince him of the qualities of the hull he had thus designed, the half model might not be changed at all. In the case of the *Katie*, it was probably changed only a little, for Cock's yard was already acquiring a reputation for building wooden ships of just this type and size, and a two-masted schooner only a foot and a quarter shorter and in all other respects very similar to the *Katie* had been launched only a year earlier. This schooner was called the *Madeleine* and was so like the *Katie*, and one or two others of the series of schooners which were built in the Bell Inn yard after her, that it is possible that they were built from the same half model.

This method of building straight from the half model was only possible when there were very well-established shipbuilding traditions. Nevertheless it was not very common for more than one schooner to be built from the same model, though it did happen from time to time, for the owners of these ships were individualists and each had his own ideas about the sort of vessel he required. Even in the rare case where many vessels were gathered together under the management of one man, he did not often commission the same yard to build him two ships in a short space of time to fulfil approximately the same requirements. But it did sometimes happen among the merchant schooners that, when a particular builder was known as the designer of a particular type of vessel, a shipowner commissioning a new schooner might ask that she be built as a replica of a fine ship recently launched. Or, in building for speculation, a yard might produce a ship to sell for its own account that was identical to one recently completed and already of good local repute. Paul Rogers, a great schooner builder at Carrickfergus in Northern Ireland, did this. We know that the Cock brothers did build more than one vessel from the same model later, for two schooners which followed the *Katie* two and three years later from the same slip, the *Rose* and the *Geisha*, were in dimensions identical to one another. At the request of her master and part owner, the *Rose* had two fewer flat floors than the *Geisha* and the *Katie*. In consequence her run was longer and she needed more ballast when sailing light.

At Cock's yard the half model was carved out from a block of wood with sharp gouges and chisels and it was, of course, a miniature of the finished vessel to scale to the outside of her frames inside the planking. The model was between three and four feet long. The block from which it was cut was itself constructed from layers of planking a half or three-quarters of an inch in thickness. Very probably these laminations would be of yellow pine, but if it was intended that the finished model should be kept for a record or for decoration, the alternate layers might be of some darker wood so that when polished they would show up the lines of the vessel. The planks were fastened together with wooden pins driven into holes drilled right through the whole, so that the finished block was as strong and could be carved as easily as a piece of the natural wood.

There was purpose in this system. When the half model was finished to the satisfaction of everybody who was concerned with the new vessel, the pins were knocked out so that the laminations of which the model was built fell apart. Each plank then represented a 'waterline' of the future vessel and from these scale waterline sections all the main measurements necessary for the moulding loft could be obtained. This method of building from a laminated half model was usual in North Devon and in other parts of the west coast but it was a comparatively sophisticated system and quite different methods were used in other parts of the United Kingdom. On the south-east coast, in some of the yards where the sailing barges were built, and in South Cornwall thirty years before (wooden schooners had long ceased to be built in South Cornwall when the *Katie* was laid down), ships were built from models made up of solid frame half sections cut from half to one and a half inch planking and fastened to a base plank cut to the schooner's profile. One solid half rib was used for every two or three frames of the future schooner and light stringers, called 'ribbands', of half or one inch batten were tacked along the ribs to give an idea of the shape and run of the planks on the finished vessel. These frame models were called bracket models.

These solid frame models seem to have tended to be built to a rather larger scale than the carved kind and one of the few that survive is about twelve feet long and eighteen inches thick at the deck level. Such models were much easier to make and alter than the carved kind, but they did not provide such complete information about the finished vessel, nor can they have formed so convenient a basis of work. At some yards, both types of model were used concurrently and sometimes, even, models of each type would be made in the course of development of the same vessel. Sometimes, also, special detail models of a ship's bows or counter would be cut from the solid for the information of shipwrights working on that particularly difficult part of the hull. Sometimes a full hull model would be cut into a number of slices, each representing a few feet of the vessel's hull and providing about those few feet the basic data required in the mould loft for the development of the finished schooner. Simon Jones of Portmadoc built the small barque *Pride of Wales* from a half model to a scale of eight feet to the inch. The model was mounted on a flat board and a saw cut was made at intervals of five to ten eights from the skin to the mounting board, through which cut the requisite measurements could be made. Where the curves of the hull were acute, forward and aft, the saw cuts were at more frequent intervals because the rapid changes in shape needed more complete measurement if they were to be conveyed accurately to the mould loft. All these methods and variations of them were used in the

United States and Canada and in Scandinavia. In Canada, schooners were sometimes built from solid block models from which half sections were obtained by bending soft wire around the model. Whatever method was used in modelling, the purpose was the same, to ease the conception and design of the vessel and to produce that design in such a form as to provide the basic data from which the full-sized vessel could be built.

The methods of design, that is, the principles upon which the half model was carved or built, were almost always entirely traditional in the case of the merchant schooners. No tank tests were made to give basic data under controlled conditions, and no mathematical formulas derived from such data were used to indicate the line of development of the various parts of the hull. Rather each model was a little different from the one that went before it, different in a way that might, under analysis in terms of the hydrodynamics of ship design or of seagoing experience, be better or worse. If there came back to the moulder evidence of his ship's behaviour at sea which confirmed the desirability of certain factors which had not been in his previous creations, then the novel quality he had given to that hull would be incorporated in many more, and be adopted by his successors so that it became part of the tradition of building so far as that particular type of vessel was concerned in that locality. Some moulders used the same half model all their lives, at least as the basis of every design, if not in literal fact. Some experimented and produced widely differing types of schooners in a short space of years. Others slowly evolved, benefiting from experience but adapting that experience in the service of the different types of vessel they wished to produce.

A few of these half models have survived, many more in North America than in Britain. Sometimes models were kept for decorative purposes; they were polished, mounted on base boards, and perhaps fitted with stump masts, deckhouses and bulwarks. A few builders kept their half models as a basis of comparison with future designs and, in time, formed considerable collections. But with most of the yards have gone the collection of models, discarded with the passing of unheeding generations, burned, or thrown away. Laminated models once split up in the normal process of their use were not often put together again; the bits, once they had been measured up, went as fuel for the mould-loft fire.

If few half models have survived, they are still numerous in comparison with the surviving drawings. I have heard of very few yards at which drawings were certainly used instead of a half model as the basis of design. It is certain that very few wooden merchant schooners were built from drawings. Indeed at no stage in their construction did scale drawings, or the detailed structural drawings which were used in the yards where large wooden ships were built, enter in at all, even in the very last days of schooner building in the first two decades of this century. At Cock's yard drawings, even blueprints, were in use at the time the *Katie* was under construction. Some of these still exist, but they relate to the building of barges and steamers and steel schooners in the Iron yard near the Bell Inn yard, by methods learned by one of the Cock brothers in an apprenticeship in a North Country steel shipbuilding yard.

The late Mr Emrys Hughes of Portmadoc could remember that David Williams and David Jones of that port built schooners from drawings, but it is not certain whether these were the scale drawings of design, or structural drawings used at a later stage. One sheer plan used in an Aberystwyth yard was still in existence some years ago. At only one yard is it certain that complete drawings, sheer plan, body plan and half breadth plan, were used always, and that the vessels were designed on paper in this fashion instead of in three dimensions on the half model. This was the yard of the Ashburners of Barrow. Here Richard Ashburner, one of the three brothers who ran the yard, was a trained naval architect and in designing his vessels he began, not with a half model cut from the solid, but with architects' drawings upon paper. Very fortunately, three of these sets of plans have been preserved. They show the *Result*, *Mary Ashburner* (Fig 5) and a vessel which is most probably the *William Ashburner*. The history of these ships will be discussed later. In original, the drawings are beautifully executed with the diagonals and waterlines drawn in coloured inks, and the ships that were built from them were beautiful, too.

Such was the quality of the vessels launched from this yard that a number of them survived until the 1950s. The Ashburners made half models sometimes, but, like the models made at shipyards nowadays, they were for decorative and record purposes. I have a decorative half model in my possession which was made by the late Mr Harold Underhill from the lines of the *Mary Ashburner* and it is a source of constant pleasure.

But however the design of the vessel began, whether it was on paper or in the half model, the next stage in her construction was the same, the making of full-scale drawings, starting with the half-breadth plan, on the vast dark floor of the mould loft. This mould-loft floor—which, in Cock's yard was in existence until the building was burned down in 1948—was usually situated as a second storey above a blacksmith's shop or a timber store, and it was here that the true shape of the full-sized schooner first became apparent.

A series of lines was drawn across the deck of the half model, evenly and widely spaced amidships, closer together at bow and stern. An exactly corresponding series was drawn on the second lamination of the model and on each of them in turn. If the model was of the solid frame variety, it was merely a matter of measuring the breadth of each of the templates at deck level and then taking a series of breadth measurements at the same distances from the rabbet of the keel up each of the solid frames.

Along the mould-loft floor was drawn a chalk line of the length of the finished vessel, or of a definite portion of its length if (as was usually the case) the loft was too small for the plan to be drawn out in its entirety. From this chalk line, other lines were drawn out at right angles, each of a length standing in relation to the length of the central line as did one of the lines on the deck of the half model to the length of that model. Thus the basis of a full-scale deck plan was produced on the floor. Then the loftsman, who was in charge of these operations, took a long, flexible batten and placed its head at the head of the central chalk line, which represented the mid-deck length of the schooner. Next, he bent the batten to lie along the floor with its inner edge just touching the ends of the widths and drew along it in chalk, thus producing the outer line of the schooner at deck level. He relied upon the natural curve taken up by the batten under stress to give him a line natural and suited to its function, to be the shape of a vessel to make its way through the sea. Where, at bow and stern, the shape changed more rapidly and the batten had to be forced to meet a greater number of breadth lines in a shorter length, the reliance on its curve was less. Amidships, where a long easy flow of line was required, the final shape of the vessel was that of the curve taken up by a long timber held at a few points under stress.

The natural curve of the batten was an important factor in the design of small wooden ships. Not at Cock's yard, but at some yards a generation or so earlier, moulders sometimes worked without a half-model, working out their breadths on the floor as they went along. They relied upon their intimate knowledge of ships they had worked on during long years of apprenticeship and experience for the outlines of their plan, and upon the curves of their battens for the details of the half-breadth shape. It is hard for the modern shipbuilder to believe, but nevertheless a fact that in such yards the mould loft was sometimes a stretch of sandy and sheltered beach near the building slip, and the lines drawn would be furrows made by walking backwards drawing a sharp stick through the sand.

When the loftsman had obtained his deck plan he measured off along each of his widths distances corresponding in scale to the widths of the second layer of the laminated model, or the second series of measurements he had made on the solid frames. These widths he joined up likewise, with curves drawn along the length of the strained batten. In this way, measuring off on his chalk widths for each of the measurements he had made on the model, or scaling up his drawn plans in exactly the same

17.   The *M. A. James* after conversion to a motor schooner

18.   The *William Pritchard*, built at Portmadoc in 1903, lying deep laden in Cumberland Basin, Bristol. She is an excellent example of a later Atlantic schooner

19. The *Snowflake*, built at Runcorn in 1880, drying her sails in Mevagissey

way, the moulder produced on the floor of his loft a full-scale, half-breadth plan of the schooner in which the irregularities and imperfections not perceptible in the miniature had been ironed out. His next job, and the function which gave him his name in Appledore, was to develop the shape of his frames.

He knew how many frames there should be and how they should be spaced, because he knew from experience what strengths were needed to meet the strains to which this vessel would be subject. He also knew the timbers that were to go into her construction, the sort of wood and the quality of the particular sample concerned. Along the waterlines of his half-breadth plan, therefore, he marked off the positions of the centres of the frames; perhaps the space between the frames would be eight inches, perhaps only six. In the *Katie*, the frames were of eight-inch square timber at deck level, so their centres were sixteen inches apart along the centre line of the vessel. The moulder marked off his frame breadths for each frame for each of the waterlines of his half-breadth plan and the measurement he took was that of the broader of the two outer edges of the frame, since that length represented the greatest breadth of the frame later, when its fore or after edge—depending upon whether it be a frame of the bow or of the stern of the vessel—was bevelled away to take the run of the planking.

On the mould-loft floor the moulder laid off each of these frame breadths for each waterline from a centre line which now represented the vertical centre of the vessel from mid-keel to mid-deck. In this way he produced on his floor in chalk the profile of each half frame in turn, the shape in outline of each of the eighty or so of the frames of the finished schooner. He could not always have eighty such drawings on the mould-loft floor at once, as well as the half-breadth plan from which he was working, but this was not necessary and the frame drawings would be made in batches of a few at a time, almost always on top of one another, so that the finished drawing was a sort of full-sized body plan of a part of the vessel.

F

DIFFERENCES IN BUILDING METHODS

These were the methods used in Cock's yard at Appledore while the *Katie* was being built as they were described to me between thirty and forty years later by men who worked at the building. But every district in Britain differed in the details of its building methods and what was customary at one yard was not recognised as good practice in others near by. Sometimes a moulder at work on the loft floor began his waterlines with the deck line and sometimes with the lowest waterline of all. At the yard of J. & W. B. Harvey at Littlehampton (Plate 23) and many others, diagonals and buttock lines were used extensively in the fairing up of the hull drawing and the bevels were obtained from diagonals. In contrast, in some West Country yards vessels were built with square frames which were adzed to shape after the ships were fully framed up on the slipway by men who had probably never heard of diagonals. The methods used at Harvey's yard were relatively sophisticated. A shipwright who had worked there wrote of the mould loft process as follows :

Many people hear of bow and buttock lines without knowledge of their prime purpose in the mould loft, which is to reveal any unfairness of shape which may still be there, however carefully the half model has been made, and the level, or so-called water-lines, transferred to the floor. The frame stations were all marked on the several beams of the model, which was screwed together and therefore easily detachable. Half an inch to the foot was the scale commonly used, so everything was magnified twenty-four times in the laying off and previously imperceptible irregularities became very obvious.

All the waterlines were dealt with in turn from the lowest to the deck line. All having been faired, attention was directed to the body plan. Here the level lines were straight, and being set off at the required intervals, one only had to mark the intersections of the square stations with the curved level lines in half breadth in order to obtain the contours of the cross sections. Now, although every care had been taken to fair the curves of the level lines, when the spline was pinned into place in the body plan unsuspected deformities were revealed which had to be corrected by alteration at the half breadth at corresponding points. Frequent readjustments and obliterations were necessary. This was called 'fairing the body' and gave an indication of the frame shapes.

By this time the mould-loft floor was a maze of intricate lines because we used to superimpose the after part of the half breadth on top of the fore part and put the two halves of the body plan on top of one another over all so as to save space.

Now the diagonals were put in. They gave the true bevel of the frames, more or less, and from them the bevel for the sawyers was obtained. They appeared as straight lines diagonally in the body and as curved lines both in the sheer and half breadth, where they used to be distinguished by coloured chalks and, in order to avoid having to tamper with them after having run them in, we applied a further test of fairness by means of bow and buttock lines. If any unsightly hollows or bulges were discovered, the needful alterations had to be made to the half breadth and body plans, however perfect they had seemed to be, and only when they were completed were the diagonals put on the floor.

We depended on the buttocks a great deal for showing us if any awkward curves had developed in the shape of the vessel. Builders who did not use buttock lines often made bad mistakes, although their laying off was perfect. The *Waterwitch* was a good example of this, and her after body contained bad kinks in the buttock lines.

We had to be especially careful in the case of shallow and beamy ships with any pretensions to symmetry, because both the contours and bevellings changed so steeply. In order to modify the acuteness of the bevels in the vessel's ends, it was the practice to cant the frames at bow and stern. This threw their heads away from the last squarely-cut frame and brought their heels into bevelled contact with the deadwoods above the keel.

These more sophisticated methods were used by schooner builders in Denmark. Danish builders varied amongst themselves and in detail from the English yards, but on the whole the tradition they carried on was more developed than that of the small British shipyards. They began their ships, not with half models but with line drawings on paper, sheer, half breadth and body plan, beautifully finished, with diagonals and buttocks picked out in coloured inks. Even in the nineteenth century, when drawings of this kind were almost unknown in small British schooner building yards, the Danes seem to have worked from them and some of the older yards still in existence have collections of drawings covering most, if not all, the ships built there. For this reason the information available about Danish schooners and their evolution is far more complete than is the case with ships from the United Kingdom. Danish builders made half models, but they were usually of the decorative kind and often made after the ship was launched. The homes of yard managers are sometimes filled with beautiful half models of this sort.

Mould lofts seem to have been used relatively little by builders of schooners in North America. The custom instead was to erect a platform of softwood planks on trestles immediately in front of the stem timbers of the growing vessel. On this platform—the scrieve board—the frame shapes were scored out with steel points one after another, so that the complete body plan was scratched out when the last frame had been erected. The frames themselves were laid on this platform as they were made up. Often they were not bevelled until they had been erected. Often, too, the scrieve board was used in conjunction with the loft floor as a source of ready direct reference by the craftsman building the ship. To complicate the issue, at Appledore the local dialect form of the term scrieve board, 'screed board', was sometimes used for the loft floor itself.

From the drawings on the loft floor, however they had been made, the moulds from which the loft and its master drew their their name in Appledore were made up. From light rough timber, a quarter, perhaps a half-inch in thickness, sometimes with the bark still attached to it, the dross of the saw pits, full-sized two-dimensional patterns for the frames were made up in the mould loft. They were tacked together, shaped so that the outer edge represented the shape to be taken by the outer edge of the frame and numbered each in turn in order as they lay from bow to stern of the vessel. These were the moulds, the patterns from which the ribs of the ship were made and upon them, given the design, depended in the main the success or failure of the yard. Their function was to convey to the sawyers the information for translating into a full-sized ship the ideas for the shape of the schooner conceived first in miniature in the half model.

But the function of the moulders went far beyond this. They were responsible for and had an intimate knowledge of the timber stocks in the yard. In the years before the *Katie* was laid down, in the slack periods when there was little repair work or building going forward or when the ground was hard and particularly good for hauling, gangs of men, the yard sawyers and the labourers, had gone out into the countryside of North Devon to the estates of the Taw and Torridge valleys to fell trees previously bought by one of the Cock brothers.

Walking through the woods with the estate agent or the squire, he had personally chosen the trees as particularly suited to his purpose and they had been marked for felling. The men who cut the wood into shape for building the schooner in the ship-yard by the river had, months or years earlier, felled some of her timber in the woodland glades, lopped it and topped it, dragged it to the cart rides, manhandled it on to great timber carriers which were part of the equipment of the yard, and ridden with it on its way to the sea. They became expert lumber-men, they had rounds to chant as they cut with axes at the bole of the tree, they knew all the trade of the woodsman and some of their expeditions kept them a fortnight from the yard. When, a few years later, the last wooden ships were launched and the sawyers turned from the yard, many of them took to lumbering and stayed in this business for the rest of their lives.

In the yard were built up the stocks of timber—oak, elm and beech from England, pitch pine, Oregon and yellow pine, spruce, hackmatack and birch from North America and Scandinavia. Some of it lay out in the river in chain-bound rafts for years, or in the seasoning piles about the yard, slowly losing its sap. As foreseen demand and circumstances allowed, planks were cut at the saw pits from logs, and curved pieces, selected on the tree because of their possible suitability for framing, cut into rough frame shapes and piled in pattern for seasoning so that the air could move freely between them (Plate 24). At some yards twenty years earlier, at Poole and on Chichester Harbour, at Plymouth and in the barge yards near Chatham, these timber stocks were augmented in a particular fashion. At intervals, there would be sales at the nearby Royal Docks of odds and ends of sawn timber left over from the days of wooden warship building, or too small for use in the wooden parts of contemporary building projects. This 'government oak' as it was called was bought cheaply and, although some of it had been condemned by naval standards, was always reckoned to contain fine stuff for building small schooners.

Another way in which the timber stocks of a yard might be increased was by purchase of the old, hard, long-seasoned timber derived from the destruction of large old wooden merchant or warships in some nearby yard. Ships built of this wood would have against them in *Lloyd's Register* (if they appeared there) the qualifications that they were built from partially old, or partially secondhand material. Such timber was often doubtful in quality and seldom used for the major part of a vessel's framing. I have heard of only one vessel said to have been built entirely from such timber, the *Julie*, a small ketch forty tons gross, and the last vessel to be built at the Scoble & Davies shipyard at Malpas in Cornwall. Her timber is said to have come from a wooden man-of-war concurrently breaking up at Plymouth, and to have been brought round to Malpas by sailing barge.

Not all the timber that went into merchant schooners was carefully seasoned at the time it was put into them. Throughout the history of wooden shipbuilding, the obtaining of adequate supplies of good timber was a continuous problem, the problem of having adequate seasoned timber available for a building project greater still. Much poor and inadequately seasoned timber went into wooden ships in the eighteenth and nineteenth centuries and the modern popular idea that ship timber was always of fine quality is little more than a myth.

At Cock's yard when the *Katie* was built, schooners were being launched fairly rapidly, as these things went, and the slips were producing an average of more than two ships a year. But very often schooners were built in a much more leisurely

fashion. Repair work in normal times paid better than new building and many ships were built on speculation to the yard's
account to keep the men busy in periods when repair work fell
slack and there were few vessels on the grids. Such a ship might
be worked on at intervals for years before she was launched, and
timber put into her framing that had been felled only a few
weeks before for that specific purpose would be matured and
seasoned by the time the vessel was planked up. The *P. T. Harris*,
a three-masted schooner built at Appledore to designs by Richard
Ashburner and Philip Kelly Harris and launched in 1912, and
the last merchant schooner to be built at Appledore, was so long
in building that she was whitewashed in frame on the slips (Plate
25). The ketch *Irene*, the last vessel to be launched at Bridgwater
(Plate 21), lay three years on the slipway, so that small boys used
to clamber over her and drive pounds of nails (carelessly left open
in the yard) into her exposed deadwood. The ketch *Garlandstone*
launched in 1909 took about five years to build at the yard of
James Goss at Calstock. In the later days of the merchant
schooners when few vessels were being built and the rest, growing
older, required more repair, such delays in building were natural.
But even in the nineteenth century, when trade was good and
cargoes available in many trades, owners were often in no hurry
for their new ships, particularly during adverse swings of the
trade cycle. Craftsmen, using only hand tools and heirs to an
ancient tradition of leisurely quality and slow industry, were not
in a hurry to build them. At small yards, even in the 70s and
80s, schooners could often be years in the building.

THE SLIPS

While the complex pattern of the half-breadth plan was growing on the loft floor and the flimsy structures of the moulds were
being made, men were working out on the slip fifty yards away.
Outside the Bell Inn today, in the high wall on the opposite
side of the road, are two great doors, now never opened, that
lead on to the site of the Bell Inn yard. Fifty yards away, down

by the water's edge, where today there is a modern building slip for large steel vessels, the bank was hollowed out and the wall cut down where the foot of the old slip rested in the tidewater. Here the *Katie* grew.

First came the keel blocks four feet apart, three feet deep, so that a man could work between them. On these keel blocks the keel was laid to dimensions scaled up from the half model. This keel was of elm, unseasoned, stinking, and in three pieces, scarfed together. It was of elm because elm was a cheap local timber obtainable in the large sizes required and stood up exceptionally well to immersion in sea water, unseasoned because it did not deteriorate as the sap dried out of it. Supervised by the loftsman and yard manager, gangs of sawyers and yard labourers turned over the piles of seasoning timber so that oak beams and bends could be selected for the bow and stern structures, the frames and the deck beams. Sometimes the selection of the stem and sternpost pieces from the piles of seasoning oak brought forth loftsman, head shipwright, manager and yard owner, if two or more of these functions were not fulfilled by the same man, as they were at Cock's yard. Then, as the moulds became available from the loft floor, they were taken by a lad to one particular shipwright who spent most of his time at this period of the vessel's construction selecting from the seasoning piles of sawn but unfinished grown oak bends the timber best suited to match each part of each mould. This man, trained in years of wood shipbuilding, knew just what materials he wanted and selected his timbers for their grain, size, bend and quality to minimise waste and the work of the sawyers.

Knowing the timber available, the moulder made a detailed sketch in chalk of the structure of the deadwood of his stem and sternpost and from this sketch moulds were also made. Moulds and timber were then fed to the pit sawyers who cut out the timber to the shapes demanded. On the keel, the stem and sternpost were hoist with derricks and around them the deadwood was built up in massive strength many feet in depth. The stem and sternpost were scarfed to the keel and secured with copper bolts, the deadwood itself on the *Katie* was fastened with bolts of galvanised iron. To insert these bolts, auger shafts were drilled through the mass of timber. Some of the bolt shafts were eight feet long, drilled with augers of increasing length to a diameter of one-sixteenth of an inch less than that of the bolt which was to go through them. Men drilled these holes for hours, taking turns at the twisting of the horizontal bar at the auger head, and then the copper bolt was driven through. These copper bolts were, in fact, nothing but bar copper an inch to an inch and a half in diameter, cut to length, and at the building of the *Katie* were driven through the augered hole by gangs of three or four men with sledge-hammers, seven, ten, or fourteen pounds in weight. Soft copper would be ruined by a misdirected blow, and the skilled labourers in the driving gangs had to hit the head of the bolt fair and square. As they drove they called a round—the same round the sawyers used in axe work when felling :

> 'Oh—lee—ram im up !
> 'Oh—lee—ram im up !
> ram im up !
> ram im up !
> Lam away—Oh !'

When the bolt was driven, the ends were clenched off over a rove so that the whole was, in effect, a great copper rivet through the keel and deadwood.

The *Katie* was to have an elliptical counter stern, but some of the schooners built by the Cocks at this time had a transom counter. When a transom was to be fitted, this massive boarding, made up by the shipwrights from material sawn to moulds at the pits, was fitted into place straight after the sternpost and the whole supported, as was the stem, by a scaffold structure around the growing bow and stern. With the transom came the aprons and knightheads, the latter massive timbers, perhaps fifteen feet long, three feet wide and nine inches thick, rising from keel to above the bulwarks. No part of their surface was flat, no line in them straight. They were one of the most exacting tests of the shipwrights' skill in construction.

All this time the frames had been growing on the ground around the pits and slipway. The sawyers at the pits were fed with the moulds from the mould loft, and with the unfinished sawn timbers selected against the moulds by the selecting shipwright, and with certain instructions as to the bevel of the frame on which they were at work. This bevel was the change in direction of the angle of the face of the frame on its outer surface, the first rough shaping of the frame to take the run of the planking and to be the basis of the shape of the ship itself. In the midships frames there was no bevel, in fact the eight midships frames on the *Katie* were called in the usual terminology of the industry at the place and period 'the dead flats'. As the frames moved towards bow and stern, so the bevel became steeper until it was perhaps of thirty degrees. From the waterlines of the half-breadth plan, knowing the position of the centre of each frame, it was easy for the moulder to measure roughly the angle of bevel of a frame for each successive waterline, so that he would have in the end as many angle readings as there had been layers in the original half model. These readings he set out on a bevel board by means of which the instructions were passed down to the sawyers. They were only very rough bevels, of course, because they were derived from waterlines or level lines, and not from diagonals. Despite the practices at Harvey's and many other yards, many of the schooner builders had never heard of diagonals.

There might be five or seven pieces of timber in a completed frame. The bottom timber was called the floor and was made in one piece athwart the keel. It was cut to taper each side of the keel, sloping fairly steeply upwards each side underneath and more gently on the upper side. Each floor was cut with a shallow slot amidships where it took the run of the keelson. On each side of the floors were the first futtocks, the sections of the rib where it bent steeply upwards. There were probably two of these, cut from grown oak bends of approximately the right curve. They were scarfed to the floors and, on the *Katie*, were of eight-inch square timber. The floors were heavier, perhaps a foot square at the keel and tapering to eight inches where they joined the futtocks. Very occasionally a frame in a small ship might be made up from a single solid piece of grown timber on each side of the keel. An Appledore motor barge, the *Nellie*, is said to have had one such solid frame in her amidships.

The finished frame was a massive object. The pieces cut to mould and bevel by the sawyers were laid out near the slip and by fitting the scarfs made into completed frames. Although at Cock's yard the sawyers put on a preliminary bevel, it was more usual for the frame to be made up as a dead flat and for the bevel to be put on afterwards as it lay on the ground by shipwrights working with adzes from the bevel board. Even at Cock's yard the sawyers' bevel was, of course, only a comparatively rough one and was finished off by adze work after the frame was erected. This adzing of the bevel was a highly skilled occupation since the variation in bevel was continuous all the way down the frame and the shipwright had to judge how the degrees of change were distributed over those parts of the rib lying between the dozen or so different readings on the bevel board.

As the frames were finished around the slipway, they were hoisted into position athwart the keel with derricks and bolted there. The positioning of each frame relative to the keel and to the others called for skilled judgment. In later years, when wood shipbuilding was revived during the second world war, it proved difficult to train enough men for this job in the time available. Consequently, in the few surviving West Country yards and those new ones which were established for the purpose, wooden motor fishing vessels were sometimes built up to the moulds. That is to say that the moulds themselves, tacked together to make full ribs, were erected on the keel and, being light, could be easily and rapidly adjusted into position under the supervision of a skilled craftsman. The less experienced gangs could then follow and place the frames in position against these templates, or even assemble them from floors and futtocks after the floor had been bolted to the keel. Sometimes, even in the building of the schooners, only a few evenly spaced frames were made up from the loft floor, and, when they had been erected and light battens called ribbands tacked into place around them, the moulds of the other frames were made up to fit the ribbands on the slip. Such a method of moulding depended largely upon the natural curve of the batten for the shape of the finished vessel in all but her main dimensions.

In most yards in the days when the schooners were built the moulds, as soon as the frames were made up, were returned to the mould loft and there used to light the stove on winter mornings. In some yards the moulds were treated more seriously, carefully made from good timber and kept for years. At Cock's yard they were kept in the loft and used in the building of the later, very similar, vessels, but they must have ended in the same fashion eventually. Very few moulds are to be found in the surviving mould lofts for that reason. They were essentially temporary devices, conveyers of information from the mould loft to the men who built the schooners.

The frames were bolted to the keel with copper bolts right through both timbers. The bolts were headed and mushroomed with hand hammers, the countersinking packed with oakum and white lead putty and the whole sandpapered off so that it was difficult to tell where the bolt heads lay. Some years ago I bought a floor timber from a schooner that was being broken up. The copper bolts had been cut to lift the floor from the keel and I wanted to draw them in order to cut my timber, but, although they were only slightly corroded, they had become part of the wood itself. In the end they had to be cut on the saw bench with the timber and remain embedded in it still.

At Cock's yard, two or three gangs worked on the erection of the frames, bow, stern and amidships, at the same time. They raced one another to get the frames into position on the keel. Meanwhile, shipwrights tapered and curved the stempiece with adzes to give to the schooner a sweet entry. As soon as the *Katie* was framed up, the bevels were finished with adzes likewise. The shipwrights tacked battens along the run of the frames and adzed away the face of the frame until the battens sat comfortably. Had the frame been erected unbevelled the shipwrights would have tacked the battens along the more projecting edge of the frame, the forward edge in the bow half of the schooner, the after edge astern, and would then have adzed at that edge until the batten sat comfortably all the way along, making full contact with each frame face in turn. In this way a smooth run and good seating for the planking was assured. On this system, bevelling was purely a matter of judgment and no bevels were taken in the mould loft. It was a highly skilled function of the shipwright, since batten runs could only be taken at intervals on each set of frames and the rate of twist of the frame face had to be estimated. When wooden schooners were broken up, you could often find the marks of the bevelling adze still impressed on the frame faces.

All this time the loftsman, with his men of the loft floor, was watching and supervising around the slipway, fulfilling his function in the building of the schooner, supervision of the development of her curved surfaces. They were especially concerned with the complexity of the framing at the stern. Here, as the framing developed and the intended shape of the schooner became apparent, the shipwrights made box moulds, hollow dummy frames made up in position in the counter of the vessel and passed to the sawyers for cutting out in the solid. Adze and chisel would be used for the final shaping. The frames of the counter stern ran into the deadwood from all directions and those of the Cornish stern ran into the last frames fore and aft. Much fitting was done before the skeletons of bow and stern were shaped to the moulder's liking.

While this process of building the stern was going on, the pitch pine or greenheart keelson was scarfed from several lengths, and copper-bolted. The timber was so made up that the scarfs did not coincide with those in the keel, since if they had done so the whole would have provided a natural hinge round which the vessel would have worked in a seaway. Once the keelson was in place, the deck beams and waterways could be fitted. First, the frame tops were levelled off with adze and plane, then the beam shelf and clamp were bolted into place. This shelf was a massive line of timbers scarfed into a solid whole, eight inches

thick and ten inches deep, stretching right round the vessel below
deck level inside the frames, fastened with copper or galvanised
bolts sixteen to twenty inches long. The clamp was a thinner
line of timber beneath it. Wedge-shaped slots were cut into the
beam shelf and into these slots were dropped the wedge ends of

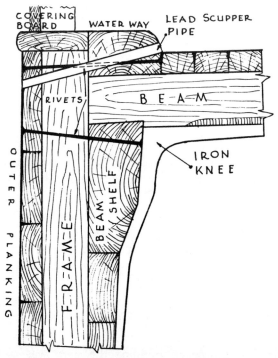

Fig 8   Beam shelf, clamp and waterway

the eight-inch square deck beams, each cut to a camber of perhaps two inches from straight-grained oak timbers. The beams
were packed close together in the bows of the schooner but
spaced out to a full four feet in the *Katie* amidships. They were
bolted into place and further strengthened with galvanised iron
knees on each side bolted to the beam shelf and the clamp piece
beneath it. Thirty years before, these knees would have been
made of timber.

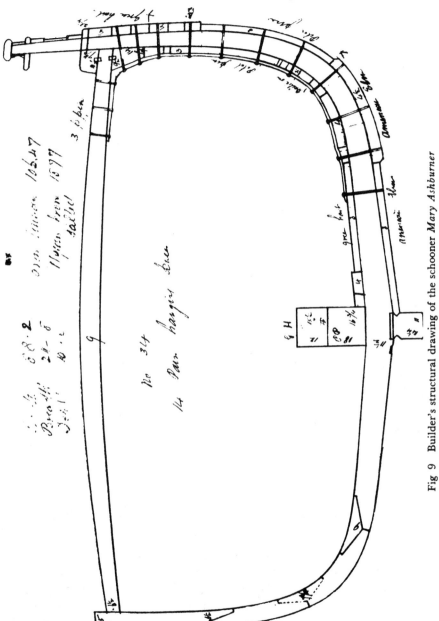

Fig 9 Builder's structural drawing of the schooner *Mary Ashburner*

Above the deck beams was bolted the waterway, a thick timber projecting above deck level all the way round the vessel for further strength, and over the heads of the frames the covering board ran round. Bolts ran right through waterway, frames and outer planking, and the whole was pierced with lead scupper pipes at intervals. The form of the whole massive assembly can be seen in Fig 8 and Fig 9 and in Plate 26.

The short beams in the way of the hatch coamings were spaced only three feet apart. They were secured with eight-inch square fore and aft timbers bolted to the beam ends and to the transverse beams at either end of the hatchway, and further strengthened with iron knees. Inside the frame thus made the hatch coamings were bolted, two and a half inch oak, reinforced with iron at the corners. These hatchways were very small by modern standards and indeed, were one of the major factors operating against the merchant schooners in later years. During and after the second world war, many motor schooners and ketches were refitted with larger hatchways of modern pattern and do not seem to have suffered, so perhaps the immense strength of the deck structure of the *Katie* and generations of her predecessors was in some degree superfluous.

The ribs about the bows were packed solid with oak timber scrap, the pawl post morticed to the keelson and bolted and bound with angle irons to the deck beams above. The structures of knees and strengthening blocks around the points where the masts were to pierce the decks were built up and the rabbet for the garboard strake was cut, perhaps a hundred feet long, each side of the keel, of varying depth and angle fore and aft of the dead flats and continued up on each side of the stem and stern-post as the rabbet to take the plank ends. For this the largest chisels and mallets were used.

Some schooners had, in addition, a final strengthening of diagonal iron bands let into the face of the frames running forward and upward from the keel to the frame heads. The ketch *Progress* had such bands in her, and they made a problem for the repair gangs when she was on the grids in later years, for an

20. Stern of the *Clara May*, built at Plymouth in 1891

21. Hull of the *Irene*, built at Bridgwater in 1907

22.   Stern of the *Kathleen & May*, built at Connah's Quay in 1903

23.   The men and boys employed at the yard of J. & W. B. Harvey, Littlehampton, at the beginning of the century. A ketch is under construction in the background

auger was apt suddenly to strike iron where there should be only timber.

The complex mass of timber which now stood on the slipway was liable to early destruction from rot if neglected. Rot was always the enemy of the wood shipbuilder and the shipowner, and one device intermittently used to try to combat it was the process of salting. This might take the form of soaking timbers in brine, or of spraying the frames in brine after they had been erected, or of packing the spaces between the timbers with rocksalt. Salting in various forms was used in the United States at the end of the eighteenth century. It was adopted later in Britain and seems to have been used more in the merchant schooners than in other types of wooden sailing ships.

The schooner was then ready for planking. The planks, stored in the yard's seasoning piles, had been cut out months or years before by the pit sawyers from squared bulk pitch pine brought by rail from Plymouth to Bideford and rafted down the Torridge on the ebb to Appledore. In earlier years it would have been imported direct from Prince Edward Island or New Brunswick in the ships of James Yeo, who made the shipyard where the *Katie* was built. In the yards where big wooden ships were built in the middle years of the last century, plank plans were worked out on paper beforehand and showed on a plane surface the shape and run of each plank. Thus the total area of timber required could be estimated and the curve and taper of each plank measured and passed down to the sawpits.

Builders of small wooden schooners used no such refined methods. The taper of the planks at bow and stern was calculated by the shipwrights of each planking gang and passed to the sawyers. The planks were often tried out against the frames while in preparation, the fore end of the bow planks shaped to the rabbet and the plank hollowed out on the inner side to take the curve of the frame. The planks in the *Katie* were two and a half inches thick and eleven or twelve inches wide, while some of the bow planks tapered to six inches. There was a band of planks three inches thick along the length about the waterline and these heavier timbers were to take the strains of rubbing at quay sides, at boats alongside, and at the beams of other vessels lying chock-a-block in dock or at loading barges. They were the vestiges of the thick whale bands of very heavy timber which surrounded small merchant ships in the eighteenth and early nineteenth centuries.

When they were shaped, the planks were steamed in the steam chest, a heavy wooden trunk two feet square and perhaps forty or fifty feet long. Steam was led into the chest from a boiler, fired with sawpit refuse, alongside. When thoroughly soaked in this fashion the planks became relatively soft and pliable; they were drawn from the chest by the planking gang and rushed over to the framed-up schooner where they were shoved and shouldered and wedged and shored and clamped into place (Plate 27). The planking gangs worked at high speed while their planks cooled; it was a point of professional pride and of good practice never to send the same plank twice to the steam chest. To protect themselves from the face of the boiled timber the gangs would snatch up anything that was handy to them, sacks, shavings, or the jackets of their fellow workers. Each plank gang was divided into three parties. The first forced the plank into position with the help of the others, then they secured it with shores and clamps while the drillers augered out the fastening holes and the fasteners drove in the copper or galvanised iron bolts or treenails. On the *Katie*, copper was used for fastening below the waterline, wooden treenails between wind and water, galvanized iron above.

There were six planking gangs, two forward, two aft, and two amidships. Each started at the garboard strake, next the keel, and worked upwards. The bow planks were fastened first at the rabbet and led backwards; the stern party worked forward. Experienced shipwrights were put in the bow and stern gangs, while journeymen and men just out of their time worked amidships. The bow and stern gangs raced one another, the journeymen, working on the dead flats amidships, lagged behind the other gangs because they had to fit their planks so as to meet the others, creeping along the frames backwards and forwards. The plank ends were always butted together on a frame. Before steaming, the inside edges of those planks which were to lie on the more steeply curved frames of the schooner were chamfered with adzes. The gap between the planks was wedge shaped and the chamfering so done as to leave a very small gap on the outside edge for the caulking, the inner edges of the planks touching. All this planking work called for great skill and it was here that the shipwrights' powers were best displayed. The judgment in plank shaping before steaming, in timber selection, and the practical skill used in bringing the plank home into its final position, were acquired only by long years of practice in the arts of wood shipbuilding. Sometimes, when the run of planks could not be brought to a full curved surface on bow or stern, 'stealers', tapered short planks, filling gaps in the run of the main timbers, were used. Such stealers were apparently used in Cock's yard, but in earlier years and in some yards even at the present day such devices are considered bad practice and out of the tradition of good shipwrighting.

The deck planks presented no comparable problem and were fastened with six-inch spikes. The work was started amidships and carried outwards and sternwards and forwards, the outer planks being tapered off to shape (Plate 28). Next the stanchions were put in, one in every third or fourth rib and made of light timber perhaps six inches square driven down between the frames about three feet and fastened from the outside of the planking by galvanised iron bolts or treenails. The rail was mounted on top of the stanchions and the whole boarded up, the stanchions first bevelled with adzes and the boarding, softwood an inch thick, spiked into place. But before the rail was finished the coveringboard, an assembly of oak beams two or three inches thick and perhaps two feet wide, was bolted into position over the waterway, frame heads and planking and caulked around the stanchions with oakum and pitched. The stanchions were a recognised place of weakness in any wooden vessel, and if they were carried away the sea would pour below through the holes in the covering board between planking and ceiling. These holes, being at the very edge of the vessel, were difficult to plug in a seaway, and more than one schooner was nearly lost through trouble starting in this fashion.

Now the decks were planed off to a smooth cambered surface, the slip was cleared of all surplus timber and caulking began. Caulkers used pitch and oakum, and the oakum used in the *Katie* came from Exeter gaol, which fed all the shipyards of southwestern England with this very necessary material. Skilled caulkers did little or nothing else in the shipyard. Each had his own selection of irons, some curved, some straight, some broad, some narrow, to meet each contingency in different parts of the vessel (Plate 29). The blow of caulking mallet on the iron produced a distinctive and musical note. At some yards the caulkers used to cut slots in the mallet head so that a clear note was produced, and each caulker would cut his mallet differently so that when a group were at work a whole succession of notes and combinations of notes came from the slipway. This musical play of the caulking mallets was one of the most characteristic sounds of the small seaport towns in the days of the building of the schooners and for generations before.

When the caulkers had finished, the boys went round the schooner clearing off the quarter-inch surplus of pitch. Finally, the shipwrights rounded off the run of the planking with plane and adze so that you could draw your hand down the side of the schooner as she lay on the slipway and feel no sudden change in the development of any of her subtle and complex curves. The finishing of the caulking was sometimes closely watched by the master or the owner who, when a ship was being recaulked after repair, would give the apprentices a few pence for tidying up the surplus pitch when work had ended in the yard in the evening. A stylish master would have the after deck payed with white lead instead of pitch.

If the schooner was to be sheathed, this was the stage when the metal was put on. Usually, merchant schooners were sheathed with felt and yellow metal, and indeed every southern-going wooden vessel had to be so treated, else, after a month or so, her planks would begin to be drilled away. In those days when modern anti-fouling compositions were unknown it was said that a schooner could be ruined in one Mediterranean voyage. First the hull below the load waterline was tarred heavily and then felt sheets, themselves soaked in tar, were pressed on top of the tar close to the vessel's shape. Light-gauge, yellow metal sheets were pressed on top of the felt and secured with copper nails, and this yellow metal was sometimes painted on top with a green copper anti-fouling which gave the hull a characteristic and attractive appearance. Sometimes, in early days, copper sheet was used instead of yellow metal and a few schooners were sheathed with zinc, which was less expensive than copper and possessed the same properties. When a vessel had been sheathed, the notation 'felted and yellow metalled' and the year were inserted in *Lloyd's Register*. Often the date of her sheathing was years after her date of build, for a schooner in the home trade would not be sheathed until she was taken up for a deep-water cargo. These sheathing notations are today a most valuable record of a vessel's activities, for if there is no record in the *Register* of a schooner having been sheathed it is most unlikely that she ever went beyond the limits of home trade, since it was not possible for a classed vessel to keep her class if she went on deep water with an unprotected bottom. So if a schooner was sheathed, it is almost certain that she went deep water.

The ceiling was fitted while the vessel was still on the slip, the job being kept for wet weather when the softening ground did not allow of other work about the yard. Then the shipwrights and labourers would be turned on to the lining of the schooner's hold with two and a half inch timber fastened to the insides of the frames, shaped to the bevel with adzes. It was fastened with galvanised iron bolts, one in every three of which went right through outer planking, frames and ceiling. This ceiling was not subjected to the direct strains applied to the outer planking, but was nevertheless a stressed surface and an integral part of the vessel; without it the schooner was not strong enough for seafaring. The whole structure of ceiling, deck beams, hatchway, iron strengthening knees, keelson, hogpiece and pump well, can be seen very clearly in the photograph of the hold of the ketch *Hobah*, built at Trelew Creek in 1878 (Plate 30). The keelson was protected with iron strips against cargo grabs and the bowsprit shipped. A couple of light poles were lashed in place where fore and mainmast were to be stepped and the schooner was then ready for launching (Plate 31, Fig 10).

The *Katie* was on the slipway for six months, and few schooners can have been there for less; most vessels took longer and some stayed on the slipway for years. At the time the *Katie* was being built, the Cocks were launching ships so rapidly in the terms of this industry that some of their vessels left the slipway without even their ceiling, which was put on afterwards in the Richmond drydock. The *Katie* was launched with no deck fittings beyond her stanchions and bowsprit; everything else was left to the drydock and a new schooner was laid down in the Bell Inn yard as soon as she had left it. Such methods were exceptional, even vessels built as a main interest of the yard were usually largely fitted out on the slipway, some were even rigged. The schooner *Rhoda Mary*, for example, was launched at John Stephens' yard at Point in South Cornwall with her lower masts standing, and the *Trevellas* was launched fully rigged (Plate 32).

If a vessel was being built to special survey, as very many of the first-class schooners were, the yard was liable to a visit from the local Lloyd's surveyor all the time she was on the slip. He tested the quality of the materials that went into the schooner, condemned bad timbers, bad workmanship, unsatisfactory methods, and his presence was a guarantee to merchants that the vessel was such as was likely to deliver their merchandise quickly and with the minimum of trouble and damage. The Maltese Cross against her name in *Lloyd's Register* was the symbol of the highest maritime quality. Surveyor's sometimes drove moulders and yard managers to despair and bankruptcy with wholesale condemnations, and sly yardmen sometimes built bad timbers into a schooner which were easy to replace so that the surveyor would condemn them and, feeling that he had conscientiously

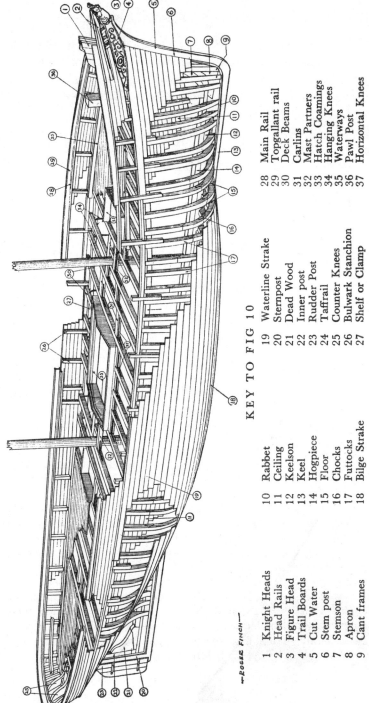

—ROGER FINCH—

KEY TO FIG 10

1	Knight Heads	10	Rabbet
2	Head Rails	11	Ceiling
3	Figure Head	12	Keelson
4	Trail Boards	13	Keel
5	Cut Water	14	Hogpiece
6	Stem post	15	Floor
7	Stemson	16	Chocks
8	Apron	17	Futtocks
9	Cant frames	18	Bilge Strake

19	Waterline Strake	28	Main Rail
20	Sternpost	29	Topgallant rail
21	Dead Wood	30	Deck Beams
22	Inner post	31	Carlins
23	Rudder Post	32	Mast Partners
24	Taffrail	33	Hatch Coamings
25	Counter Knees	34	Hanging Knees
26	Bulwark Stanchion	35	Waterways
27	Shelf or Clamp	36	Pawl Post
		37	Horizontal Knees

Fig 10 Simplified structural drawing of a three-masted schooner (many frames have been omitted, as has also navel piece on the bow which carried the hawse pipe)

fulfilled his function, would not condemn less questionable material elsewhere. I am not suggesting that Lloyd's surveyors were ever easily fooled, merely describing a method by which, tradition has it, a moulder sometimes combated acknowledged over-conscientiousness.

The classification rules regulated the schooner's being. The date of her birth was determined by them, since it was the year and month in which she finally passed survey that was recorded, as far as Lloyd's was concerned, as her date of build. Not even when she was away to sea did she escape them, for it was the constant and evenly spaced inspections for the maintenance of her class that brought her most frequently to the shipyards. It was this work—the inspection and refitting of vessels to fulfill the rules of their classification—that provided the main occupation of most of the schooner building yards, and the background against which the schooners slowly grew on slips behind the grids that were the heart of the yard, as the mould loft was its brain.

The grids and gravel repair beaches provided places to inspect and work upon a vessel's hull between tides. Most minor repairs on small vessels are made on grids to this day. Henry Hughes in his splendid book about the history of Portmadoc, *Immortal Sails*, describes the survey and repair work carried on at Portmadoc in the late nineteenth century, twenty years before the launch of the *Katie*:

> It may be asked how did the shipbuilders and the craftsmen of the ancillary trades occupy themselves during the lull which prevailed almost uninterruptedly for a period of twelve years. The answer is not far to seek. A wood-built vessel's initial classification as A1 has to be renewed after a lapse of the first twelve years of her life. Many vessels, some of importance, were falling due for the major overhaul about this time, and this was an extensive and expensive undertaking. Spars had to be 'struck' to the lower-masts, the rigging and standing gear overhauled; timbers were removed at recurring intervals so that a thorough examination could be made of the hull. All the deep-water ships, too, were copper covered underneath the waterline, and this, together with its underlay of felt, had to be stripped and renewed, a tedious and highly specialized procedure. . . .

24. Potential frame timbers lying seasoning in the shipyard at Appledore. This photograph was taken during a revival of wood shipbuilding which occurred in the second world war

25. The schooner *P. T. Harris*, launched in 1912, framed up in the Appledore yard

26. Beam shelf, clamp, waterway, covering board and some remaining deck beams (not cut wedge-shaped at the ends) framing and ceiling. Ketch *Ade* (ex-*Annie Christian*) built at Barnstaple in 1881 and broken up in 1950

27. The planks were 'shoved and shouldered and wedged and shored and clamped into place'. Planking gang at work in a Danish shipyard in 1950

28. Laying new deck planks, schooner *Kathleen & May*. The watching figure is the master and owner, Thomas Jewell

29. Caulker with irons and oakum at work on the decks of *Kathleen & May*

30. Hold of the ketch *Hobah*

31. Launch of the *Madeleine* from the Bell Inn yard. *Madeleine* was built immediately before the *Katie* on the same slipway

A dozen ships, their sides slung with pitch-stained stages, lined the muddy shores of the harbour, the metallic clink of numberless caulking mallets chimed their noisy tunes from dawn to dusk; that was the 'call note' of these halcyon days of sail and wooden ship. Mingled with the rustle and bustle of Glaslyn's escaping floods, it will for ever ring in my ears as the music of days now buried in the past.

Such repairs on the grids set many problems. The space between the muddy beach and the underpart of the vessel on the grids would often be only two or three feet deep. To overcome this lack of space, jointed augers, bent and shortened tools and many other locally developed devices were used.

And, of course, there were multitudinous other repairs. Ships were dismasted, stove in their bulwarks, lost galleys and deckhouses, they leaked, they were too deep or too shallow, they couldn't steer or wouldn't go about, or they needed structural modification in other ways. As they grew older they rotted and fastenings wept, they hogged, they sat on anchors, lay in foul berths, they picked up worm. Later they needed engines, new spars and improved sail plan, new hatches and redesigned decks and accommodation. There was at all times plenty for the repair yards to do. Sometimes an old vessel would be sheathed completely by being covered with two-inch planking over her original outer skin. Such treatment sometimes made them too heavy, spoiled their looks and handiness and did not much lengthen their lives. Sometimes, too, a vessel was rerigged. In the late nineteenth century many brigs were converted into barquentines and three-masted topsail schooners, as these sail plans proved their worth on deep water and at home. In the late nineteenth and early twentieth centuries, too, and for the same reasons, a fashion for three-masted vessels arose and many two-masted schooners and ketches were rerigged in this fashion (Plate 3). As late as 1935, the ketch *Maud Mary* was rerigged as a three-masted schooner at P. K. Harris' yard in Appledore.

Moreover, there were jobs of major repair and rebuilding. Old schooners were quite often rebuilt entirely and came off the beaches as almost new vessels. Often schooners were replanked, partially reframed, given a new keel or keelson, or new ceiling and such work was not considered important enough to justify the term rebuilding. Sometimes they would be padded out under the frames so that even their shape was materially altered. Small ketches and smacks were sometimes cut in half with pit saws as they lay high and dry on a shelving beach and the bow end dragged a few feet away from the stern by a team of horses. Into the gap thus made would be scarfed a new section of keel and on to that section would be built frames and deck beams so that the vessel emerged longer, faster and of greater capacity than before. In an article in Volume 45 of *The Mariners' Mirror*, Grahame Farr recorded the words in which the men who did the jobs described how they rebuilt the ketches *Ceres*, *Ant*, *Lady Acland* and *Iron King*.

Some shipowners built up considerable fleets of schooners by buying wrecked or damaged vessels at nominal prices and rebuilding them into new ships. Such enterprise paid because, providing the main timbers were sound, repairs had to be very extensive indeed before their costs equalled the cost of a new building. Schooners so treated were noted in *Lloyd's Register* as 'Rebuilt' or 'Almost Rebuilt' in the appropriate month and year. Right down to the very last days of the merchant schooners, this rebuilding and modification went on; even in 1947 the wooden ketch, *Emily Barratt*, which had served the war as a hulk of the balloon barrage in Falmouth Harbour, was rebuilt with a new keel and keelson and rerigged in a dry dock half a mile from the slip where the *Katie* was launched; a year later the *Progress* was extensively repaired. So extensive and frequent were these modifications that, in deck plan and fittings at least, very few of the schooners and ketches which survived until the last years of the merchant schooners bore any close resemblance to their original form.

I have described here, very briefly, and in a very simple form, something of the building of the hull of a wooden schooner, but the *Katie* was one of the last wooden merchant schooners to be built in this country, and only ten years afterwards the last few schooners of all were launched. The yard in which she was constructed was one of the finest and most up to date of all the schooner building yards. While the *Katie* was growing in the Bell Inn yard, in the Iron yard a few hundred yards away steel barges were being built by modern methods and soon fine steel sailing ships like the *Annie Reece* and large steamships were to be launched. Though the methods used by the Cock brothers in the construction of *Katie* and her sister ships were traditional and representative of the methods which had been used for centuries in building wooden ships in small yards, their approach to the problem, their attitudes towards shipbuilding as a business and to the organisation of their yard were, if still liberal and leisurely by modern standards, far removed from the ideas of the builders of the majority of the vessels mentioned in this history.

Wooden sailing ships were built by these methods, or by methods very similar, at the big yards where the vessels were of sufficient size to employ many men on the slips, at Bridport and Harwich, Littlehampton, Falmouth and Flushing, Par, Portmadoc and Connah's Quay. There were great variations in the methods of moulding and building, and practices invariably used in some districts were unknown in yards only a county's breadth away. Even in such fundamentals as the distribution of strength between frames and planking, there were wide variations. Compare the framing of the Barnstaple-built ship in Plate 26 with that of the ship built a few miles away at Appledore in Plate 25. Cornish-built ships were often lightly framed and thickly planked. The schooner *Alpha* built by Charles Dyer at Sunny Corner, near Truro, had two and a quarter inch planks with three and a quarter inch rubbing strakes. The *Heather Bell*, built at Barnstaple by John Westacott, had two and a quarter inch planks throughout, but her framing had double the wood of the *Alpha's*. The Barrow flats built in Cumberland were among the most massively constructed of small merchant sailing ships. The *Millom Castle*, built by William White of Ulverston, had two and a half inch pine topsides, elm below the bilges. The beam shelf was of nine-inch timber and she had three sternposts. The framing in the first twenty-five feet of her and the last twenty-five feet of her run—fifty feet out of her length of eighty feet—was almost solid. Her upper frames were six and a half inches square and her floors and futtocks nine inches square and all of oak. Her ten-inch deckbeams were of hackmatack. Her deck planking and ceiling were two and a half inch throughout. No wonder she has survived a hard life of almost a century!

Right until the very last days of their construction in the present century, the greater number of merchant schooners, and certainly nearly all the small ketches and sloops which stayed within the limits of the home trade, were built under conditions far more primitive than those at Cock's yard. Very often only a few men were employed in the yard; the owner, his sons, and a few sawyers and labourers. No mould loft was used, nor any draw-ings or half model; the schooner or ketch was built by eye alone. The yard owner bought his timber from local dealers, from estates and from larger shipyards, and selected it with a view to its natural shape. When a ship was built, the small and closely-knit team of craftsmen and skilled labourers, working under the super-vision of the owner or head man of the yard and disciplined by long and hard apprenticeship to the methods and ancient traditions of their craft, selected and formed each timber in turn as it was built into the fabric of the vessel. Moulds might perhaps be made up on the slip, fitted into place on the keel, and subse-quently modified until they fulfilled the moulder's ideas of what they should be. In such a yard, there would be at the most two and perhaps only one sawpit with a single pair of sawyers; these men, themselves skilled, could readily understand the cuts the moulder required of them. In such a case there was never any plan of the vessel other than that which existed in the builder's head, yet the yard would produce closely similar vessels, for such conditions of building depended for their success upon the general appreciation of traditional forms and were not conducive to ex-periment. In some cases it is said that the moulder of such a yard worked always from the same midships frames, working out the shape of his vessel as she grew on the slip with moulds and adze and pit saw from the datum lines of keel and end posts in the one plane and centre frame in the other. Such methods of building could sometimes produce odd results. The very successful and fast schooner *Ulelia*, built by Charles Dyer at Sunny Corner, near Truro, for the Newfoundland trade had one more deck plan on her port side than on the starboard. She was not symmetrical.

Yet even these conditions were not the most primitive, for here we have assumed at least a yard and a team of craftsmen producing together, albeit very slowly, a number of vessels. But in earlier years, and in the last days of the large-scale building of small wooden ships in the 60s and early 70s, hundreds of brigs and schooners, ketches and sloops were launched where there had been no yard at all before and would be none again. A sheltered cove, a creek of a tidal haven, the high beach of an exposed coast, these were the birthplaces of a great many ships built in isolation and under conditions completely primitive. In Prince Edward Island, ships were built on the sandy beaches from softwoods cut in the adjacent forest. In Britain, given the impetus of the desire to invest in a schooner expressed on behalf of a group of local men of small substance by the future master or manager, a group of craftsmen, who thought of themselves as the shipwrights of a particular district and not as men of a yard, would be gathered together. They would dig a sawpit and put up a shack or two at some generally convenient point on the coast, or where ships had been launched traditionally, and there they would build the vessel. Most often such a site would be found upon a beach between cliff and spring tide flood, for the ownership of such ground was most often uncertain or common, and there were no rates to pay on huts erected there (Plate 32).

Such were the traditional methods of building, and perhaps until the 1870s the majority of small merchant sailing ships had always been built in this way. Small wonder then that today it is so frequently impossible to trace the sites of the yards in which these ships were constructed or, even with the best of them—the ships that are to be found recorded in *Lloyd's Regis-*

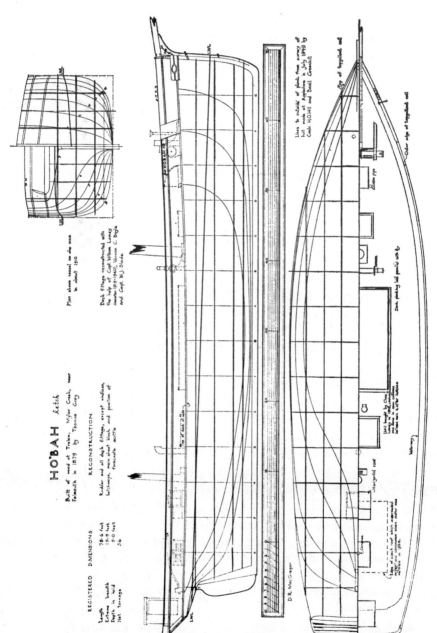

HO'BAH *Ketch*

Built of wood at Tresless, Mylor Creek, near
Falmouth in 1879 by Thomas Gray

RECONSTRUCTION

Rudder and all deck fittings, except windlass,
hatchways, main sheet block, and position of
forecastle scuttle

REGISTERED DIMENSIONS

Length	78·6 feet
Extreme breadth	19·9 feet
Depth in hold	9·0 feet
Net tonnage	56

Plan shown vessel as she was
in about 1910

Deck fittings reconstructed with
the help of Capt. William Lamey
(master 1919–1940), Vernon C. Boyle
and Capt. W.J. Slade.

Lines to outside of plank from survey of
hull made at Appledore in July 1949 by
Cmdr. H.O.Hill and Basil Greenhill

D. R. MacGregor

Fig 11   The ketch *Hobah*

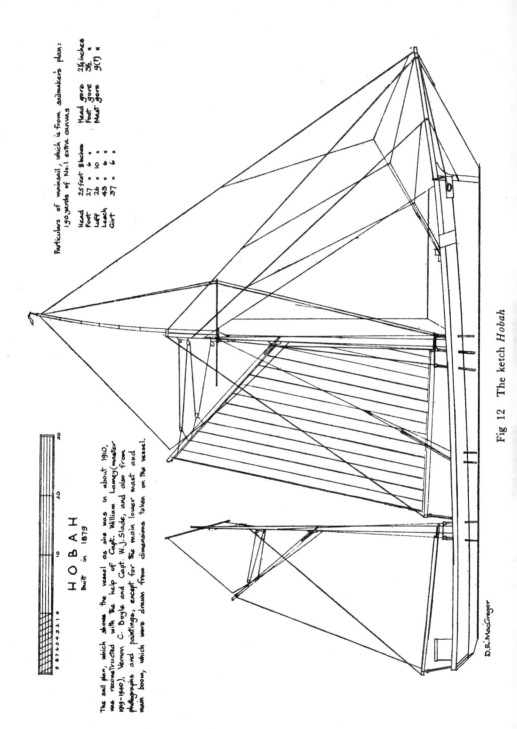

HOBAH
Built in 1879

The sail plan, which shows the vessel as she was in about 1910, was reconstructed with the help of Capt. William Lamey (master 1919-1940), Vernon C. Boyle and Capt. W. J. Slade, and also from photographs and paintings, except for the main lower mast and main boom, which were drawn from dimensions taken on the vessel.

Particulars of mainsail, which is from sailmakers' plan; 150 yards of No.1 extra canvas

Head	25 feet	8 inches		Head gore	2½ inches	
Foot	27	6	"	Foot gore	3½	"
Luff	26	10	"	Mast gore	9(?)	"
Leach	43	6	"			
Girt	37	6	"			

D.R.MacGregor

Fig 12   The ketch *Hobah*

ter—to unravel the puzzled clerk's efforts to record their place of building. Sometimes they are attributed to a county, or a district; sometimes to the local name of a creek or stretch of beach which is to be found on no ordnance map; frequently to the official customs port of registration. Thus schooners launched as far apart as Point and Sunny Corner are attributed impartially to Truro in contemporary registers. Moreover, in such registers as the *Mercantile List* which are prepared from Custom House records, the local names, often given in terms understood only in the parish concerned, are misspelt, so further complicating the issue. Already only by careful research is it possible to determine th eexact place of origin of many even of the later merchant schooners.

As an example of this form of building let us take the ketch *Hobah*, seventy-seven tons gross (Plates 30 and 33, Figs 11 and 12). Mr Thomas Gray, a master shipwright of South Cornwall who had probably been employed previously in one of the yards at Falmouth, set up and built a vessel on his own account in 1878. At Trelew Creek, a tiny steep-banked tributary of the Mylor Creek, he hired a labourer or two and dug a sawpit at the back of the beach on the western side, fifty feet from where the present roadway crosses the water. A few yards farther down keel blocks were laid across the beach, a hut was erected and a store of timber built up behind. In the sawpit two sawyers, Edward Drew and his son William of the parish of Mylor, who had previously worked in Trethowan's shipyard at Little Falmouth, cut out all the timber for the new ketch. With shipwrights and labourers, she was slowly built at the creek's edge and duly launched and fitted out. Her form was more or less traditional in South Cornwall with a straight stem and a long, steeply-sloping transom over a deep sternpost, the Cornish stern. She was sold to owners in Falmouth and set to work in trade to the western coast of France.

When she was finished the little yard was abandoned, the hut dismantled, the sawpit filled in by the slow tides; and for generations it has been forgotten locally that there was ever a

32. The schooner *Trevellas* ready for launching at St Agnes in 1876

33. The ketch *Hobah* moored in the Torridge

34. The *Lafrowda* of Penzance

ship built at Trelew Creek, though the *Hobah* herself survived
until the end of the second world war. Thomas Gray moved to
Falmouth and there set up another yard at the end of the High
Street, on Penryn river. Here he repaired his own *Hobah* and
the famous schooner *Rhoda Mary* after she had collided with a
trawler. Sawyer Drew and his son moved with him and there they
cut out the timbers for another ketch. But she was never finished,
and shortly afterwards Mr Gray was forced to retire from business.

In tracing the history of the builders of the wooden schooners,
it is almost the rule to find that the business ends in bankruptcy,
not merely in the later days when the industry was dead or
advanced in dying but also in the 70s and 80s when, if not on its
former scale, it was still prosperous and developing. Even in the
boom periods, when much new construction was going forward,
reputable builders were forced out of business. The risks attendant upon carrying large stocks of timber, the high standards of
the surveyors of vessels built to Lloyd's Rules, who would sometimes force the reconstruction of parts of vessels on the slips
again and again because of faulty timbers, and lack of knowledge
of the cause, treatment and prevention of the various forms of
fungal decay in timbers, were among the causes. The small capital
involved in most of the businesses meant that their continued life
depended on the timing of one or two orders, and many of the
practical men who set up in small yards of their own were almost
completely lacking in business skill. All these, and the fact that no
industry reflects the variations of the trade cycle more faithfully
than shipbuilding in all its forms, meant that most of the men
who built these ships ended their business days in liquidation,
many of them when the schooners they had launched were still
only at the beginning of a long sea career.

THE FITTING-OUT BERTH

Two hundred yards from the site of the slip where the *Katie*
grew, and lying parallel with it but further downstream, is the

H

Richmond drydock, built in 1856 by the great James Yeo of Richmond Bay, Prince Edward Island, and his son William, who set up in Appledore as his father's British agent (see Chapter 6). It is a large dock and the *Katie* could fit very well into the head of it and leave room for another vessel to be moved in for repairs behind. Here she was moved as soon as she was launched and here she lay for some months slowly fitting out.

For some time the sawyers had been working on the cutting out of the masts. Square blocks of pitch pine, drawn from seasoning pools in the river, were cut into octagonals, and then 'sixteen squared'. Below the deck level they were left unfinished. At the foot of the mast was cut the tenon heel to fit into the heel slot in the keelson. Above deck level, the mast was finished with draw knives and planes to a cylinder sixty feet long. It was left square at its head to take the cheeks and the doubling, and rounded off again at the cap. The mast was fitted with eyebolts and battens at the crosstrees and cranes for throat halyards and for the yards on the fore. The mast was stepped with sheerlegs. The standing rigging, shrouds, backstays and forestays, was hoisted with a gantline and fitted to the mast after it was stepped. The master rigger took over at the rigging of the sheerlegs. The riggers were Alfred Galsworth, Bob Cooksley, Jack Taylor and Billie Johns. It was said that Jack Taylor's fingers were so hard he could splice a piece of flexible steel wire without using a marline spike.

The *Katie* was rigged as a three-masted schooner with standing topgallant yard above double topsails on the fore, and a single spar bowsprit. Fitted jibbooms began to pass out of fashion in these vessels before the end of the nineteenth century and were rare in their later days. The last schooner to have the full headgear was the *Minnie*, lost in 1938; the last to set a jibboom, and probably one of the last merchant sailing ships in Northern Europe to do so, was the ketch *Mary Stewart* of Braunton, which was still equipped in this fashion in 1948, although her bowsprit and jibboom together were no more than a spike at this time.

The *Katie* had studdingsails from the upper topsail yardarm down to the rail, with the usual studdingsail booms on the fore yardarm. Many of these later standing topgallant-rigged schooners were fitted with studdingsails. The sails they developed were triangular and are shown with the rigging in Fig 13. Fowey schooners also set a simple triangular studdingsail with its head at the topsail yardarm and its boom on the lower yardarm. Sometimes gaff topsails were set out as make-do studdingsails. The barquentines which preceded the standing topgallant schooners set rather similar sails as additional canvas. All schooners carried a light running sail under the foreyard and many ketches a flying yard for the same purpose. Every Bridgwater ketch carried this yard in her port bulwarks.

There were five different combinations of square sails in customary use in British schooners at the end of the nineteenth century. In the words of Captain W. J. Slade:

1. *The double topsail schooner* had on the foremast foreyard, lower topsail yard and upper topsail yard. The foreyard was secured to a spider band below the eyes of the foremast rigging and hung in the centre by a strong single chain fastened to an eyebolt under the trestletrees. The lower topsail yard was secured to the cap and held up by an iron bar or truss from under the centre band on the yard to a cup on the fore side of the topmast. This kept the weight of the yard up from underneath. The upper topsail yard was secured to the topmast above the cap by a band which travelled up and down the topmast. The lifts were on the upper yard and ran from the eyes of topmast rigging to the yard arms on either side. There were no lifts on the lower yard. (Plates 14, 16, 19, Vol. 1; and 3, 4, 25, 31, 33, Vol. 2.)

2. *The double topsail and standing topgallant-yard schooner* was exactly like No 1 with an extra yard above the eyes of the topmast rigging with lifts from the topgallant eyes of rigging to the topgallant yard arms on either side. It was secured to the topgallant mast by a band which travelled up and down in the same way as the upper topsail, but when the sail was stowed the topgallant yard never came below the eyes of the topmast rigging. (Plates 18, 32, 39 and 40, Vol. 1.)

3. *The single topsail and standing topgallant-yard schooner* consisted of one single topsail with the yard travelling up and down the topmast like the upper topsail yard of a double topsail

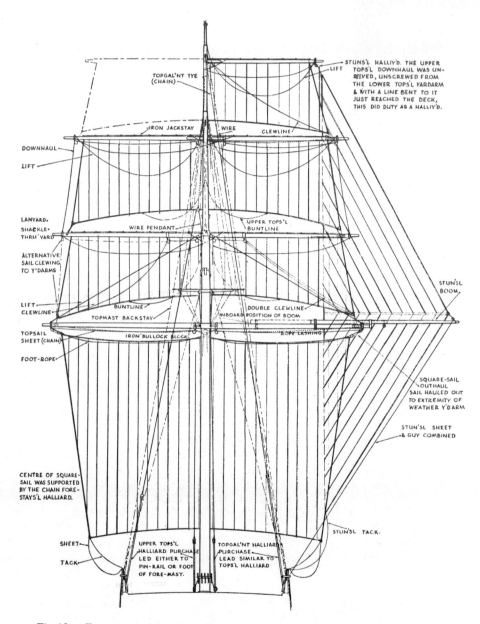

Fig 13   Foremast rigging of standing topgallant schooner (right hand). The vessel is rigged in the style used in Portmadoc. The left hand part of the diagram shows an alternative arrangement for the clewlines sometimes adopted in double topsail schooners on the coast. The footrope stirrups have been omitted in both cases for simplicity.

schooner (see No 1). There was nothing on the cap. It was one single topsail with a reef in it. The topgallant was the same as the one mentioned in No 2 and always above the eyes of the topmast rigging. This was a comparatively rare rig.

4. *The single topsail schooner* had a yard hoisting up and down the topmast and secured to the topmast by a travelling band. It was known as a 'Garibaldi schooner' and had point reefing. In French schooners, it had roller reefing gear. (Plates 34, Vol. 1; and 32, Vol. 2.)

5. *The flying topgallant-yard schooner* was similar to No 4 but the topgallant yard was set flying above the topsail like a boat's lug sail, except that when set the yard was level. A traveller ran up and down the topgallant mast above the eyes of the topmast rigging. It never came below this point but the halyards ran through a bow on the foreside. This allowed the yard to run down to the topsail yard and in harbour both yards and sails were often stowed together. The lifts, were on the lower yard in this case. (Plates 7, 8, 11, Vol 1; and 25, 27, 34, Vol. 2.)

The late Harold A. Underhill in his book, *Masting and Rigging—The Clipper Ship and Ocean Carrier*, illustrated in diagrams some practices in the rigging of schooners. From these and the diagrams which illustrate this chapter (Figs 14 to 21 inclusive), it will be possible to reconstruct the rigging of some of the five types of square topsail schooner, always bearing in mind that there were great variations from port to port and even from ship to ship in what was considered good practice.

The setting of gaff topsails was another matter in which there was much variation from port to port. Captain W. J. Slade describes Appledore practices in detail in Appendix 3 to this volume. Only four British schooners were fitted with the patent roller-reefing topsail almost universal in French schooners. This equipment, the Système Bruard, described in Bulletin 13 of the *Amis du Musee de Marine* in Paris, was most efficient and satisfactory, and one of the four British ships equipped with it retained it for thirty-five years (Page 185). The system was admired in Appledore, and the chief reason it was not adopted there and in other British schooner-owning places was probably because the iron-work was not readily available. The widespread adoption of

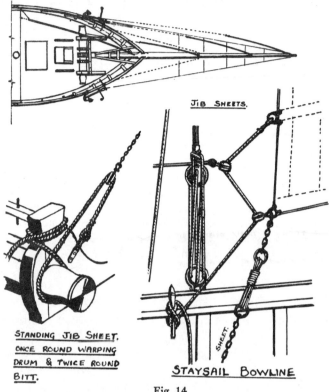

JIB SHEETS.

STANDING JIB SHEET.
ONCE ROUND WARPING
DRUM & TWICE ROUND
BITT.

STAYSAIL BOWLINE

Fig 14

the ketch rig at the end of the nineteenth century, a time when it might have been economic to produce the equipment, finally ensured that the roller-reefing topsail was not adopted even by the most go-ahead of British schooner-owning communities. Apart from a few Portmadoc schooners, the staysail schooner was not adopted as a rig for commercial vessels in Britain either, though it was used in two-masters without square topsails in Norway in the 1870s. The Bideford polacca brigantines (Chapter 6 in this volume) were, in effect, staysail schooners with square sails added and they remained popular locally for many years.

Sometimes triangular raffees were used above square topsails by way of a topgallant. The photograph of the *Lafrowda* (Plate

Fig 15   Rigging of a two-masted schooner with flying topgallant yard

34) shows such a sail set. In later years, after motors had been installed, triangular sails set from a single yard were sometimes used instead of square sails. Both the *Mary Barrow* and the *William Ashburner*, three-masted schooners, were so equipped before the second world war.

In the local sail loft in Appledore (Plate 35) work was going forward on the making of the sails for the *Katie*. The spar dimensions were given to the master sailmaker and a rough draft was sketched and then filled in with straight edge and heavy pencil on any large piece of white card that was available. Often the backs of placard railway timetables were used for this purpose, and I have many such drafts of sails of well-known West Country schooners. The sailmaker and his men and boys worked from these drafts, which showed the distribution of the canvas, the stitching, the cut of the sail and all the various finishings in the way of bolt ropes, bands, reef points, eyes, cringles and so forth that had to be worked into it. The master sailmaker at Appledore kept account books of all the making and repair work he did for the local ketches and schooners. I have one of those books in front of me now, and each vessel is given a numbered page down which is recorded the canvas work of the years between 1910 and 1921. During those eleven years, the ketch *Hobah* is credited with no less than eighty-two entries, during which the price of heavy canvas for her main and squaresails rose from 1s 7½d to 5s 6d per yard, so that at the end of this period a new mainsail for the two-masted schooner *Ythan* cost no less than £32 8s 5d. From this book it is apparent that the *Rosie,* a sister to the *Katie,* had in her mainsail 233 yards of No 1 cotton canvas costing 2s 4d per yard in 1916. In addition, the sail was barked for £1 15s 0d. The costs of sailmaking are split up into their various parts, cost of canvas, wood fittings, bolt ropes, twine and labour, the latter a very small sum in the early years of the period. The names of all the well-known schooners and ketches of the western coast and of their owners and masters are in this book, together with a record of their canvas work and the miscellaneous services they had done for them over the years—mast and sail covers,

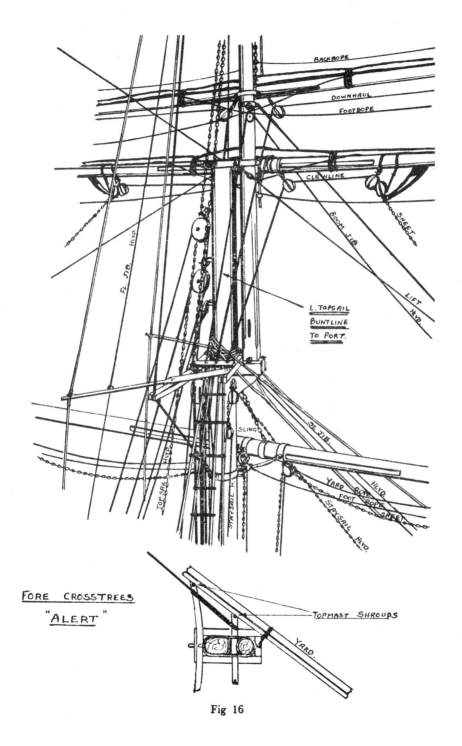

FORE CROSSTREES
"ALERT"

Fig 16

hatch covers, skylight covers, boat sails, oil, rope, cane baskets at 2s 9d each, twine and the making and constant repair of the main canvas. In the latter years, the entry 'to repairing with second-hand canvas'—the necessary make-do and mend of hard economy—becomes more and more frequent.

The number of repairs recorded in this book shows that in contrast to the custom in big ships little or no canvas work was done on board schooners at sea even on deep-water passages. For their sails, the schooners were dependent upon the shore. This was perhaps due to a number of reasons : the smallness of their deck space and the fact that decks were rarely completely dry at sea; the smallness of the crews, which did not justify carrying a specialist in canvas work; and the fact that their voyages, on the whole, even in deep water, were shorter—there was no schooner equivalent of the barque's hundred days by way of Cape Horn.

The sail lofts were a part of the life of the small seaport towns in the days of the sailing ships. Each loft had its polished floor, its men at palm and needle seated on the benches, its smell of tar and new canvas, its great bolts of material lying perhaps in racks to one side, or in a basement below. Later, heavy-gauge machines were introduced, and in the last days even female labour to work these machines. The sail lofts, because of the demand for sails for yachts and canvaswork for tents, awnings, covers and so forth, remained in existence for years after the last schooners had been launched; indeed, many ports still have a loft in commission.

The *Katie* was given roller reefing on fore and main, with point reefing on mizzen. Already in the early twentieth century, roller reefing on at least one mast was universal and many vessels were equipped entirely in this fashion. Before long the older method of reducing canvas had dropped out of use altogether and many seamen of the later days of the merchant schooners had no first-hand experience of point reefing, regarding it as an anachronism. In the 80s and 90s, many schooners adopted roller reefing for the heavy canvas of the main, leaving the points on the lighter fore and mizzen. With roller-reefing gear, a thimble

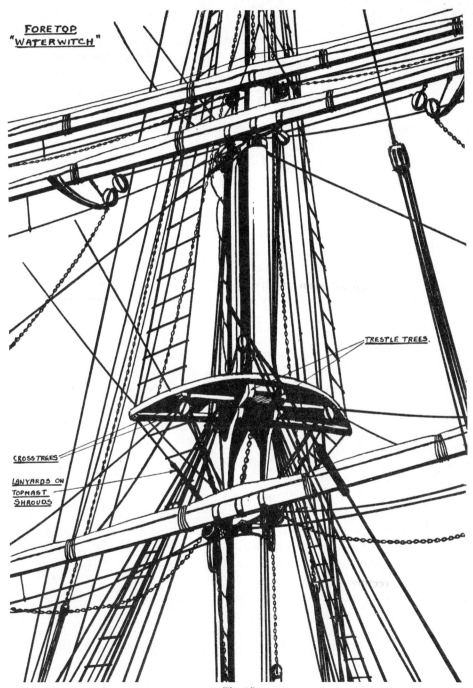

FORETOP
"WATERWITCH"

TRESTLE TREES.

CROSS TREES

LANYARDS ON
TOPMAST
SHROUDS

Fig 17

was worked in the doublings close to the weather rope of the sail and another in the leach rope with brass eyelet holes in each cloth of the sail where they joined. These were up about the double reef mark and were there in case the roller gave out or the boom carried away. Point-reefing sails in British schooners were loose-footed and secured to the boom at tack and clew only. Roller sails were fastened with robands to a jackstay which ran along the top of the spar. Every combination of point and roller system is to be seen in photographs of schooners taken in the last fifty years. The roller system, besides being easier to work at sea, was more efficient in that the sail, rigidly held to the boom, did not sag to leeward and could be of better cut. Roller-reefing gea ˜ were of two main kinds, Appledore and Jersey. The Appledore gear, invented by Williams, was a five-thread worm gear with which it was possible to handle almost any sail in almost any weather. The Jersey gear depended on a drum rotated by a chain and tackle.

While the sails were being made, in the loft, in the *Katie* carpenters and joiners were at work. Even in a small schooner there was a great amount of light woodwork to be done and the carpenter's shop was an important and profitable part of the yard. The panelling of the wedge-shaped cabin immediately in front of the stern-post, where most of the master's life on board was spent and the crew usually ate together; the tiny state rooms of the master and the mate, which were little more than enclosed bunks; the mess room forward of them, if there was one; the forecastle and the companion ways, all had to be fitted out and equipped with the miscellaneous gear required for their life at sea. On deck, companion hatches of teak and mahogany, the whaleback wheelhouse with its latrine and lamp locker, hatch covers, deck lights, ventilators, harness casks, dolly winches, fife and pin rails and the great structure of the pump handle windlass forward, all had to be fitted. Much of the windlass consisted of ironwork beyond a blacksmith's capacity, and the dolly winches, apart from the wooden drums, were made entirely of cast iron. This foundry work was made up at the nearest iron works; many of the small

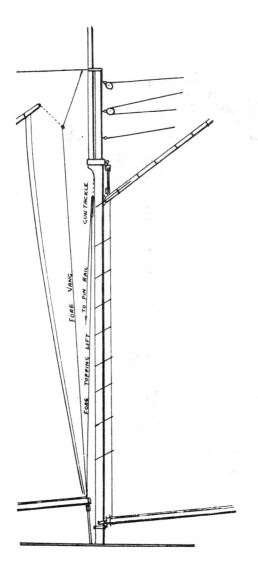

FORE VANG & TOPPING LIFT
"ALERT"

NO VANG ON MAIN.

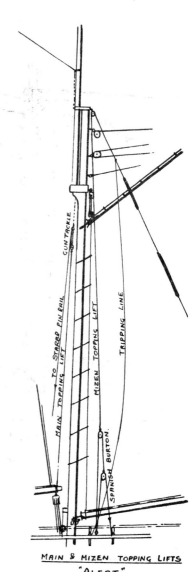

MAIN & MIZEN TOPPING LIFTS
"ALERT"

Fig 18

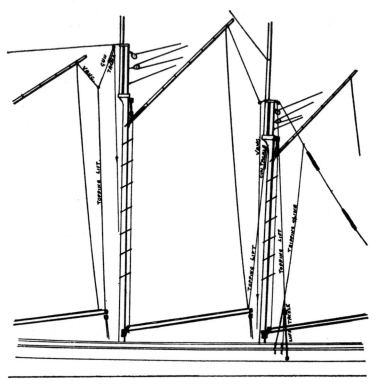

TOPPING LIFTS & VANGS
"BROOKLANDS"

Fig 19

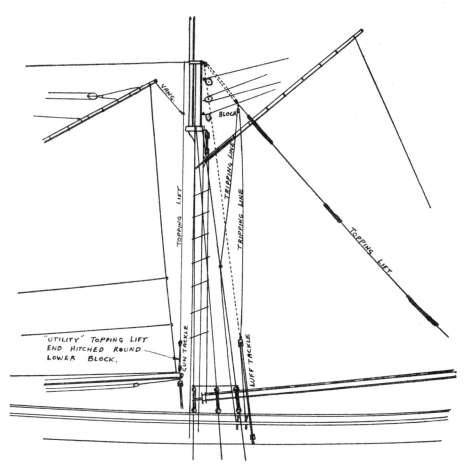

VANGS.

BLOCK.

TOPPING LIFT

TRIPPING LINE

TRIPPING LINE

TOPPING LIFT

"UTILITY" TOPPING LIFT
END HITCHED ROUND
LOWER BLOCK.

GUN TACKLE

LUFF TACKLE

FORE & MAIN TOPPING LIFTS.
"SNOWFLAKE"

"FLYING FOAM" & "MARY SINCLAIR" SIMILAR. MAIN
TOPPING LIFTS OF KETCHES "HENRIETTA" "GARLANDSTONE"
& "EMILY BARRATT" SIMILAR.

"MARY MILLER" HAD A SIMILAR SET UP ON THE MIZEN
WITH WIRE INSTEAD OF CHAIN, BUT WITH A SINGLE
TRIPPING LINE.

Fig 20

seaport towns had foundries which fed not only the shipyards but the mines and farms and small factories in the countryside for miles around. There was the Bassett foundry at Devoran which served the Stephens' yard at Point, and the Lidstone foundry for W. Date of Kingsbridge. But the ironwork of the *Katie* was most probably made up in the Iron yard next door to the slip.

The rope for the *Katie's* rigging was manufactured at the rope-walks at Bideford and Appledore. Both establishments were three hundred yards long, the one at Appledore open and that at Bideford partially covered in. The ropewalk was always an important feature of the business life of a seaport town and was often owned by the shipyard master in close conjunction with his business. The blocks, deadeyes, hearts, bullseyes and other wooden equipment for the rigging were manufactured with lathes and drills in the 'block shop', an old stone building standing at the back of a small courtyard opposite the high wall that skirts the Richmond dock. This building, Docton House, is probably the oldest in Appledore.

An important piece of the *Katie's* furniture which was made up at this time was the figurehead (Plates 36 and 37). At Appledore it was customary to employ one man, Tom Owen, who for years had carved head ornaments for ships launched on the Torridge river. In other yards, the job would often be given to a shipwright particularly skilled with the chisel, who took pleasure in such detailed fancy work. The figureheads of most merchant schooners were small half-length feminine figures, and were well draped since they were often modelled on the wives and daughters of masters and managers. Some were crude, roughly-hewn blocks of wood and of no merit either as portraits or carvings; others were beautiful pieces of folk art carved in detail and emerging from a carved and decorated stem head. One of the most beautiful of the figureheads of small wooden sailing ships was that of the ketch *Sunshine* of Bridgwater, a detailed half-length of a woman in a broad-brimmed sun hat. Of a much earlier period and rougher, but of a certain typical

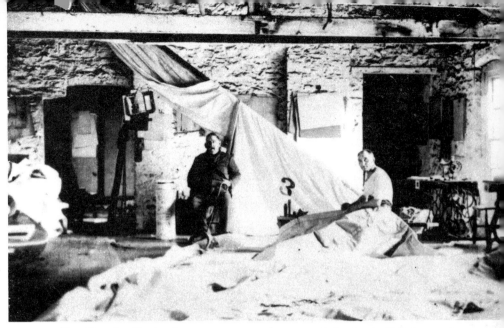

35. Captain Charles Lamey, master and owner of the ketch *Hobah*, watches sailmaker Pen Oatway at work on a mizzen for the *Hobah*

36. Bows, headgear and figurehead of the *M. A. James*

37. Figurehead of the *William Ashburner* of Barrow, built at Barrow in 1876

38. Appledore from Instow. The ketch is the *Annie*, locally dubbed the *American Annie*. She was built, almost certainly as a schooner, in Nova Scotia in 1859

charm, was the figurehead of the *Alice Williams,* which stood for some years on the cliffs above the south haven of Skokholm Island. It is sometimes said that it was a point of professional pride among the carvers of wooden figureheads for small ships that they should work from one piece of timber, but the figurehead of the *Alice Williams* was a compound of several woods, as is the fiddle head decoration of the schooner *Annie Christian* which is in my possession.

This fiddle head shows another aspect of the figurehead, its colour, for covering it is a leatherlike jacket of layer upon layer of paint, the whole perhaps an eighth of an inch in thickness. In this jacket is to be found every colour—blue, yellow, reds from dull to scarlet, orange and white—and the whole is so thick as to have obscured completely all the delicacy of the carved scroll work underneath. In its sixty-five years of life upon the bows of the schooner about the seas and shores of Europe, this ornament had been repainted again and again and rarely had the previous layer first been removed. Some masters in the nineteenth century, however, allowed no colours but white and pale blue, and some schooners, the famous *Rhoda Mary* among them, retained this custom to the end of their days.

The fiddle head of the *Annie Christian* surmounted a prettily curved stem decorated on each side with scroll work, growing thicker at its head and ending in a rough-shaped swelling shield which must in the course of its life have borne a number of devices. Usually, the figurehead concluded a pattern in two planes, the rise of the stem in the vertical, the backwards flow of the trail boards in the horizontal. These trail boards were customarily checker-pattern painted in white but sometimes, after it became a legal requirement to show a ship's name on her bows, the schooner's name would be carved upon them in small letters. More often, however, the name was further aft, in the rail at either side, though in wooden schooners it was never over-prominently displayed. Astern, the name and port of registry would be cut into the counter or transom in V-shaped chisel slots filled in with paint. When a schooner changed her port of registry the old

I

lettering, no longer painted in, remained; sometimes the change threw out the balance of the design and the name had to be recut as well. On the sloping transom of the *M. A. James* as she lay on the mud of the Torridge in 1948 were visible the letters of no less than three ports of registry, Bideford, Plymouth and Caernarvon. Sometimes when a ship came from a place not dignified by a Custom House, and therefore not a place of registration, the locally patriotic owner would display the names of both havens, and a schooner might voyage over the seas of the world bearing upon her stern the double legend 'Portmadoc, Port of Caernarvon'. In 1947 the stern of the ketch *Agnes*, owned in Braunton, bore the pleasant conceit 'Agnes, Bude, Port of Bideford'.

The masters and owners of most schooners and ketches took pride in their vessel's decoration. Even if neither figurehead nor carved ornament were fitted, the stem head was usually picked out in yellow or white paint. This decorative work received renewed attention in the last days of the merchant schooners when, after the second world war, there seemed to be a sort of brief recrudescence of pride amongst the crews of these ships. Paint work was carefully maintained, carved ropes on counter sterns were filled in where they had long been broken, and name plates restored. When the bows of the *Kathleen & May* were rebuilt after she had been cut down by a trawler in 1947 the carved head ornament was carefully reconstructed from the fragments and bolted into place once more upon the new bow. Sometimes, when a schooner had no figurehead of her own, a particularly proud master would buy one from a wrecked or broken up vessel and fix it into place on his own stem head. The figurehead of the schooner *William Ashburner* shown in Plate 37 was not her own but was bought in a junk shop in a West Country haven and restored for her use. Quite probably it was taken from the two-masted schooner *Cadwalader Jones* of Portmadoc, before that vessel sank off the west coast in 1933.

In drydock, the *Katie* was painted white, her teak and mahogany deck fittings polished, the panelling of her whaleback picked out in light blue—which was also used on the covering board around her scrubbed decks—and her ironwork was painted green. White inner bulwarks and blue covering boards remained the traditional lining of the deck of a merchant schooner all their years, but a white hull was unusual; they were mostly black above water and green of copper or anti-fouling beneath. In later years between the wars, when paint was an expensive item of upkeep, nearly every remaining schooner and ketch took to the black of tar topsides, but after the second world war many of the survivors reappeared again in blue-grey, and one, the iron ketch *Mary Stewart*, was smart in black and white. Masts were scraped and coated with linseed oil and tallow melted down together. This mixture made the gaff travel up and down more easily.

THE LIFE OF THE YARD

At the time of the building of the *Katie*, Cock's yard employed eighty or ninety men and boys. There was no machinery in the yard and all the work of building was done by hand labour. Shortly after her launch, a single steam-driven circular saw was installed and all the remaining wooden ships that were to be built at the yard were constructed with the aid of this device alone.

When an apprentice joined the yard, he was given thirty shillings' worth of tools and no further assistance. The remaining equipment he used in his seven years of studentship had to be found by him. On joining the yard, his fellow apprentices initiated him in a manner that was a relic of more brutal times, which ceremony was officially suspended about the time the *Katie* was launched. Henceforth he was a member of the yard and must learn his trade; for so doing he was paid 4s 6d per week.

An apprentice of seven years became a journeyman, and then, after further experience, a master shipwright. He was the craftsman of the yard. But the number of shipwrights can never have been very large and the practice of their trade depended upon a social pyramid. In its lower levels were the labourers skilled and unskilled, and principal amongst these were the sawyers.

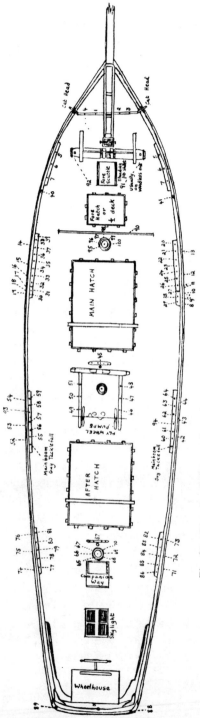

Fig 21 Pinrail diagram of a three-masted schooner with standing top-gallant sail

KEY TO FIG 21 (By Captain W. J. Slade)

1 Standing jib downhaul.
2 Fore staysail downhaul.
3 Boom jib downhaul.
4 Flying jib downhaul.
5 Pin for chain shank for anchor flukes.
6 Spare.
7 Boom jib sheet.

25 Spare.
26 Peak halliards (fore).
27 Topgallantsail downhaul.
28 Boom jib halliards.
29 Topgallant halliards.
30 Flying jib halliards.
31 Upper topsail halliards.
32 Spare.

52 Port main shrouds.
53 Port main shrouds.
54 Port main shrouds.
55 Peak halliards main.
56 Topgallant brace.
57 Upper topsail brace.
58 Lower topsail brace.
59 Fore brace (port).
60 Main halliards (main).

78 Mizzen topmast back-stays.
79 Mizzen main halliards.
80 Tackle.
81 Spare.
82 Spare.
83 Mizzen peak halliards.
84 Mizzen topmast back-stays.

8 Topgallant backstay shroud, starboard side.
9 Topmast backstay shroud, starboard side.
10 Starboard fore shrouds.
11 Starboard fore shrouds.
12 Starboard fore shrouds.
13 Starboard fore shrouds.
14 Port fore shrouds.
15 Port fore shrouds.
16 Port fore shrouds.
17 Port fore shrouds.
18 Port topmast backstay shroud.
19 Port topgallant backstay shroud.
20 Purchase tackle for catting bower anchor (belaying pin).
21 Fore staysail halliards.
22 Lower topsail clewline.
23 Upper topsail downhaul.
24 Lower topsail buntline.
33 Topgallant downhaul.
34 Fore main halliards.
35 Spare as required.
36 Upper topsail downhaul.
37 Lower topsail clewline.
38 Fore reefing tackle.
39 Standing jib halliards.
40 Flying jib sheet.
41 Flying jib sheet.
42 Starboard main shrouds.
43 Starboard main shrouds.
44 Starboard main shrouds.
45 Horse for foresail sheet.
46 Main reefing tackle.
47 Gaff topsail halliards.
48 Topping lift for fore boom.
49 Gaff topsail tack (main).
50 Gaff topsail jackstay (main).
51 Gaff topsail sheet (main).
61 Topgallant brace.
62 Upper topsail brace.
63 Lower topsail brace.
64 Fore brace (starboard).
65 Spare.
66 Mizzen gaff topsail halliards.
67 Topping lift for main boom.
68 Gaff topsail tack (mizzen).
69 Gaff topsail jackstay (mizzen).
70 Mizzen gaff topsail sheet.
71 Starboard mizzen shrouds.
72 Starboard mizzen shrouds.
73 Starboard mizzen shrouds.
74 Port mizzen shrouds.
75 Port mizzen shrouds.
76 Port mizzen shrouds.
77 Guy tackle fall mizzen boom.
85 Mizzen topping lift and fall.
86 Mizzen guy tackle fall.
87 Horse for main sheet.
88 Mizzen sheets single blocks each side.
89 Mizzen sheets single blocks each side.
90 Fore horse.
91 Standing jib sheet starboard.
92 Standing jib sheet port.
93 Main topmast backstays (port).
94 Main topmast backstay (starboard).
95 Topgallant sheets (port).
96 Squaresail halliards (port side).
97 Lower topsail sheets.
98 Lower topsail sheets.
99 Squaresail halliards (starboard).
100 Topgallant sheets (starboard).

The sawyers manned the pits which were, with the piles of seasoning timber and the gaunt frames of half-finished schooners on the slips, the most apparent feature of the wood shipbuilding yards. Long and narrow and about eight feet deep, these pits were either stone lined, or lined with packed logs through which, if the pit was near the foreshore, the water was always oozing. Relics of them are to be seen to this day; there was recently one two-thirds filled in, but quite clearly a sawpit, on the site of Trethowan's first yard at Roundwood on the Truro river; there are depressions in the bank at Yard Point near Mylor where John Stephens had his slips; there are a number traceable in the timber yards of villages far inland. Pits survive almost intact in the new growth of spruce above the red sand beaches of old ship-building sites on Prince Edward Island. Each pit was manned by two men, the top sawyer and the pit boy. The saw cut, a three-inch bite, was made on the downward stroke; the work fell to the pit boy, the top sawyer's function being largely to guide the blade. A boy would serve for years under a constant rain of sawdust in the pit and he would become a top sawyer only when he was physically fully developed. The sawyers found their own saws and it was the top sawyer's responsibility to select and buy them. For every pound they earned the top man took eleven shillings, the pit boy nine. At the yard of Scoble & Davies at Malpas in the late 90s, a top sawyer could earn £1 a week steadily. At the same time and at the same yard a shipwright was paid 4s a day for a six-day week. Whatever the state of building, there was almost always work for the sawyers to do, but a shipwright might find himself without work from day to day as repairs and building fluctuated. His greater wage was the less reliable.

The sawyers did all the cutting of the yards. They were men of great skill and delicacy in working within small limits with large and heavy tools. An old, skilled top sawyer would cut heavy timber for many feet with nothing save the scratch of his own thumbnail as a guide. They shared the shipwrights' facility for predicting the shape to be assumed by a timber between two measured points. They were men of great physical strength and endurance, they cut thousands of feet of the hardest timber, sometimes three feet square, the timber being moved across the pit on rollers, wedged if it was cut to a bevel. Aged men, once sawyers, whom I met in my own youth were witnesses to having had great frames.

There were many legends of the endurance of sawyers current in small seaport towns quite recently. One team in Cock's yard at the time of the building of the *Katie* is said to have worked for sixteen hours without a break. At night, they worked by the light of naphtha flares suspended above the pit. At Portmadoc at the time of the schooner building boom of the 90s the whole yard was lit by these flares and shipwrights and labourers worked in shifts among the misshapen shadows of the growing frames.

In earlier days some sawyers were itinerant men, and at the turn of the century there were legends among them of the days when their work was done by roving gangs, hired for a season. These gangs of men, who must have been among the most physically tough ever to roam the face of England, were regarded with respect and some fear by the villagers where they pitched at shipyard or timber stacks. There is little doubt but that in the middle of the last century there were female sawyers working in the pits of many yards. There was an aged shipwright at Saul in Gloucestershire, alive twenty-five years ago, who told me his father had seen women teams at work in the yards of Burt & Davies by the Berkeley canal.

At Cock's yard the pits were stone-lined, and at the bottom of each there stood always a half-gallon pitcher of beer. The day began with a light breakfast before six in the morning, and from six to twelve the men of the yard worked without food. At midday they had a heavy meal: beef, fried in the blacksmith's shop, bread and cheese, beer. At four they had a light meal, and at six the day ended. When they reached home the sawyers would wash down outside, as miners used to do. In the summer evenings, when they had cleaned and eaten their last meal of the day, sawyers and shipwrights would play golf on Northam Burrows (for golf was a proletarian game in North Devon in those days), or fish, or sail their boats. Many shipwrights had boats built as privilege with yard materials. On Sundays, they would take their children on to Northam Burrows and light fires among the sandhills and make picnic teas. Bideford Regatta day was an annual holiday and in the evening, when the rowing and sailing was over, 'try your strength' machines at the fair were smashed to pieces and brawls were frequent.

The shipyard worker's life was incredibly hard by late twentieth-century standards. He worked from six to six from Monday to Friday, six to four on Saturday. He began the day with morning tea boiled on a fire of the chips that were the sawyer's perquisite and kindled on the open hearth of a stone-floored, waterless, cottage. From five to six he walked four or five miles, from Bideford or Northam to Appledore. There is still the shipwrights' path from Bideford through Cleave Houses, across Limers Lane on to the cliffs above the Torridge, through woods and fields to Appledore. This walk is one of the most beautiful I know around the shores of England, but it is used hardly at all nowadays. Yet there were men alive a few years ago who could remember gangs of thirty men of the yard walking to their work along this path, singing in the complete darkness of a still, cold winter's morning, the ice in the pools cracking beneath their feet, each man knowing every foot of his daily journey. On Friday, when each worker received his pay in gold wrapped in an envelope, the young men went courting. They would walk four or five miles to their sweetheart's cottage, spend the evening and walk home in the small hours, rising at five for the shift next morning. Sometimes there was a dance in Appledore, or across the water at Instow. On moonlit nights, the young men and women would sing as they slipped back across the flood of the Torridge from the Instow side in 'Daddy' John's sprit-rigged ferry boat (Plate 38).

The distances these men walked to work in those days of very limited public transport were often remarkable—from St

Clements and Truro to Malpas, from Devoran and Perrana-worthal to Yard Point, from Burton Bradstock to Bridport. But there was another side to the picture, a side which came from no relaxation and hard poverty. 'Us never saw father except of a Sunday, the rest of the week it was always yard or pub,' said the son of one Cornish shipwright. Until the 'Lloyd George' of 1906, if a man fell sick there was no help for him but a club round among his workmates; if he died his family were thrown back on grandparents or destitution. Unemployment was frequent and when it came there was no choice but to find more work at any distance or starve. When Mr Gray was forced to close down his shipbuilding business at Falmouth in the early 1880s, his own sawyers were without work. One of them told me sixty years later :

Those were the days when a man had to work or starve. Mileage did not count. Father went to see Mr John Thomas Rapson, shipbuilder, of Penryn, who had a yard close to Penryn Church, on the riverside, just underneath the cemetery. Father had worked for him previously when he built vessels there. On this occasion there was no work to do. After doing some work for country wheelwrights, we went to work at Ponsharden yard between Penryn and Falmouth for Mr Emmanuel Martin who carried on the shipbuilding there. We built a ketch called, I think, *Irene*, also another called the *Leader*, also repairs to others whose names I don't remember. Work fell off and we moved to the Bar, Falmouth, where Mr Charles Burt had a shipbuilding yard. We agreed to work and cut the timber necessary to put twenty feet in the centre of a schooner called the *Pearl*. We did this and a few other jobs of repairs. All this time Mr William Henry Lean was calling upon us to help him in the building of schooners in a yard close by. We went to his assistance and after a time back to Ponsharden again. It was now time for me to consider breaking away from pit sawyer to go on top. My opportunity soon occurred and I went to the shipbuilding yard and foundry carried on by Mr Walter Cox, saying, 'I heard you want a top sawyer,' and he said, 'Come on !' There they built tugs, cargo and Government ships for foreign rivers; these latter were iron, sheathed over all with timber. It was there I first saw iron ships leave the ways, and I realized more than ever the old wooden walls were doomed and that my future was not pit sawing. I left Mr Cox at the end of 1892 (when the schooner *Viking* was leaving the ways of Messrs Pool, Skinner & Williams, the first iron sailing ship to be launched at Falmouth) with thanks to him for the finest written character I ever received.

Not until the 90s did young men think to leave the trade of wood shipbuilding in the West Country, and fifteen years later there was still at Appledore a complete community of builders of wooden ships. The town, with its shipyard and dry docks, rope walk and sail lofts, shipchandlers, merchants, pilots and boatmen, was still dedicated to the construction and management of small merchant sailing ships. Six years more had yet to pass before the first engine was installed to make the first auxiliary ketch, and of this perpetuating device the Appledore men were to be the pioneers and most successful exploiters in home water. The yards at Appledore had not the facilities to build a ship of the size and quality of Robert Falcon Scott's *Discovery*, but here and in other West Country villages, as at Portmadoc, there remained still in good measure the ancient skills, seven years after Scott had found them nearly forgotten on the Tay.

At all the schooner building yards, a launch was a pleasant ceremony. At Millom, on the Duddon in Cumberland, the school-children were given a day off to watch a ship leave the ways and many yards declared a holiday when a launch was to be made. The names these vessels were given were varied in the extreme. Family names were common, particularly those borne by the young children of the managers or masters, *Little Fred, Francis & Jane, Kathleen & May, Peter & Sarah, Saidie R.* Sometimes ships were named after their owner's mother, like the *Jane Banks*, or their girl friends, like the *Katie* herself. Sometimes names had a religious bias, like that of the *Hobah*, though in the latter half of the nineteenth century these were few, as were also the names of royalty, though there were many schooners *Victoria* and at least six called *Prince of Wales*. Battles, in particular that of *Alma*, and the ensuing peace, were celebrated, and there were many schooners named *Olive Branch*. Some abstract names were perennially popular, *Harmony*, *Economy*, *Gratitude*, *Favourite*; some ships had odd names, like the Bristol ketch *Electric*, some unconventional like the Newfoundland schooner *Devil*. In early days, ships were often called the 'packet' of the towns they regularly served and this custom was continued among the trows of the Severn until the late nineteenth century. Small ketches and sloops that traded among the creeks and rivers of the west coast to lane-side quays and farms had homely names as befitted their calling, *Minnie Flossie*, *Maggie Annie*, *Gwendoline*, *Maud Mary*. There were place-names like *Garlandstone* and *Cantick Head*, and lines of schooners had their own trade marks in names like the 'little' ships of Stephens of Fowey and the *My Lady* and the *My Beauty* of John Westcott of Plymouth. Initial names were common, made up either of the first letters of the owner's names, like the *W.M.L.*, named after William Montague Lawdey, a local merchant of Appledore, or of the initials of a group of owners, like the *W.J.C.*, built near Truro in the 1880s, and named after William Martin, John Burley, and Charles Dyer, her owners and builder. Dozens of ships were named in full after their owners and their families, such as the Warbricks and Barrows and Pritchards and Morrisses and Evans, and perhaps these were the most popular names of all. Many schooners were given foreign names by way of compliment to the Continental merchants from whom it was hoped they would take cargoes in the home trade, such as the *Frau Minna Petersen*, *Fanny Breslauer*, *Tony Krogmann* and *Anna Braunsweg*. The lists of these vessels are lists of the female names of their period; there are dozens of *Marys*, many named *Minnie* and *Ann*, now forgotten names like *Ermenilda* and *Hetty*, *Lydia* and *Ada*, and many *Isobells* and *Isabellas*. There are also names that date completely, like the *Girl of the Period*, or place completely, like the *Malpas Belle*.

Some of the schooners had beautiful names, among them the *Spinaway* of Fowey, the *Crystal Stream* built at Par, the *Sparkling Glance*, the *Lively Oak*, the *Flying Foam* of Bridgwater, the *Ocean Swell*, the *Forest Deer*, the *Queen of the Chase*, the *Vil-*

lage Belle, the *Pass-by*, the *Driving Mist*, and, loveliest named of all, the little *Startled Fawn*.

The launch was always noticed in the local press and the following report from a Bridgwater newspaper gives a good account of the way these things were done in 1907.

THE LAUNCH OF A VESSEL AT BRIDGWATER
MESSRS CARVER AND SON'S PREMIER SHIP
THE LAUNCH CELEBRATED BY A DINNER

Although Messrs F. J. Carver and Sons, the well-known Bridgwater shipbuilders, have turned out many excellent vessels in the past, it is doubtful whether they have previously built a more shapely and graceful ship than the *Irene*, which was successfully launched on Wednesday morning last. It is some years since a new craft was locally made, and consequently more than ordinary interest was taken in the launching proceedings. The *Irene* is a ketch of very smart and useful appearance, her dimensions being : length 85 feet; breadth 21 feet; and depth 9 feet; and she is registered to carry 165 tons. The *Irene*, which has been purchased by Messrs Clifford J. Symons (Taunton-road), Clifford Symons (Camden-road), and Captain Wm. Lee (her future skipper), will be employed in the general trade of the port. The weather on Wednesday morning was chilly, but bright, and large crowds assembled on both banks of the river to watch the launch, whilst numbers occupied points of vantage on the shipping with which the river was fairly sprinkled. Photographers abounded, and many excellent snapshots of the vessel taking the water were secured. A considerable number of people were on the deck of the vessel, and the scene was one of considerable animation when just before eight o'clock the workmen removed the stays. A slight lift by a hydraulic jack at the vessel's bow caused the *Irene* to move, and she at once gracefully glided down the ways, saluting her future home with a generous splash which caused a wave to wash the opposite bank, much to the discomforture of those stand-ing at the water's edge. The launch was in every way a complete success, and hearty cheers were raised as the *Irene* swung round to the tide and slowly drifted to the side of the *Sunshine*. Just as the vessel was moving from the yard, Miss Gladys Symons with a suspended bottle of wine christened the ketch as the *Irene*, and wished it *bon voyage*. The vessel is now alongside the east quay, and is being rapidly rigged up for her first voyage.

The *Irene* (Plate 21) survived at work at sea until 1960 and was the last British trading ketch in commission. The *Katie* herself (Plate 39) made many crossings of the North Atlantic before she was lost off Puerto Rico in February 1914. She had been bound for Garston with a cargo of copper ore loaded at Tucacas.

CHAPTER SIX

BARMEN AND BRIDGWATERMEN

APPLEDORE is now and has always been a place of ship-building. In the last two centuries, William Record, William Barrow, Thomas Geen, William Clibbett and his son of the same name, Thomas Peter Cook, James Cock, his sons and grandsons, the Hinks, Waters and Ford families, William Pickard, John Westacott, Phillip Kelly Harris and his sons, and latterly joint stock companies operating on larger capital, have built and repaired every kind of ship to the limit of size imposed by the building sites.

Until 1850 there were two principal sites. The first was the sheltered triangular bay which then existed stretching from what is now the Bell Inn yard to the head of the present Richmond drydock and round to the south end of Appledore quay. Here on the eighteenth-century Benson's New Quay, William Clibbett and his son and Thomas Peter Cook built ships. At the other end of Appledore, between the village and the hamlet of Irsha, another bay stretched up towards the church and here was Churchfield, the yard of Thomas Geen.

In the early 1850s, big changes took place. William Cock, a member of a family which had moved into the district from the neighbourhood of South Molton, took over the Churchfield yard. A year later he died in one of the periodic epidemics of cholera which swept Appledore in the mid-nineteenth century, but his family continued to occupy the yard for fifty years. In the late 1840s, James Yeo of Port Hill, Prince Edward Island, paid a visit to his son William who lived in Appledore and acted as his father's British agent. James Yeo began life as a labourer and later became a carrier working between Kilkhampton and

Bideford. In 1819, he emigrated to Prince Edward Island and by the middle of the century was the colony's greatest merchant and shipbuilder and on his way to becoming its most powerful man. The result of his visit to his son was a scheme to turn Appledore's sheltered bay, for centuries the traditional safe, free mooring place on the river, into the British headquarters of James Yeo's great shipbuilding and lumber-trading business. In *West-countrymen in Prince Edward's Isle* Ann Giffard and I have described in detail what happened. Land was bought and filched, the great Richmond dry-dock was built and roughly-finished ships began to pour across the Atlantic from the beaches of Prince Edward Island into the dock where they were caulked, refastened, partly re-rigged and classed by Lloyd's surveyors. Then they were sold in the British tonnage market. Appledore became one of the busiest and most prosperous places in south-western England, though at a price. The whole neighbourhood was dominated by William Yeo, who as employer, landowner, banker, quarry-owner, merchant, large shipowner and his father's voice in England, controlled the lives of half the population.

When he died in 1872 the area fell into a depression from which it took ten years to recover. Then Robert Cock took the lease of the Richmond dry dock and John Westacott, son of a Barnstaple shipbuilder, that of the second dock William Yeo had built a little further up the river. They had great difficulty at first because the skilled labour for which Appledore had become famous had moved away and men had to be persuaded back into the neighbourhood and new men recruited. Robert Cock succeeded and his son built the *Katie*. John Westacott went bankrupt and in due course set up a new business at Cleave Houses, three-quarters of the way up-river to Bideford.

Robert Cock acquired the Iron yard, as it was called, between the two dry docks and here in the twentieth century the Cock brothers built steel schooners and steamers of various kinds. Before this venture was started, one of the Cock brothers had served his apprenticeship in steel shipbuilding in a north country yard and although the Cock family themselves did not long survive the first world war as shipbuilders, their enterprise in bringing the yard at Appledore into line with modern sea economy enabled it to survive to become the prosperous shipbuilding centre of today.

In the Richmond yard, Robert Cock and his sons after him built, in the last years of the old century and the first years of this, the series of wooden schooners of which the *Katie* was one. They were somewhat like the Portmadoc schooners of the same period in size, rig and appearance and were probably built under the influence of developments which were taking place at that port. There were a dozen or more of these schooners, among them the *Maud* of 1896, the *Sydney*, the *Madeleine* (Plate 31), the *Virginia*, the *Banshee*, the *A. M. Fox* (Plate 40), the *Rose* and the *Geisha*, and some were commissioned by Portmadoc shipowners.

Maud, was owned in Jersey. *Sydney*, built in the following year, was still afloat in 1932, owned in Lorient and fitted with an oil motor. *Madeleine* was owned in Plymouth, and her successor, the *Katie*, in Portmadoc. She was a fast schooner, and Basil Lubbock records that in the winter of 1911-12 she went from Civita Vecchia to London in twenty days, and in the summer of 1912 from Hull to Bermuda and back in two months fourteen days, including the time in port. The *Virginia*, sheathed at her launch, was owned in Newfoundland. Both *Banshee* and *Geisha* were also sheathed at their launch, were both owned in Braunton by Claude W. S. Gould and were both out of the register books before the first world war. The *A. M. Fox*, owned by Captain Fox and registered at Plymouth, was well known in Newfoundland waters.

So none of the later Appledore-built wooden schooners lasted for very long. But after the building of the last of them the Cocks launched three steel ships, the *Annie Reece*, the *W.M.L.* and the *Lucy Johns*, all three-masted topsail schooners. *Annie Reece*, renamed *Diolinda*, was trading on deep water in the Indian Ocean in the 1950s. The *W.M.L.* was less fortunate; she was caught at the outbreak of the first world war in a Spanish port,

39. *Katie*, soon after completion, alongside Appledore quay

40. The *A. M. Fox* drying her sails in Dover harbour

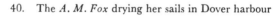

41. *Esmeralda* and *Lily* discharging coal at St Ives

42. Polacca brigantines, from a drawing by J. Jobbins, probably of the 1830s

where she was discharging hides from the Argentine. Her master died and her crew filtered home one by one. In 1917, the American four-masted schooner *Agnes Manning* (Chapter 2) came into Appledore after stranding off Lynmouth. She was sold, her partly Negro crew was paid off while her master, liking the place, settled down in Appledore as landlord of one of the local inns. There he won fame for his prowess with the revolvers he brought from on board his schooner; it is said he would toss a penny in the air and shoot through it before it reached the ground. He promised to bring home the *W.M.L.* and with an Appledore mate he set out to do so. A Spanish crew was enlisted and they had reached the Bay of Biscay when they were intercepted by a German submarine. On being ordered to abandon ship, the crew left but the master and mate stayed behind to fight her. Neither of them survived.

After the *W.M.L.*, only one large schooner was built at Appledore, the *P. T. Harris* (Plate 25) of 1912. At that time Phillip Kelly Harris was running the New Quay yard, having taken it over from John Westacott years before. When the fleet of Thomas Ashburner was dispersed at Connah's Quay in 1909, men from Braunton and Appledore were among the buyers at the sale and it had been agreed among them that Clarke of Braunton should bid for the *Result*, and Harris for the *M. E. Johnson*. Mr Clarke obtained the *Result*, but the bidding for the *M. E. Johnson* went above Mr Harris' limit and she was sold to the Kearons and Tyrells of Arklow. By way of compensation the aged Richard Ashburner advised Mr Harris on the building of a new schooner, like the *M. E. Johnson* but with a counter stern. This vessel, the *P. T. Harris*, was slowly built and eventually launched in 1912. She was lost five years later when, on a voyage down the Welsh coast in company with the ketch *Bessie Ellen*, she vanished in a squall and no sign of her was ever seen again.

Centre of shipbuilding though Appledore is and always has been, it is as a shipowning place, a port of small sailing ships in the home trade, that it was famous over the seaboard of England. There were no big fleets in Appledore and every skipper had his

K

own small vessel, ketch (for the ketch was *par excellence* the ship of North Devon), sloop, or small schooner, or at least had shares in her. Though from 1816 until the death of William Yeo, Appledore ships traded in every ocean of the world and were deeply involved in the American trade, from the late 1870s it became almost entirely a coasting port. The capital accumulated in the prosperous times of William Yeo, and the great seafaring tradition built up in the Prince Edward Island trade, meant that there were many families ready to turn to small investment in coasting ships manned by their own members, and this ensured Appledore continuing as a shipping place for many years. The ketches and smacks took open beach charters, lying out on every beach on the north coast of Cornwall and Devon, risking onshore gales, discharging Lydney coal over a 'gun' into farm carts (Plate 41). The 'gun' was supplied by the local farmer who took the cargo and who was also the local coal merchant. In this way most of the domestic coal of Cornwall was supplied. The Appledore men received an extra shilling or two shillings a ton on a four-shilling fixture for beach work, and thus each master built up money to buy his own small vessel. Where the master was an employed man, without shares, the master's surplus under the two-thirds system was the basis of his small fortune.

The Slade family, whose remarkable rise was so well recorded by Captain W. J. Slade in *Out of Appledore*, provide an excellent example of how the system worked at its best. Starting in 1888 with the small capital saved by a woman who worked with her sewing machine far into the night to enable her to buy a small ketch for her husband to run, the family never looked back and were the last owners of a fleet of motor sailing ships in Britain. Altogether, twenty-two sailing ships passed through the family's hands before the last of them was sold after the second world war.

With its narrow cobbled streets of small brightly-painted cottages between the river and the headland, its salmon boats and small luggers, and its watermen who used to sail for pleasure, Appledore was a town of individual shipowner masters. Across the pool and up the broad Taw, behind the Burrows, is Braunton pill and, at its head, the lonely quay of Wrafton, where once two limekilns stood. Behind, under the lip of the downs, with outliers of Exmoor visible far behind, is the village of Braunton itself. An inland market village, it has nothing of the sea or shipping about it but is a farmer's centre in all its atmosphere.

But though there are no shipyards or quays at Braunton, this village has been important in the history of the home trade. Though Braunton started late as a shipping place, many men of Braunton in the late nineteenth and early twentieth centuries were both seamen and farmers (and so dubbed 'grasshoppers' in Appledore). They would first buy a small sloop for the local trade, then a larger sloop or a small ketch, and finally a big ketch or a schooner to sail all over the seas of Europe. In later days, more ships were owned in Braunton than in Appledore and, looking across the Taw from Instow or the quay, a forest of masts could be seen rising above the seawalls at the entrance to the pill. Led by the enterprise of the late H. G. G. Clarke, who held an interest in many of the ships owned there, the Braunton men were the first in Britain to adopt the auxiliary motor and their intelligent exploitation of this device led to the prolonging of the last years of the merchant sailing ship in home waters. But this is another story and has its place later.

Appledore and Braunton between them were then the homes of a great number of small vessels and over 100 ketches and schooners are said to have sailed out over the bar on one tide. Before the ketches became fashionable after 1870, the typical, small, local vessel was the polacca brigantine (Plate 42). These miniature square-rigged ships were unique in Britain. Their foremasts were in one piece instead of being divided into three parts and supported by the complicated rigging of the square-rigged ship. Their rigging was simple and they set only two squaresails. The great square topsail was set from a light yard and when it was to be taken in it could very easily be lowered right down on to the foreyard. Surviving accounts suggest the polaccas were handled like staysail schooners but had the additional advantage of the square foresail which made them relatively handy to manœuvre in rivers and at sea, even though they were beamy, deep and full-lined vessels. When working down the narrow gut which leads from Appledore to the sea, polaccas would reach across and then if they missed stays they could go astern with yards aback and fore and aft canvas taken in, except for the mainsail which was scandalised by hauling up the tack and dropping the peak, the ebb dragging them seaward as they went.

One polacca, the *Fanny*, was only forty-six feet long. Another, the *Mars*, built in Bideford in 1819, was forty-eight feet. Many, like the *Newton*, the *Friends*, the *Peter & Sarah*, and the *Sally*, were just over fifty feet long. Yet they sailed far and wide. The *Lady of the Lake* and the *John Blackwell* were Mediterranean traders, and the *Express* made at least one voyage to Santander with railway iron. The *Peter & Sarah* took the pioneer party to Prince Edward Island to establish the shipbuilding community at New Bideford in 1818 and, in consequence, a number of polacca brigantines, including the *Joe Abraham*, the *Henrietta*, the *Edith*, the *Brilliant* and the *Nugget*, were built in the island. The *Brilliant* crossed the Atlantic at least three times and the *Nugget*, seventy feet long, was a regular Atlantic trader in the 1850s.

But however far they might sail, the standby of the polacca brigantines was always the limestone trade. The limestone came from quarries at Caldy, Oxwich and the Mumbles, and was burned in kilns at the backs of many North Devon beaches and on the banks of the rivers Torridge and Taw. Women did much of the work of discharging the heavy awkward cargo on the Devon side. They worked down in the hold lifting the stones while the men on deck slung them over the side. The women would roll the heavy stones up over their knees and then lift them in their arms to a man on a plank in the hatchway who threw it on deck for another man to roll it over the side. The ship would be listed far enough for the stone to roll out through the gangway on its own.

In later years ketches went stonehacking, but the trade of

the ketch was always the gravel trade, the carrying of the yellow material of which the Burrows are made all over the Severn Sea and the west coast of England. The ketches lay out on the Neck and near the lighthouse, loading gravel directly by shovels from the beach around them and taking it to Bristol, Cardiff or Gloucester for building and road-making. Besides this trade across the bar, there was a great local trade carried on by small barges about the Torridge and the Taw.

Captain William Lamey of the *Hobah* sat down to write a list of the vessels he remembered as trading over the bar in this century and in a short while he had put down the names of 120 vessels, each the separate object of its own reminiscence. There was the ketch *May Queen* of Bude, which once came over the bar from Spain loaded with a cargo of nuts; there was the ancient ketch *Purveyor* which, at a very advanced age, sailed out to South Africa. There was the *Thomasine & Mary*, built at Boscastle, a little tiller-steering ketch whose wreck in Walton Bay during a thunderstorm in 1926 is one of my own earliest memories. There was the *Aneroid*, a brigantine built in Prince Edward Island which, sailing from Bideford, was probably the last British merchant brigantine at work (Plate 43) and the *Hilda* a barquentine built at Appledore by William Pickard, an associate of James and William Yeo (Plate 44). There was the *Bonita*, Captain Reuben Chichester, which was never fitted with a motor and which on 14 April, 1933, was observed from West Appledore being rowed with two sweeps in a flat calm in over the bar and the following morning was rowed up to Bideford on the flood tide. There was the *Driving Mist*, ex-schooner, which was dismasted and foundered off the Old Head of Kinsale on her first voyage as a ketch. Fittings to her main rigging proved unsatisfactory. Captain Lamey could also remember the *Thistle*, the *Ranger* and the *Orestes*, ketches which used to sail from Minehead, the smack *May* of Lynmouth, and the *Herbert* and *Penguin* of Porlock Weir. He could remember when ketches worked the Axe to Lympsham Quay (which the *New Design* visited as late as 1935). He could recall ketches lying side by side on the beach at Weston-super-Mare to discharge their coal cargoes and unloading at the wooden quays on the now utterly abandoned Congresbury Yeo. He could recollect the days when Appledore ketches and smacks used to lie behind the old training ship *Formidable*, anchored in King Road off Portishead to await the tide to go up to Bristol and he remembered that on 6 January, 1900, a fleet of vessels sailed out over the bar bound up the Bristol Channel and four of them, the *Sir Francis Drake*, the *Jane & Sarah*, the *Watermouth* and the *Dahlia* were lost in a breeze that followed.

Across the Severn Sea, Milford Haven was a sister port into which many of the bar ships traded and many men of Braunton and Appledore have made family connections in Pembrokeshire and in South Wales generally. The ketches used to trade to Dale, to Saundersfoot, and to the islands off the coast, where there are still the remains of limekilns, and into Solva Haven and St Davids. The last Devon ship to trade into Solva was the ketch *Dolphin*. They carried the necessary goods for the farmers of the creeks of the Haven straight to their own quaysides from the ports of England. The cargo book of the *Alford*, reproduced as Appendix 2 to this volume, shows this kind of trade. In the Haven there were shipbuilders, too, on a large scale, and Goddarn, Lewis, Hogan, Jones, Ackford and a dozen others launched schooners, brigs, barques and ketches.

Best known of these Milford Haven shipbuilders were J. & W. Frances of Castle Pill. All through the late nineteenth century they were launching schooners and ketches of good repute, and they continued in business until 1909 when they launched the *Democrat* for owners in Braunton. Another of their ketches, the pretty little *Enid*, was still afloat in the 1950s.

Life on board the small vessels was hard, but the owner masters loved their small ships and took great pride in their maintenance. In 1908, the *Hobah* was bought from her Falmouth owners by Captain C. Lamey of Appledore and Mr L. H. Hyett. She had already served twenty-six years on deep water and on the narrow seas and needed a certain amount doing to her. She was dry-docked at Appledore and given a special survey from which she emerged classed A1 for six years, then she sailed to Lydney to pick up a coal cargo. Times were hard and freights difficult to get, so she waited at Lydney for some time. The only cargoes offering were destined for Bude Canal at 4s a ton, and although Charles Lamey made numerous visits to the pits nothing else was offered to him. His son William asked him : 'Other people take Bude cargoes, so why not the *Hobah*?' And his father, tiring of inaction, in the end said : 'Right, my son, you shall see what is wrong with them !'

The *Hobah* loaded her coal and left Lydney on 29 November. She sailed down to the bar, and in and out and over the bar many times, and she sailed around Hartland many times too, but never once could she get into the Bude Canal. In the end it was 29 January when she entered and, once in, she could not get out. After three weeks the paid hand started off at six in the morning and walked home to Appledore. His wages for nearly three months were the wages for the voyage, £2, and he had a family to keep. By and by the young Lamey wished to go home as well and in the end his father hired a jingle to take them back to Appledore.

But such a voyage was unusual, and the bar ships in general did well enough in trade to make small capitalists of the sturdy populations of Appledore and Braunton. They carried sand, gravel, limestone, manure, hay, bullocks, granite, and coal for the beaches as well as for Braunton potteries and Fremington Pill, where there was once a wooden drawbridge past which schooners with cockbilled yards could kedge to the now vanished quays inside.

There was a shipyard of great repute at Barnstaple where William Westacott built wooden sailing ships of all rigs and sizes. In 1880, at least fifty ships built by Westacott were afloat. He built the schooner *Snaefell*, noted for her Atlantic passages, the barques *Spirit of the Age* and *Standard Bearer*, two swift and famous schooners almost identical in size and appearance, the *Old Head* and the *T. Crowley*, both launched for T. Crowley

& Company and registered at Kinsale. He was, also, a builder of sloops for the local trade, for the Chuggs and Goulds who have always been great owners of small sailing ships on the banks of the Taw. Such vessels as the *Telegraph* and *Telephone, Electric* and *Bessie Gould* were all of his building; all sloops of sixty or so feet in length which later became ketches.

Among his last ships were three of particular importance, the schooners *Village Belle, Annie Christian,* later *Ade* (Plate 3) and *Emma Louise*. The first was fast and long lived; her figurehead is still to be seen high over a street in Arklow. *Annie Christian* was built as a two-masted schooner for a trade with general cargo between Liverpool and Dalbeattie and was at first commanded by Captain Christian. When she was two years old, it is said, she was sunk in the Mersey and, on being salved, was sold and refitted as a ketch. As a ketch, she remained in the home trade for sixty-six years, for nearly all of which she sailed first from Bridgwater and then from Appledore. She was reduced to a hulk at Appledore in 1947.

Very similar to the *Annie Christian*, indeed so similar in size and appearance that the two vessels were probably built from the same moulds, was the *Emma Louise* (Fig 22). The last of Westacott's ships, she was still in commission in the summer of 1948, trading between Lydney and Minehead, and had become one of the features of that place through an association of many years. William Westacott's son John, after he had failed at the New Quay yard, moved to lower Cleave Houses where he had grids below the bank at the bottom of Limer's Lane. A succession of financial disasters finally drove him altogether out of business but he did not launch his last ship, the pilot boat *Frolic*, until 1905.

The industry of building small wooden ships on the estuaries of the Torridge and the Taw had grown to such a size by the late nineteenth century that at one time the various yards at Barnstaple, Appledore and Bideford were said to be launching a ship a week between them. It is very doubtful, however, if this rate of launching was maintained for long, for even if each yard had

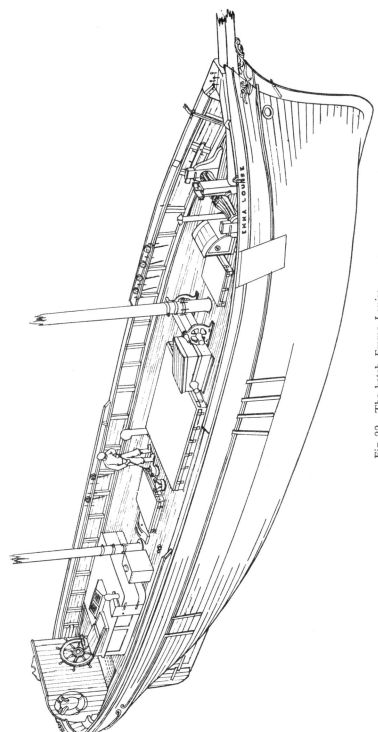

Fig 22 The ketch *Emma Louise*

two slips in production at once, at no time could they have achieved this feat for more than four weeks in succession.

The greatest of Bideford shipbuilders was Richard Chapman of Cleave Houses, and though he ceased to build ships in 1818 he is still part of this story because at least one of his ships survived into the 1880s. Thomas Evans succeeded him and then George and later John Cox, H. M. Restarick, Hansen and Company, M. W. Blackmore & Sons and today The Bideford Shipbuilding Company are still building ships on or very near the site where Richard Chapman's father Emmanuel was building 200 years ago.

H. M. Restarick had a yard at Bideford East-the-Water, as well as the one at Cleave Houses. Before him, John Johnson built ships there. John Johnson's best known vessel was the *H. F. Bolt*, an ugly ketch which was one of the last engineless vessels in the home trade. His last ship was the ketch *Julia*, and after her launch the yard was taken over by H. M. Restarick. A year later the new owner's first vessel, the smack *Kitten*, was launched. She was the first of a series of vessels for North Sea fishing which Restarick launched in succeeding years, a series which ended with the *Fair Fanny* in September 1876. Besides these fishermen, trading vessels were launched at this yard; the *Bessie Clark*, a round-bowed, straight-stemmed ketch which was probably the second merchant sailing vessel in home waters to be fitted with an auxiliary motor and certainly the pioneer in the West Country; the *Alford*, the Bude ketch whose cargo book appears among the appendices and the barquentine *Winifred*, the largest vessel built at the yard. Restarick, who was a builder of great repute, also launched two beautiful ketches for the North Sea fishrmen's mission service, the *Cholmondley* and the *Edward Birkbeck*. His yard closed in November 1886.

From time to time from the 1820s to 1868, seagoing ships were built at Weare Giffard, near the head of the Torridge tidal water. At first, building took place on the west bank right by the bridge and, later, a little downstream where the river makes a loop to the east. A series of vessels were launched, from the

Louisa, a brig of 1829, to the barquentine *Sedwell Jane* of 1868. These ships were floated down the winding stream without even bulwarks, and passed, according to contemporary accounts, through the fourth arch of Bideford Bridge to be fitted out at one of the yards below.

THE PARRET

From Braunton to Minehead there is a stretch of cliff many miles long, the sea front of Exmoor, which rises, grey, brown and solitary, terraced behind it. From the cliff roads, the whole stretch of the mouth of the great estuary is clear on a summer's day, dotted with ships and patched with every shade of blue and green. This cliff coast has four harbours and several approachable beaches. Ketches traded into Combe Martin until the second war; the last to do so was the *Ann*, built by Date at Salcombe and at least one vessel, the *Cruiser*, was built at Watermouth in 1866, by Symons, probably a Symons of Bridgwater.

Lynmouth was a harbour as well, and ketches and smacks lay behind the narrow mole at the mouth of the Lyn. Schooners still worked into Ilfracombe in the 1950s and the *Emma Louise* was the last of many small vessels owned in Minehead. Watchet had a shipyard where the ketch *Friendship* was built and many sailing ships were owned there, including the beautiful Prince Edward Island-built schooner *Kelso*. One of the last Watchet sailing ships was the schooner *Naiad*, built of iron by the Neville Brothers at Llanelly in 1867, which nearly turned over at Calstock in the great gale of 1891. She was lost at Looe when she was sixty years old. But the greatest port of small ships east of Appledore bar was Bridgwater on the Parret.

The Parret is a very muddy river. It winds many miles between its first bridge and the sea, across flat country so that on high tides the schooners seemed to be riding above the meadows. Once it was dotted with quays, at Combwich, at Dunball and all the way through Bridgwater town itself. Their gaunt ruins, buried in the growing mud, were still there a few years ago, but it is difficult to imagine what the river was like fifty years before when it was lined with shipping all the way from the bridge to below the old slip where Carver built his schooners and ketches. The site of Carver's yard was still visible in the late nineteen-forties and nearby was the dry dock where, as late as the 1930s, two ships, the *Irene* and the *Fanny Jane*, were repaired. There were grids in the river bed below the dry dock where ships were constantly lying under repair. Mr Clifford S. Carver of Bridgwater, who sailed in five Bridgwater vessels, remembered for me years ago the days when there were hundreds of small ships in and out of the river. An average of 120 ships a month traded into the Parret between 1864 and 1929. A large number of these vessels were owned in Bridgwater, and many were built there at the yards of Prosser, Gough and Carver. Gough's yard was downstream on the river bank near Dunball Wharf, and here small ships were built through much of the nineteenth century, smacks, sloops, schooners and ketches. Carver was trained in Gough's yard and was the principal ship repairer at the end of the old century and the beginning of the new.

Bridgwater ships were home traders, though a few went on deep water to South America for hides and to New York. They carried all cargoes about the narrow seas, but chiefly the bricks of their native port to Liverpool, Antwerp, the Elbe and to Danish ports. They used to visit every small haven around the west and south coasts of Eire, Youghal, Clonakilty, Waterford, Kinsale, Baltimore, Killaloe, Limerick, Fenit, Galway, the Aran Isles, penetrating far inland to the banks of small creeks. They carried anthracite from Hook, Saundersfoot and Swansea, coal from Liverpool and Lydney, granite from Penmaenmawr, Porth Gain, Porthoustock and Newlyn and timber from the Baltic ports. In 1913 the *Florrie*, built at Bridgwater in 1892, sailed to Dublin, Glasgow, Newport, Porthleven, Newlyn, Limerick, Llanelly, Guernsey, Rotterdam, Caen, Alderney and Southampton.

There were many hundreds of these vessels, each with its own world, its adventures and peculiarities, its owners, masters, builders and mates. Mr Carver wrote of them :

I happen to have sailed in a number of Bridgwater vessels. First, the *New Design*, one of the prettiest little ketches on the coast. Secondly, the *Annie Christian*, now re-named the *Ade*. I made many voyages in this vessel when she belonged to Bridgwater, under Captain J. Brightwell. She was later sold to Appledore and re-named. Next the *Sunshine*. I sailed in her under the late Captain Herod, long before she became auxiliary. She was then a beautiful vessel and could outsail and out-weather all comers. I made many fine and fast passages in her. The fourth vessel was the *Good Intent*. The *Irene* was the last vessel built in Bridgwater and was built by a relative of mine. Others were also built by the late F. J. Carver, including the *Florrie, Sunrise, Swan, Beatrice Hannah, Kate and Annie* and *Maggie Annie*.

Of these, I should say the *Kate and Annie* (sunk by enemy action in the first world war) was perhaps the best. Many others were also built in Bridgwater, some by Gough & Son and some by other builders also.

To name a few : *Coronella, New Fancy, Clara, Ellen, Clara Felicity, Octavius, Crowpill*. This is by no means a complete list. I could name many more. It seemed fitting and appropriate that some should come back to lay their bones in the river that gave them birth. The ketch *Marian*, now ending her days on the mud on Highbridge river. The *Severn*, now rotting out in Combwich Pill. The remains of the *Fame* and *Tender* both lay on the east bank of the river above Dunball Wharf, where they discharged many of their cargoes.

Mention of the *C. & F. Nurse* reminds me that I was one of the crew who took her to her graveyard to be broken up at Newport. Actually, she was not broken up but re-sold to Gloucester. Curiously enough she, too, has gone to her original home to end her days. The *Conquest*, a smart little ketch, was lost in crossing Poole Bar. Some have just disappeared. Among these may be mentioned the *R.K.P.*, lost while on a voyage from Gloucester to Bantry with salt. After sailing from Cardiff Roads she was never heard of again. The schooner *Sarah Jane* was another that just vanished. Quite a number were lost in the 1914-18 war including the *Emma, Ermenilda, Charles, New Design No 2*. The *Sunrise* and the *Swan* were both lost in the Thames. The *Florrie* struck the Crowe Rocks and foundered in 1918. The last time I saw the *King's Oak* she was lying capsized in the river at Swansea. It should be mentioned here that both the *King's Oak* and the *Ermenilda*, neither being Bridgwater built, were both lengthened in the port of Bridgwater. The *Meridian* ended up by being abandoned somewhere near the Smalls lighthouse and although without crew sailed on, eventually to go ashore near Courtown, Ireland. The *Hilda* was a very nice vessel. What became of her I do not know. The *Young Fox* was sold to another port and was lost in an easterly gale while on a voyage from Newcastle to Portmahomack.

The *Sunshine* in particular was a fine vessel. She was built at Falmouth at the turn of the century at very high cost and was one of the largest ketch-rigged vessels. She once took bricks from the Parret to Galway in seven days, towed down to the Aran Isles and picked up kelp (she was the first vessel to call there after the 1914-18 war), carried it to Queensborough and discharged it, loaded casks at Woolwich and returned to Bridgwater, all in forty days. After many years of sailing from Bridgwater, she was sold to Appledore and then, again, immediately after the second world war, to trade on the North African coast.

From Bridgwater also there sailed the *Flying Foam*, built at Jersey in 1879 and never fitted with power. She was a pretty little schooner and was not lost until driven ashore at Llandudno during a gale in January 1936. Another famous Bridgwater ship was the ketch *Good Intent*, which carried around her taffrail the text 'The Sea is His and He Made it' for over 130 years from her launch in 1790 to her breaking up at Pill between the wars.

At the beginning of the first world war there were still thirty small sailing ships in Bridgwater. Of these, some were lost in that first war, nearly a score by the normal hazards of the trade of the narrow seas and a few were sold to other harbours. The goods they carried are today moved by lorries and by small motorships owned on the Continent and in other home ports. The quiet Somerset river no longer knows the keels of these ships which once took the name of its harbour all over the seaboard of England.

THE GLOUCESTERSHIRE SCHOONERS

The Forest of Dean is a stretch of woodland occupying that

part of Gloucestershire which lies between the Severn and the Monmouth border. It is contained in a space between Ross-on-Wye in the north and Lydney to the south, between Mitcheldean to the east and Monmouth to the west. Or, if you don't mind breaks in the woodland, the Forest stretches all the way from Queen's Wood near Newent to Went Wood above Newport.

It is an attractive stretch of woodland, for there are pools in the quiet glades and from the hilltops sudden views of the grey sweep of the estuary, far away to the eastward, with black dots which are shipping and the grey dock behind Sharpness Island. Among the woods are signs of an old industry, for the dark shapes of small pit heaps loom among the trees of the deeper valleys.

The Forest of Dean coalfield is an old one and outlines South Wales; the pits, though shallow, have extensive workings. The coal used to be taken by rail from the pits down through the small market town of Lydney to Lydney dock at the head of a long canal of yellow water. It is a small harbour, miles from the town, flanked by trees and red cliffs that drop down into the estuary.

For a number of reasons, including the smallness of Lydney dock and the local connections built up by Appledore masters, the Lydney trade remained a job for the sailing coaster until the end of her days. Even in 1939, you could be sure when visiting Lydney of seeing an Appledore ketch or an Irish schooner loading or waiting to load (Plate 45). In the January of that year I went into the haven one night tide in a vessel in company with four ketches and found two large three-masted schooners inside lying under the shoots. Nearly all the schooners left in trade took Lydney cargoes from time to time; I remember two years earlier watching the ketches come slipping out of the harbour in the first light of a dawn tide, chugging out under power and setting their canvas, brown tanned, patched and weathered, to go forging down-stream with the tide, Devon-bound with cargoes for Braunton Pill, Ilfracombe, Minehead and Bideford.

The few surviving sailing coasters that used the harbour in

the last years of their trading were the remnants of a mighty host, for Lydney had always been a great coal exporting place, and in earlier years the whole dock and the canal behind throughout its length were sometimes packed with small sailing ships. There are men alive today who say that they have seen dozens of vessels packed into that small stretch of water, vessels from all the west coast of England, but chiefly from the north coast of Devon, and from the estuary itself—for the estuary was the home of some fine schooners.

These ships came from Gloucester, from Frampton and Saul and Arlingham, villages on and near the canal, and from Bristol. Alexander Watkins of Saul was a trowman's boy—the trow was one of the local craft of the Severn and was once to it as the spritsail barge was to the Thames (Plate 46)—who rose to command two trows and who, when he retired from active seafaring, bought an old Bridgwater ketch, the *Selina Jane* of eighty tons, which had been built by Gough in 1872. This vessel was eventually lost in the Youghal river when she stranded on the crest of the tide. The wreck was raised and brought back to the Severn where the *Selina Jane* ended her days as an accommodation ship for stevedores. Shortly after the purchase of his first vessel, Watkins bought the *Pearl*, a brigantine which had been launched at Whitehaven in 1867 and converted to be a topsail schooner when she was first brought to the Severn Sea. She is supposed to have been built for the South American copper ore trade and to have made passages round the Horn in her youth. She certainly went deep water, for she was felted and yellow metalled in 1875. She was wrecked in Courtmacsherry Bay in 1927, the last of the numerous merchant schooners to be called *Pearl*.

The next vessel to enter Captain Watkins' fleet was the *Kindly Light*, an iron ketch built at Falmouth in 1894 which was laid down for Captain Cook of Bude. It is said that when she was on the slips it was noticed that she was going to be too long for the lock at that inconvenient port and that she had to be altered accordingly. If this is so, her appearance did not suffer from the change for she was a singularly attractive vessel. She set a jack-

43. *Aneroid*, of Bideford, 229 tons. This vessel built by David C. Ramsay at West Point, Lot 8, Prince Edward Island, in 1894, was typical of the scores of brigantines which were built in the Island for British owners. She was probably the last merchant brigantine to work from a British home port

44. *Hilda*, a barquentine built at Appledore in 1879 by William Pickard

45. The old Newfoundland trade ketch *Progress* of Bideford, built by W. Date at Kingsbridge, loading coal at Lydney in 1937

46. The flush-decked ketch-rigged trow *Jonadab* off Portishead Pier

yard topsail on the mizzen and had a wheelhouse from the time of her launch. On the last day of January 1917 she was lost by submarine gunfire. She was followed under Watkins' management by the *Yarra*, a big flush-decked trow. *Yarra*, which was so developed in her hull form that she was usually spoken of by the trowmen as being a trading ketch with a trow's stern, was built at Bristol in 1880. For Watkins, she sailed in the Irish trade and was still afloat on the river in 1949 as a towing barge. After the *Yarra* came the *Dispatch*, a fine two-masted topsail schooner built at Garmouth in 1888. She was launched, with three other schooners, the *Amy*, the *Lark* and the *Ythan*, for the Newfoundland trade and all four at first were fitted with a patent reefing square topsail of the French type. She survived the longest of these vessels, for the other three were all lost, the *Ythan* off the Irish coast in 1924. At that time the *Ythan* sailed from Appledore and was the last of these four schooners to retain her patent gear.

The *Dispatch* had a particularly beautiful white-painted figurehead and, in Gloucestershire days, double topsails on the fore. On one occasion, when on a voyage from Tralee to Gloucester, she was blown 500 miles out into the Atlantic and only a transhipment of stores from a Portuguese trawler saved the crew from starvation during their long beat back to the land. The voyage as a whole took thirty-eight days. *Dispatch* was not sold until Mr Watkins' death in 1935, when she became a hulk at Avonmouth.

Watkins' last vessel was the schooner *Earl Cairns*. Launched by Ferguson & Baird at Connah's Quay in April 1884 for George Raynes of Liverpool, she was a big wooden three-masted schooner of 127 tons. Before Mr Watkins bought her she had sailed from Flint and from Fowey. This fine vessel, which traded in the Severn Sea for very many years, was later badly damaged by a fire in the engine room and passed in this fashion to Philip Kelly Harris of Appledore, who repaired her and fitted a second-hand motor, sending down her topsail yards from the fore. She was given a gaff topsail on the foremast and sailed for a long time

L

as a fully-rigged fore-and-aft schooner, in the trade to Ireland from Lydney. At the outbreak of the second world war, the *Earl Cairns* was one of the schooners commandeered for balloon barrage duties at Falmouth; there she lay throughout the war and at the end of it she was condemned where she lay.

Stanley Harper of Saul ran Stephens' *Hetty* (Chapter 2, Volume 2), at one stage in her career, and the *Welcome Home*. The latter, a two-masted topsail schooner of 115 tons, was built at Stornoway in 1881. *Welcome Home* ended her days with the *Dispatch* as a hulk in Avonmouth docks. Mr Harper also ran the *Kate*, built at Appledore in 1865. At an earlier date the Harper family had managed the *Via* of Brixham built by J. Upham in 1864. This schooner was owned by her builders for some time and later at Padstow, Llanelly and Glasgow. She came to the estuary in 1892 and sailed out of Bridgwater for nearly thirty years. At the end of the first world war she was bought by F. H. Harper and ran from Saul until 1927, when she was finally sold to an Irish owner. In June 1931 she was lost by stranding off Carlinford Lough.

Saul is a quiet village, scattered around the two canals which cross there. There is nothing about it that is of the sea. It lies in the broad valley, a country of rich grass and many trees and, except that you may perhaps see that the washing outside a cottage hangs on a line supported by a cut down schooner's topmast, or that there are dismantled spars by the dry dock where wooden barges are repairing, there is nothing left now to tell of the many schooners and ketches which sailed from here more than fifty years ago.

There was the *Welcome* built at Freckleton and there was the *Elizabeth Drew*. Built at Padstow in 1871 she was of 110 tons and her first owners were Sims Brothers of Tamerton Foliot, Devon. Later she went to Cornwall and to Milford Haven and, soon after the first war, she was bought by the James family of Saul for the Irish trade. She was lost in the summer of 1933 in collision with a German motor ship in the Downs. Another schooner once owned by the Sims and sailing from the estuary in her later years, was H. S. Trethowan's *John Sims*, launched at Falmouth in 1873.

The *Lucy Johns* of Gloucester, one of the schooners built at Appledore at the beginning of the present century, the *Beatrice Hannah* built at Bridgwater and the *Victoria* were all lost in December 1910. Four ships sailed north up the Irish Sea and only the fourth, the ketch *Kate* of Bridgwater, survived the gale. The *Phyllis Gray* of Gloucester, built as the *Olive Branch*, suffered a like fate, for she was found embedded bottom up in the sands below Braunton Burrows one winter's morning in 1908. The last remains of her are still there; a row of ancient ribs, seasoned iron hard and jutting out of the sands, they are known to readers of Henry Williamson as the 'Dutchman's Wreck'.

There were dozens of these Gloucestershire schooners. In the 1860s and 70s not merely trows but schooners and brigs, barquentines and large barques, were launched from the yards that lined the two canals around the inland village of Saul. At Sandfield was the yard of Miller, who built the schooners *Dorit* and *Gem*, the *Angel*, a very large vessel of 229 tons net, felted and yellow-metalled in 1875, the *Julia* and the barquentine *Carrington*, registered as a three-masted brigantine, 248 tons, felted and yellow-metalled in 1876. From Miller's yard also came the barques *M. A. Evans*, 323 tons gross, and *Jane Maria*, copper-fastened, felted and yellow-metalled, 341 tons. These vessels were launched broadside on into the canal water. Pickersgill's yard produced the barque *Anniversary*, the little brigantine *Bessie Rowe*, eighty-three feet in length, the *Mary Stowe*, which began life as a barque and was later registered as a brig and as a snow, and the big schooner *Oreala* of 187 tons net. Hunt's yard launched the barques *Star of Jamaica* and *Lizette* and the schooner *Bonnie Dunkeld*, Barnes built the schooners *Colonel Denfert*, *Conria* and *Rupert*, Jones the ketch *Anne*, Byrnes the big schooner *Maranee*, Davis the *Industry* and Hipwood the *Hafren*, launched in 1875.

These ships were felted and yellow-metalled for deep water shortly after their launch; they were built for owners in Spain and France, the Azores and Newfoundland. They were for the most part built in the 60s and early 70s and were part of the exuberant blossoming forth of coastal towns and beaches, as well as of inland villages, like Saul and Knottingley in Yorkshire in particular, which far from the coast, bred their own race of ship-builders and seamen, though there must have been people who lived and died there without ever having seen the sea.

The last owner of sailing ships on the estuary, and indeed one of the last owners of schooners in home waters, was Captain Hugh Shaw of Arlingham, the next village west of Saul. Captain Shaw at first had shares in the schooner *Kate* and in the Bridgwater ketch *Irene*, then in 1922 he bought the schooner *Camborne*. His account of his life in a manuscript in the archives of the National Maritime Museum at Greenwich is an enthralling and very valuable record.

The *Camborne*, built at Amlwch in 1884 by W. C. Paynter & Company of that port, was a three-masted double topsail schooner of graceful shape and good qualities, a working schooner with nothing spectacular about her. She was owned by Thomas Morgan & Company of Amlwch until the first world war, when she was bought by Messrs W. A. Jenkins of Swansea. In 1920, she was sold again, to the Hook Colliery Company of Haverfordwest, who intended that she should carry their anthra-cite product to the ports of northern France. They installed a semi-diesel engine of eighty horsepower and sent down the top-sail yards from the fore. She was not a success in this business. She took so long over the two trips she made to St Valery and Antwerp and had such trouble with her engine that she was laid up; Captain Shaw bought her in 1922.

A cargo of timber from Milford for Gloucester was secured and a cargo of salt was fixed from that port to Limerick. The *Camborne* arrived at Limerick in six days after meeting strong headwinds. The engine gave perfect service and the cargo was discharged in good order.

This was the time of the troubles in Ireland. For a week the *Camborne* lay alongside Limerick quay; nobody was to be seen in the town and firing went on all the time from behind barricades built in the streets. When the fighting ended, within a day the *Camborne*, as the only powered vessel in the port (remember this was in 1922) was chartered by the government forces to take troops to Cork. As many men as the ship would hold were put on board, together with several tons of food. Off Foynes, they met a Limerick steamer and the troops were transferred at sea, except for one officer who stayed on board to see the *Camborne* to Fenit where they picked up more troops and took them back to Limerick. Later, Captain Shaw spent several months taking supplies into Dingle, Valentia, Galway and other west coast ports at high freights and some degree of personal risk. In November 1922 the *Camborne* returned to England, bringing a cargo of bacon from Fenit to Liverpool.

Until 1926 Captain Shaw remembers business with his schooner as having been fairly prosperous. But for the next ten years it was only by the utmost effort that any profit could be derived from her at all. Every trade was tried, on the west coast from the clay ports of Cornwall to Glasgow, on the east coast as far north as Perth. In the end the *Camborne*, because of the reputation she had formed in her Irish days, was lucky and settled down to a run from Gloucester with salt for the bacon factories of south-west Ireland. The merchants liked their salt cargoes to be carried in a wooden vessel and the *Camborne* had a good record for delivering them dry. She shared the trade with the schooner *Haldon*, owned and commanded by Captain W. J. Slade of Appledore. With occasional return cargoes the trade was made to pay.

She was at sea throughout the great easterly gale of February 1936, the gale in which the *Nellie Fleming*, an engineless three-masted topsail schooner, vanished without trace. This gale is said to have reached 108 miles per hour in gusts and the *Camborne*, caught out on a passage from Gloucester to Tralee, was blown far out into the Atlantic, making Fenit pier four days after the gale had blown itself out. She was at that time fifty-two years old. Although heavily powered as an auxiliary, the *Camborne* was not cut down in rig; she set gaff topsails with a square running sail on her foreyard when the wind was fair. Nor was she run as a motor schooner in the modern sense. She made long passages under sail alone and although she was never meant to be a fast ship, some of these were good passages: forty-eight hours from Bridgwater to the Shannon water and twenty-six hours from Sharpness to Queenstown.

The *Camborne* was a coasting tramp; the embodiment, if you like, of the small merchant sailing ship in its last period in home waters. On the many voyages they made with him in those years Captain Shaw's sons, who were drawn to small sailing ships and the sea, took with them a small box-camera of an old pattern. With this they recorded something of the other ships they saw and the sails and the sea and the life on board the schooner and they made something of a record of that life in its last days. Some examples of their photographs appear in Volume 2 of this history.

CHAPTER SEVEN

OWNERS, MASTERS AND MEN

FRACTIONAL OWNERSHIP

THE importance of the shareholding system in the world of the merchant schooners cannot be over emphasised. The system of dividing the property in every British merchant ship into sixty-four shares was introduced in an Act of Parliament of 1824 and confirmed in subsequent Acts. It was therefore in force throughout the period with which this history deals. Though it has been shown by Rupert Jarvis that the sixty-fourths system itself had no customary foundation, the system of dividing the property in vessels into fractions, any fractions that happened to be convenient, was already long established and made it possible for a whole community to participate in providing the capital for a vessel. The account book of the schooner *Thetis*, reproduced at Appendix I, shows her as owned by twenty people in shares of from one sixty-fourth to one-eighth. Not only people with obvious maritime interests, such as shipowners, brokers, master mariners and ship chandlers owned shares in vessels but also (as in the case of the *Thetis*) many others. The local clergyman, maiden ladies, the builder, the butcher, widows, quarry owners, prosperous farmers, school masters, doctors and lawyers often dabbled in vessel property. Though many ships were owned by only a few people, many more were widely shared, so widely shared, even, that their owners were sometimes lost sight of. When the Slade family of Appledore bought the schooner *Millom Castle* from William Postlethwaite of Ulverston in 1912, twelve owners of sixty-fourths could not be traced and never were found. Instead, William Postlethwaite gave a written guarantee for the twelve shares for himself and his heirs.

These little ship-owning groups, which were particularly common in the south-west of England, were often closely tied in with the local industries. Such groups of small capitalists enabled the small, closely-knit community to create, operate and control from within itself its own mining, quarrying, manufacturing and shipping activities.

But the system of dividing vessel property into shares as small as a sixty-fourth had another and extremely important effect. Many ships had among their owners mates and even seamen, as well as masters. These men were on their way up in the local community, and often an extended family would join together to buy a vessel for several of their number to operate, one to manage, two or three others to sail. W. J. Slade's *Out of Appledore* has given a vivid picture of the way a family of this kind broke through from near poverty to relative wealth in a schooner-owning community.

But this open road to greater prosperity through shares in vessels meant that the seafaring community in the days of the schooners was fundamentally different from its agricultural equivalent. Given reasonable health, industriousness, temperate habits, a reasonable run of good fortune and, above all, a good managing wife, seamen in small maritime communities could hope to retire as shipowners, their old age provided for.

No such fluidity existed in the social structure of the agricultural hamlet. Farm workers, like fishermen, had little or no hope of acquiring capital, however hard they worked. Seamen had the means open to them to accumulate capital. Thus seafaring and agricultural communities were fundamentally different and this difference was reflected in their social structure.

At the lower levels, of course, the seafaring communities were just as poor as the agricultural communities described so vividly in Flora Thompson's *Lark Rise to Candleford*. In bad periods life for many people was so hard that, in the vivid terminology of Appledore, 'they had to work for their breakfast before they could eat it'. But at the other end of the scale there were many success stories of families who, in two generations, became prosperous from nothing and even, a few of them, very rich.

THE MASTER

The job of sailing a small schooner was a skilled one in the highest sense of that much abused term. It is not too much to say that everything depended on the master. Given identical conditions, the same ship could leave one man bankrupt and acquire a reputation as a slow workshop, while for another she could make a tidy fortune and a reputation as something of a clipper. It was vitally important that the master should have no inhibitions about doing every job—from representing himself in a court case to shovelling a coal cargo. In the 1920s and 30s, when the schooners were dying, the social pattern in North Devon, where they were most successful for longest, was the working master who owned part of the ship himself and was prepared to do every job on board. In South Devon, where the masters tended to be hired men and the owners stayed at home and managed, the industry faded out of existence.

Masters of schooners were men of many different kinds. Some were the sons of hardworking, independent owner masters and such boys began their sea career very early. W. J. Slade first went to sea with his mother at the age of three months and he spent at least a month at sea every year with his father after he was able to wash and dress himself. Captain William Lamey of the *Hobah* could remember going round the land in his father's ketch before he was five years old.

Others were sons of prosperous shipowners or shipping families and began their careers at twelve or fourteen years as boys in a schooner belonging to their family, or to friends. A great number of them were young men who had shown more energy and intelligence than their fellow seamen, had earned a good name and eventually won command of a schooner or ketch in which they often had shares. They had no paper qualifications and they did not require any as long as they stayed within the limits of the home trade and did not command ships carrying passengers. They reached responsible positions at a very early age. In 1913, no member of the crew of the *Millom Castle*, including the master, was over twenty-one.

Under the Merchant Shipping Acts, if the schooner cleared from a British port for a voyage taking her outside the limits of the home trade, the master had to have some kind of qualification. Most regularly ocean-going schooners were, therefore, commanded by men who had passed the necessary examinations or who held the Certificates of Servitude granted to men already experienced in command when the examination system was first introduced.

When a schooner normally in the home trade and commanded by a master qualified only by experience was fixed for a deep-water passage, various expedients were adopted to overcome his disabilities. If the master had some knowledge of stellar navigation, and if the owners and the insurance authority had confidence in his ability to make a deep-water passage, the ship might clear from the United Kingdom to a foreign port within home trade limits and from there clear overseas. Sometimes a second master was employed for the voyage, appearing on the papers as in command. This second master might be an unsuccessful qualified master, who would in fact work as mate, or even as a seaman, or he might, in the early part of the period, hold a Certificate of Servitude. Shoreham brigs in trade to the Baltic and the Mediterranean used this method, as did many schooners in the Newfoundland trade. The official master in such cases was sometimes referred to as a 'nurse'.

Occasionally, when the usual master of a schooner in the home trade was not able to navigate and yet the owners wished to retain him in command on a deep-sea voyage, a second qualified master was employed in nominal charge and with full powers as a navigator, the ship's usual captain acting as sailing master. All these expedients were used on board schooners occasionally taken up for deep-sea fixtures and on board ships seasonally employed outside the limits of the home trade, in the Baltic or Mediterranean trades, or making one voyage a year to Newfoundland. They were used sometimes in schooners regularly employed on deep water where the master was a part-owner, or a man particularly commanding the confidence of owners, merchants and insurance society. When the schooner was of more than a certain size the problem was doubled; she had to carry a qualified mate as well.

Charles Henry Deacon (Plate 8, Volume 2) was a good example of an 'unqualified' master. He was born at Beesands in Devon in 1862 and began life by working on a farm. In later life he often used to say that no seaman could know what work could mean until he had served on the land. At eighteen, he went to sea in a Brixham schooner, but, although he was always proud of being a Devon man, he soon took to sailing in Cornish vessels. He joined the Stephens fleet, was put in charge of a schooner at the age of thirty-two, and remained in command for forty years with the same employers. In this time he lost no ships by accident, thought two were sunk under him during the first world war. After the war he was given the barquentine *Waterwitch* and stayed with her for seventeen years. He had a bronzed, gypsy-like face and wore a fur cap, gold earrings and old-fashioned leather thigh boots. To test the speed of his ship in light airs, he would drop small pieces of paper over the bows and then walk alongside them to the stern; when becalmed he could be seen standing by the break of the little quarterdeck of his old barquentine lighting matches to see which way the coming wind would move the flame.

On board the *Waterwitch*, which was built to be an ocean trading brig, there was good accommodation for the master. Most of the schooners were well fitted out aft. A twisted companionway, turning through 180 degrees in the eight or ten feet of its fall, led down to the cabin, a panelled triangular apartment built into the stern of the ship (Plate 9, Volume 2). The two long sides of the triangle were lined with narrow, hard, upholstered seats backed by panels rising three feet above the deck. Above this was a shelf, packed usually with all kinds of sea junk and rimmed with a low rail on miniature turned stanchions. Above this shelf, panelled lockers sloped back to the deck head. Aft, above the shelf, was a square mirror let into the panelling. Between the upholstered seats was a small triangular table, shaped to fit the small cabin and usually supported by a single leg rising from the deck amidships. The forward, broad end of this table folded downwards to give passage before the fireplace that was built into the forward bulkhead between the door to the companionway and the door to the master's cabin on the other, starboard side. This fireplace was often of the late-Victorian cast-iron pattern and looked strangely out of place in a schooner's cabin. The earlier, and the poorer, ships had a coal stove in the same position.

The mate had a small cabin at the foot of the companionway. Immediately forward in some schooners there was a mess room where the whole crew ate, but in most schooners they ate in the cabin in a manner described later. The tall, hollow structure of the skylight occupied most of the deckhead space of the cabin. Below swung the complex brasswork pattern of the great oil lamp and a tell-tale compass was fixed at the after end of the skylight. This instrument often served as binnacle compass on its reverse side. On deck, above the after end of the cabin, stood the helmsman, his hollow footfalls echoing above the master's head, as did also the ceaseless grate and rattle of the steering gear. In some tiller-steering schooners the compass was in a hole on the after side of the companion, which was entered from the starboard side.

The master lived beneath the tell-tale compass and the swinging oil lamp. Sometimes at sea he was bent over charts on the small table, sometimes he stretched his length fully dressed on one of the hard benches, sometimes in his bunk. In harbour, he worked at his accounts on the table, or talked to his fellow shipmasters, or to shore people seated around it. I knew one such a man, the prosperous master of a lovely steel schooner, who used to sit for minutes on end at his table, doing nothing. When challenged, he would say that he was just thinking about his ship. The masters and owners of schooners and ketches used often to

watch their ships in this way. John Stephens is said to have done
so, and Captain Lamey (Plate 10, Volume 2) spoke of his father,
Charles Lamey, in these words :

> Often, towards the end of his life, after we had brought the
> *Hobah* into Appledore Quay he would go down there after the
> day's work was over and sit watching her. I would say to him,
> 'What are you doing, Father? 'Tis late now and you had best be
> coming home,' and he would say to me, 'I'm just looking at the
> *Hobah*, son, I'm just looking at the *Hobah*.' At the time I thought
> it was strange that anyone should feel that way about a ship, but
> I found myself doing the same thing before the end of my time
> with her.

Some old masters almost worshipped their vessels. Others
treated them sometimes as if they were living things. Thus Captain William Kingdon Slade, when attempting to sail the ketch
Alpha (Plate 12) through the lee of the ketch *Ulelia* seventy years
ago, was heard to say, 'Come on my little *Alpha*, I know you can
do it, come on my dear !'

The master was often the only man on board with any knowledge of navigation and on an ocean voyage the ship and her crew
were absolutely dependent upon him. This situation could arise
even in home waters. When the schooner *Hodbarrow Miner* was
lost in Mawgan Porth in March 1908 (Plate 47, Volume 2) it
was learned from the only survivor that the master had been
swept overboard, leaving the crew of three with no idea of where
they were and very little idea of how to sail the ship. They tried
to follow the course plotted on the chart by the master before
his death, but in a rising gale lost their sails and drove ashore.

Not only did the master sail the schooner, he was often her
broker and agent as well. In the words of Captain Joiner of
Whitstable, speaking of the early twentieth century :

> We always fixed our own ships and paid for everything, drew
> freight and paid insurance, wages, food, port charges, stores,
> brokerage, towage. The master was the ship's whole office. Each six
> months we had the accounts settled with the other owners, but of
> course we were part-owners ourselves. We were paid by the voy-
> age, the crew by the month of thirty days. The master got £8 10s

per voyage, the mate £5 10s per month and able seamen £3 10s.
A voyage was from Whitstable to Gravesend for chalk ballast,
then to the north-east coast for coal and back to Whitstable or
Ramsgate; we had to discharge our own cargoes when required.
If we went into London we got an extra quarter on the voyage
rate.

Such a system could be very rewarding to a careful master,
and it was even more rewarding on ocean voyages when the
master was sometimes out of touch with his owners for months
at a time. Careful management would found a fortune,
augmented by the proceeds of ballast sales, which in some ports
were traditionally the masters', and by the bonuses which appreci-
ative merchants gave to the masters of smart vessels in com-
petitive trades. Some of the Lancashire fleet-owning companies
would build a schooner for a man they liked and send him
away in her to find cargoes, requiring only that he should return
to them one-half of his running profits. In time, an energetic man
could take shares in a dozen ships, buy allied businesses and
property ashore and on this security raise capital to buy shares
in powered ships. Some of those who were fortunate and who
have died in recent years have left estates of tens of thousands
of pounds.

At the end of the last century some masters were able to take
their wives to sea with them for a few voyages in summer. Mrs
R. J. Hockin of Newquay accompanied her husband on a number
of passages in the *Ocean Queen*. She was able to enter into the
life and, in the end, to take her trick at the wheel with the rest
of the crew. Appledore owner-masters regularly took their wives
to sea with them in summer. In the 70s and 80s, on board poorer
ships, daughters sometimes worked with their brothers as crew
members. Sometimes a mate would be allowed to bring his wife
for a voyage or two, while the masters of the billyboys of the
East Coast, some of whom had no homes on shore, had their
wives and families, like the modern Groninger, with them
wherever they sailed.

NAVIGATION AND PILOTAGE

The masters of schooners differed in many respects from their contemporaries in charge of big sailing ships. They were not only navigators, but also masters of pilotage. As navigators, they were concerned in finding the way across the ocean from a point on one coast to a point on another coast perhaps five thousand miles away. As pilots, they dealt with the problems of narrow channels, littered with banks, rocks and islands; with the entrances to difficult harbours and with the berths inside them; with bad weather in narrow waters; and, above all, with tides.

Tides were almost the most important factor in the life of a schooner or ketch master in the home trade. Much of the work of these ships was not much more than controlled tidal drifting. They depended upon the tides for the speed of their passages and, given a certain quality of hull form and sail plan, the speed of a schooner in passage-working in the home trade depended more upon her master's skill with tides than upon anything else. W. J. Slade has written an account of a very early lesson in tide work.

I remember being taught a lesson as a schoolboy of tender age in handling a boat. My father's ship was lying in a berth called Skern, in the mouth of the Torridge; she had dragged her anchor and needed attention. I was called on to assist Father to row the boat one and a half miles against a strong westerly wind. As I was only eight years old my strength soon gave out, but Father soon got over that difficulty. There was a strong current running in the direction we wished to go, so an oar was fastened out over the boat's stem, with the blade on its edge to catch the wind. The stern now faced the wind and we sat in the stern pulling one oar backward on the weather side. In this way we zig-zagged from side to side of the channel just like a ship beating to windward. When it was necessary to tack, we pulled the boat's stern around to the wind by pulling the oar on the opposite side, continuing until it became necessary to go in stays again. I had to use this method on numerous occasions in the years to follow.

W. J. Slade has also written generally of tides and navigation in a schooner masters' life :

When a schooner sailed from a port such as Barry or Cardiff in a fresh head wind, the master nearly always had a goal to be reached by low water. He made the best use of the tide along shore because the first of the ebb was stronger close to the shore in his favour and in fact he would make quite a few tacks (short) in the eddy and gain a lot of distance, before the flood tide stopped running to the eastward a distance off shore. To do this he had to possess an intimate knowledge of any rocks or shoals lying close to shore. This knowledge was passed down from one generation to another and it meant miles gained towards the goal he had set himself for the tide. He might get as far as Mumbles, where he would anchor at low water to await the next ebb tide instead of being driven back again on the flood. These tactics were always used by sailing coasters wherever possible on any part of the coast. After working out tide on the ebb, a place was found close to shore or in a small cove to anchor and thus cheat the coming flood. Knowledge of this kind was simple to those born in it but was not so easy to a deep-sea sailor.

Since the 1870s, schooner and ketch masters seem always to have used charts, both on deep water and in the home trade. Even in the smallest of ketches a course was given on a compass bearing (though the compass of a small home-trade sailing ship was swung only when unavoidable). On the wind, the master might occasionally tell the helmsman to keep her full and bye, but compass courses were necessary to clear the master in case of accident. The traditional skill of the home-trade master lay in his knowledge of pilotage, tides, coasts, bottom, local weather conditions, and his ability to handle his own ship. Some of the trading-sloop masters who spent all their lives on a small section of the coast knew that coast so well that they could find their way around without any aids to pilotage. The trowmen of the Severn sailing east of Bridgwater used neither charts nor compass, the oldest men among them knew that difficult river so well that they could sound and listen their way from the Parret to Bullo Pill in the thickest weather. But west of the Parret these same men used charts and gave their helmsman a compass course.

In the middle of the last century, when the trading sloops still worked all around the coasts and most of their masters were

nearly illiterate, charts were not so widely used. There are stories
of Bridgwater seamen rounding the land on a calm night lying
in the bulwarks listening for the noise of the surf breaking on
the Longships, and of these same men sounding their way into the
Parret in the days before there were any buoys to mark the
entrance. Some masters of mid-century traders must have known
from memory the character of the bottom of much of the western
part of the North Sea.

Even in the last days of sailing ships in the home trade, the
older masters would rarely use a pilot's guide or a large-scale
harbour chart. If they traded regularly into a difficult river, they
would make up a series of notes on the passage of the channel.
Some of these home-made pilotage notes occupy a whole exercise
book. I have one in front of me now, covering the Youghal river
from the sea to the highest navigable point. It was knowledge
hard won, for there are notes on some of the sketch maps,
'stopped here ½-hour', 'remember to clear sunken rock', 'stopped
here 2 times.'

After tides, sheltering places concerned a master in the home
trade. Big, deep, powerful schooners and brigantines, and big
ketches, could draw out to sea and, in the language of the
schooner crews, 'punch out a blow'. But to small schooners and
ketches coastal voyages in autumn and winter were a succession
of hurried scuffles from sheltering place to sheltering place. Such
ships could not safely be caught without shelter in their lee. A
Bridgwater schooner, for example, making sail to the westward,
was faced with an uninviting prospect. To the south there was
no shelter except the Clovelly and the Lundy Roads. To the north
there were Cardiff Roads and Barry Roads, disliked because big
ships steamed through them, the Mumbles, Caldy and Milford.

A winter voyage might consist of a series of short passages between each of these sheltering places in turn, and then a wait
in Dale Roads for settled weather for the passage to Ireland or
to the northward. No wonder that at some ports there was a
deeply ingrained tradition of not going to sea in January and
February. In Appledore this custom of avoiding the worst weather

M

of the year can be traced back into the eighteenth century. In long periods of bad weather big schooners made the same sort of broken passages. Douglas Bennet writes :

In the noble *Alert* in August and September of 1934 we were fifty-three days from Runcorn to Falmouth, carried away our port after main channel plate, had to hurriedly shift our summer jibs and topsails at Holyhead, broke quite a few blocks aloft with the eternal flogging, chafed the gear and generally proceeded about the decks by a series of short passages from one solid object to another. *Snowflake* blew away the luff of her foresail and lost her sidelight screens. Old Deacon lost his foresail. The *Banks* also damaged some sails. At one time there were the following at Holyhead all windbound : Bound round the land : *Jane Banks*, *Alert*, *Waterwitch*, *Snowflake*. Bound for Ireland : *J. & M. Garratt*, *Volant*, *Crest* (an old Danish schooner) and *North Barrule*. There was a big ketch-rigged yacht of about 100 tons that was blown half way up the Irish Sea, and the *Garratt* with two 50 h.p. engines, the only Chester river schooner that could make Connah's Quay in one tide, had more than she wanted on more than one attempt to put out.

One evening below Bardsey we were beating into it in another attempt on the Holyhead Milford and all stations to Falmouth line, when a little two-sticker came up ahead and passed between us and the land going like a Wallasey Corporation ferry. She was the *Mary Sinclair*, which had loaded in Runcorn about a week before us, had gone south, discharged, loaded clay and was on her way back to Runcorn again. I think she did it in about fifty odd hours. Later she, too, joined the great trek south.

A year later a mate of mine in the *Banks* set off on the same royal road, the first port of call was off Ramsey I.O.M. where they sheltered under Maryhold head (another famous place for windbound schooners), then Holyhead, and finally after beating, beating endlessly in an attempt to get round the land they had to put into St Ives as they had only biscuits and tea with no sugar or milk left. The *Mary Barrow* under that famous Danish skipper 'Mad' Peter Mortensen (but definitely not to his face) with at least 150 horses in her by then, put out of the Mersey during the height of one gale, because, it transpired subsequently, one of his crew spat on the deck, but even he had to call it a day and return defeated to the Mersey with his fore and afters well round the booms.

W. J. Slade writes of amusing incidents involving his father's successful ship handling in the early 1890s :

One little episode amused me as he told it. He left St Agnes for Newport, Monmouthshire, light. The *Francis Beddoe* was rather tender without ballast and so when the wind suddenly veered north-west and blew hard he had to find a place to run her in as she wouldn't carry enough sail. She was just above Trevose coming daylight with Padstow under the lee but it was only an hour from low water. In those days the deep water was close to Stepper point on the west side of the entrance. Without hesitation he ran for it. She got inside the point where she took the baffling winds. He put the helm hard to starboard sticking her against the dreaded Doom Bar. A crowd of men were on the cliffs waiting for a signal of distress requiring the lifeboat, but none came. He wasn't giving up so easily. When the flood tide came she dropped in to the anchorage in the cove, let go both anchors, sprung the chains and prepared to ride out the gale. It was a dark winter night, and the wind fell away towards midnight. In the morning before daylight it had backed southerly. He got the anchors and sailed. On arrival to Newport he saw in the papers that an unknown ketch was ashore on the Doom Bar but had disappeared during the night. Of course it was very easy to cover up the name and it was never reported. Another voyage he was in Lydney where the crew left. He sent to Mother asking her to send a new crew. There was no one ready to go for that particular time so Mother left her children in charge of one of the females of the family and was off to Lydney by the first available train. When Mother arrived she found the vessel loaded for Bideford and Father hard at work getting ready for sea. She lost no time in joining in with the work. They sailed the following morning and with Mother's help got down to Penarth Roads to anchor. Father went to bed while Mother kept anchor watch till the tide turned in their favour at high water. They hove up the anchor, set the sails and were off again down Channel. It was Mother's turn to sleep. When she was called to get the breakfast the ship was passing Ilfracombe. They got alongside Bideford Quay that evening and were off home. No wages to pay so they were both satisfied.

When lying in shelter, ships took up position according to the ease with which they could work off shore if a sudden shift put the land under their lee. Cutters and fore-and-aft schooners lay inmost, larger schooners and ketches next, and then square-rigged vessels. At a sheltering place, hundreds of ships might gather in a few hours before the beginning of a gale. In the days of waiting at anchor the crews were severely tested. They lived together in a confined space, inactive and without intellectual diversions. Under such conditions they adopted the habits of lighthouse keepers and drew within themselves. They made picture frames and sennit mats. Every home in West Appledore has its sennit mats, born of days windbound in distant roadsteads, and wearing through generations of its maker's family.

While he was windbound, the master watched the form of the clouds, the way of the shift of the wind, considered in relation to the glass, the behaviour of birds, and the appearance of the coast about him. In later years he would wire for local forecasts, ring his friends at coastguard posts and in other ships lying in harbours on the coast towards which he was bound. Just how long these waiting periods could be is shown by the voyages some Bridgwater schooners and ketches made in the bad winter of 1911-12. The *Industry* took fifty-two days to get across Padstow bar after first sailing from Bridgwater. The *Charles* was fifty days sailing from Bridgwater to Penzance. The ketch *Meridian* took thirty-four days to sail from Plymouth to Liverpool. Most of the time on these passages was spent lying windbound.

An extreme example of lying windbound was that of the Appledore ketch *Pomona*, formerly a polacca brigantine, under Captain George Saul. He went ashore in the vessel's boat at Angle, Milford, in the early autumn and remarked to his crew, 'Well my boys, the leaves are falling and I expect they'll be growing again before we leave.' They were. George Saul's owner was a relative who could support the old man in this way as well as in any other. The *Pomona* was worth only about £150, which meant that if the owner received £10 clear a year he was satisfied. She cost next to nothing to maintain. She had the same chain main halliards for thirty years and when a link broke it was replaced by a patent connecting link. As for the crew, they got their food free and did small jobs ashore if they could find them with local farmers, fishermen, etc. Their families in Appledore had to fend for themselves. The crew could not leave the *Pomona* because they had no means of getting the fare home.

INSURANCE

Captain Joiner has been quoted as saying that 'the master was the whole ship's office'. A successful master had to be able to press a law case in a port far from home and to understand thoroughly the mass of regulations, laws and customs which governed his relations with those with whom he came into professional contact. In the twentieth century, though even fixture agreements were still often oral, the times were working against the semi-literate and the fortunes were made by men who, whatever their lack of formal education, were capable of meeting people on their own terms.

One of the most important factors in the master's life was insurance. Insurance is a part of the life blood of shipping. Not only are the standards to which ships are built and maintained imposed in the end by insurance requirements, but the whole business of ships and cargoes is greatly facilitated by a smoothly running insurance organization. The insurances of the schooner were usually borne by what are called mutual associations or, more cryptically, 'mutuals'.

The shipowners of a small port formed the association. There was often a paid, part-time secretary, but the other officials, chairman, president, and treasurer and the governing committee, usually called the 'board of directors', were not paid. Each member of the association registered each of his ships as to be insured for a given sum, often compulsorily much less than her market value in order to dissuade him from throwing her away. At Appledore and Braunton, for instance, it was stipulated that no ship was to insure for total loss above one half of her purchase price. For each ship, he paid an entrance fee of two or three per cent of her value. If the ship was lost the association called a levy, each member contributing in proportion to the total value of the ships he himself had covered by the mutual. In some associations, in the event of a total loss claim being paid, the wreck became the property of the association and the price obtained for her became part of the association funds; in others, the proceeds were divided equally between owner and club. At Braunton, the association's profits were used to build up members' deposits until they were roughly twelve per cent of the insured value of members' ships, then the surplus was returned to members each year. Sometimes, if a ship was salved and sold these returns were considerable. Salved vessels were not always disposed of. At Gloucester, it seems probable that the association itself operated vessels which it had acquired in this way for the benefit of members.

It was a very simple insurance system and a very economical one, since there was no capital, no profits, and the very small overheads were covered by occasional small levies. To work economically, the association had to be of a certain size, so that the levies on each member were small. The members were saved the annual drain on profits of ordinary insurance, and sometimes years would elapse during which they were required to pay only very small sums. At the same time they were covered, if barely, against all risks.

The working of the systems can be followed in detail from the two documents reproduced as Appendices 4 and 5 of Volume 2. It was the existence of these associations that made the development of the schooner possible, for without them it would never have been possible to attract hard-won capital to so risky a business as the ownership of small, ocean-going, wooden sailing ships. The prosperity of each small port circulated around its mutual association and where the association thrived and was efficiently run, there the small ships thrived also. There were mutuals at most of the shipping places mentioned in these volumes.

The associations had their own rules about the standards to which ships were to be maintained and the qualifications of their masters, over and above the requirements of the classification societies and the Board of Trade. Masters were examined by senior members of the association, some of whom held no certificates. Uncertificated mates were sometimes allowed to pass, while Board of Trade-passed masters might be rejected as far as ships belonging to members of the mutual were concerned.

More important even than the insurance of ships is the insurance of their cargoes. A seaworthy, highly-classed vessel attracts shippers because the insurance rates on cargoes carried in her will be low. If shippers know that cargoes carried in a particular ship or group of ships can be covered easily and cheaply, they will use those ships.

I have heard of half a dozen freight insurance societies at schooner ports, societies covering the risk of non-payment of the freight money itself. One of the most successful was the Gomerian Freight and Outfit Ship Insurance Society, significantly enough of Portmadoc. It seems very likely that the insurance facilities offered by this society played their part in the continued prosperity of that port when the schooners were in decline elsewhere.

Mutual associations existed in the great Continental small sailing ships ports. Marstal, on the island of Aero in Denmark, had a very powerful society, whose headquarters were in a square building of mellowed brick by the harbour-side. High on its seaward wall is a carved plaque in relief of a topgallant schooner under sail.

THE MASTER UNDER STRESS

In March 1891, south-western Britain was swept by a gale of exceptional ferocity, made much worse by being accompanied by heavy snow. Ships were wrecked all round the coast and scores of seamen lost their lives. Hundreds of trees were blown down and several vessels are said to have been built from gale timber bought cheap. Even at Calstock, miles from the open sea, the iron schooner *Naiad* was thrown on her beam ends on the river bank. Captain W. J. Slade has recorded the experiences of his father, William Kingdon Slade, in this gale as his father told them to him. William Kingdon Slade was master of the ketch *Francis Beddoe*, owned in Appledore.

The *Francis Beddoe* was only eight years old when she was bought so she was thoroughly good, if of only 70 tons, and he was out to get the best from her. She had been trading to St Agnes, a little pier harbour on the north coast of Cornwall since her purchase and now for the first time she was bound to Bideford with a cargo of salt from Gloucester. She sailed on 7 March 1891. One or two others left the Bristol Channel area at the same time besides some Cornish vessels and in the ensuing blizzard in which a heavy easterly gale blew, quite a number of ships were lost with all hands. Some of the sailors died from exposure. Men were found after the gale wrapped up in the sails, all dead. One of the well known Appledore sailors was Ordinary Seaman in a schooner which tried to find the land off Combmartin. She struck the rocks and sank. The crew got in the boat and followed the land wash till they reached Combmartin and were safe. These were the lucky ones. The *Jane & Sarah*, Captain Ayres, found smooth water which turned out to be Bude bay. She anchored and rode out the gale. One or two Appledore ketches got in over the bar just as it started. Again these were lucky to be home. The snow in Appledore piled up above the window sills of the houses and before the doors could be opened they had to be dug out. But what about the *Francis Beddoe*? She was out in the Bristol Channel and I can only describe my father's great ordeal as he told me of it one night on the deck of the *Alpha*.

After she left Sharpness on 7th, she ran down Channel. It started to snow heavily on the morning of 8th and it was like a blanket of snow all around. When he judged her far enough down he hauled in towards the south shore. Suddenly he realized he was in a race of tide and a heavy sea, so decided to heave to in the hope that it would soon clear, but there was no clearance so hour after hour she drove with only a balance reef mainsail and storm jib. The night wore on and then another race of tide and enormously heavy sea. His mate was Philip Quance, an elder brother of Uncle George Quance and an experienced sailor. They agreed it must be the south end of Lundy. They could do nothing but wait until it cleared and moderated enough to carry sail in order to get her under command. The mizzen was blown away and the damaged canvas furled. The night of 8th passed. She still remained hove to on the starboard tack with sea breaking on board all over her. The third hand gave up the struggle and laid down in the cabin refusing to do any more. 9th March passed and the lights were lit but the sea was so bad they couldn't be used in their proper places because of the danger of losing them. The danger of washing them away was a very real one. The mate, who wasn't a very robust man, now showed signs of exhaustion. During the night of 9th the mate laid down in the cabin and was unable to do more. There was no fire on board and water everywhere. Wet and miserable they slept not caring whether the little vessel floated or sank. Fortunately, being nearly new, she was tight as a bottle so there was no pumping to be done. From the night of 9th onward father was alone to face the elements. Altogether he was continuously on deck four days and nights. He dare not sleep because he was afraid he wouldn't wake again. The situation was indeed desperate.

On the night of 11th the sky suddenly opened and for the first time since the gale started he could see a distance from the ship. Suddenly, without warning, he saw a glaring starboard light and realized it would be dangerous. He managed to light the port side-lamp which was red. He held it up so that it could be seen by the approaching ship. They came closer and closer until just as it seemed as if she was bound to run him down he saw her port light and she passed clear but only just clear. The wash from her bow filled the lee side of the *Francis Beddoe*'s deck and father, in his own words, dropped on his knees and thanked God for his deliverance from certain death. This proved to be a big full-rigged ship running out of the Bristol Channel under her lower topsails. Soon after the sky closed in again and the remainder of the night passed with only one incident worth recording. Heavy seas had been continuously shipped and in the early hours some woodwork washed back around his legs. He saw in the darkness it was the fore scuttle and the hole left by it being washed away must be stopped to keep out the water. He had some canvas in the cabin. He got a hammer and nails. Although nearly frozen he managed to nail wood and canvas over the hole, this keeping out most of the water although not perfectly water tight. On the morning of 12th the sun broke through and the gale abated. There was nothing in sight. He managed to wear the ship to bring her round on the port tack. He lashed the helm amidships so that she would head reach slowly. He went to the cabin, rubbed some paraffin in the limbs of the crew and left them asleep. He also rubbed himself all over. He got into his bunk and went to sleep. After some hours he awoke and yelled out in agony. Every limb was cramped and stiff. Eventually they all recovered enough to set the sails. The vessel fetched in to St Ives Bay and it was decided to work up the Cornish coast. The mizzen was loosed and with palms and needles they set to work on it. It was soon in working order for fine weather only. In due course she reached Bideford bar. In the meantime the family had given up all hope of his survival. Plans were being made for the children to be shared among the other members so that mother could go out to work for a living. My grandfather had a telescope and he could often be found scanning the bay to follow the movements of ships. He could tell the name of a ship by the cut of the sails or the stand of the masts. He was doing this when he saw a strange ketch approaching the bar. The news soon travelled around and all rushed to the little yard called Ducks Alley. It was a point where the bar and a lot of the bay could be seen. Yes, they all saw this ship but the *Francis Beddoe* wasn't a ship they knew. Hope revived again but the suspense was intolerable and grandfather could stand it no longer. He went home and burst into tears. As this strange vessel approached they suddenly decided that those on board were not strangers by the way they came in. It must be local men and therefore the *Francis Beddoe* could be this ship. Well, their guess was right. The men of the family got a boat and boarded her. The crew were brought ashore and put to bed while the ship proceeded to her discharging berth at Bideford in charge of her new crew. Later, when digging down through the cargo of salt they got as far as the top of the keelson and fell down the rest, because the water had got into her and the salt had turned to brine in the bottom round the pump case.

THE CREW

I have recorded something of the life of a small seaport in the days of the schooners in *Sailing for a Living*. Whichever port she came from, the men who made up the crew of a schooner usually came from the same district and were known to one another, at least by reputation, on land. Though discipline depended upon acquaintance and tradition rather than upon the threat of force, on board some ships there were certain lines in the running rigging, sheets, halyards and braces, which were not to be cast off except by direct order of master or mate. These ropes were turned upon the pins with a half hitch. Sailing evolutions often followed a strictly maintained routine.

The boys on board were under the eyes of their patrons. Each man had lived near the ships since childhood (Plate 7, Volume 2); it is, perhaps, because of this and the fact that the schooners sailed mostly to outlandish ports overseas, that the crews were less exposed to the temptations of the contemporary maritime world than those of larger vessels.

Some schooners were almost a family affair. In the brigantine *Promise*, each of the crew of seven played some musical instrument. When the weather was quiet the crew would sometimes assemble aft and begin to play. Occasionally, in good weather, even the man at the wheel could join in. Once a passing pleasure steamer was entertained by three mandolines, a guitar, a banjo and two mouth-organs.

Boys were usually still very young when they joined their first schooners. The life to which they were introduced seems in retrospect to have been hard, but by the standards of their times it was very tolerable. Mr William Schiller of Appledore, master of the ketch *Lively* said of the initiation of these boys:

> When they first joined a ship in harbour they would have a day or two to find their way around. We would take them aloft in harbour first a little way up one side, and then to the crosstrees and then over the crosstrees and down again. At sea, they would not be allowed aloft at all at first, but soon they would be riding down the topsail in bad weather. A small boy was given special jobs to do. Outside Appledore bar in the early morning there was often a south-westerly breeze off the land which did not last very far out to sea. I have often anchored on a still night off the bar and told the boy to wake me as soon as the land breeze made. And then about four in the morning I would hear him shout, 'I can smell the hay coming off the land, master!'

In the memories of old men it is always June.

A brigantine usually carried seven men; master, mate and five hands. A brig could be worked with the same number, but the brigantine was handier and much more economical, both to build and to maintain. The barquentine, with less square canvas, was cheaper still to run and the schooner more so. A barquentine in general trade could be worked with six men. A three-masted schooner needed the same number, a two-masted schooner only four, or five when she was on deep water. Ketches were worked with three or four hands according to size, small ketches and smacks with two. These figures apply to vessels of average size. The number of men carried varied in larger and smaller vessels. Long ocean voyages were made in under-manned schooners. The *Snaefell*, built at Barnstaple in 1886, a two-masted schooner eighty-three feet in length, crossed from St John's to Liverpool with only two men on board. In 1940, Captain Murdoch sailed the ketch *Garlandstone* from a south Irish port to Lydney alone.

The seamen lived in the forecastle which, in small merchant sailings ships, was the part of the vessel below deck forward that lay between the forward bulkhead and the ceiling at the bows. It was entered by means of the forecastle scuttle and a steeply sloping ladder. In ketches and the smaller schooners, this ladder was against the after bulkhead, but in the larger schooners the scuttle was sometimes well towards the middle of the deck head and the ladder descended halfway along the forecastle floor.

At the beginning of this century, in ketches and two-masted schooners, the forecastle was furnished with a small wedge-shaped table, two bench seats on either side, frame bunks which folded back to the ceiling in port, storage for oilskins and a few shelves. On board a larger schooner, the forecastle was a more spacious apartment. There would be four or five bunks built into the white painted sides of the crew space, a big scrubbed deal table with a rough surface that made fascinating patterns in the light of a swinging oil lamp, a bookcase and some lockers. Such forecastles were well maintained places for living in. Sometimes, when the mate lived forward, there was a separate boarded-off cabin for him in the forecastle. When in later years small ships were fitted with engines and the space of the single cabin aft was given up to the motor, the master moved forward and built himself a match-boarded compartment, always on the starboard side. In these later ships, when the enlargement of hatches left no room for a galley house on deck, the cook also moved into the forecastle and that small space became congested with food, crockery, books, charts, radio, oilskins, tools and all manner of spare gear.

In the last century, forecastles did not reach these standards. They were dark and small, badly ventilated and impossible to keep clean. Mr Banks, of Folkestone, who served for years in small sailing ships, wrote to H. Oliver Hill :

> The only stove in the forecastle was a straight one with a funnel fixed on top from the deck. It was called the 'bogey' and you could do no cooking with it. The only light in the fore-castle was old fat rendered down and poured over cotton wool in a bully tin and called a 'bully light', and if someone forgot to turn it down at night we got up in the morning with black faces from the smoke. There was no table in the forecastle; you sat on the floor to have your meals, there were only two small forms for everybody to use. There were no sanitary arrangements, a wooden bucket was used, and when in harbour you fixed up a canvas in the knightheads to make it as private as possible.

In later years the 'heads' were built into the whaleback aft on the port side; the corresponding compartment to starboard was used as a lamp locker. Sometimes they were in a small box, like a cowl-headed sentry box, either in the bulwarks aft at the fore end of the quarters or forward in the shelter of the foremast fife rails.

The frequent anchor work on board schooners in the home trade wore and strained the decks forward and the forecastle deckhead often leaked. Sometimes, in bad weather, a watch in these old ships would, before turning in, heat up a poker in the forecastle stove and run it over the deck seams, so as to melt the pitch and let it fill the leaks.

The folding 'gas pipe' bunks of canvas laced on to a simple frame of one-inch steel tubing of the later small sailing ships replaced wooden bunks, sometimes surrounded by match-boarding so that they were almost like the locker bunks aft, and these in turn had replaced hammocks. Customs varied between different ports, but hammocks seem generally to have gradually given way to bunks during the second half of the last century. At the end of that period they were still common on the south and southeast coasts of England. When the ketch *Triumph* of Milton in Kent made an Atlantic passage in 1888 four of her crew of six slept in hammocks in the forecastle. The *Hobah* was not fitted with bunks until she was bought by Appledore owners in 1908.

On board ships from some ports it was the custom for the ship to supply the hammock and at Littlehampton, if a man's hammock was dirty when he left the ship, he was fined from his pay and his successor recompensed to the extent of the fine. At other ports a boy, on joining a ship for the first time, was given a hammock which remained his own property. To quote Mr Banks :

> When I signed on as an apprentice the master sent me to the sailmaker, who was the ship's husband; there I got enough canvas to make my hammock and aboard ship I was given twine, palm and needle. I made my hammock with the help of another lad because I had never done any work like that before, and when I had finished it it became my own property.

Mr Banks could remember that the barquentine *Hilda* of Faversham (Plate 44) still had hammocks in 1900 when he served on board her as an able seaman. In old ships, men preferred hammocks because they could rig an oilskin on a line above them as a flysheet to keep off the drippings of the leaking deckhead. It was difficult to keep clothes and bedding dry in such ships. In cold or wet weather the stove glowed red hot and the air in the forecastle became thick and damp. In those days the coal stoves in forecastles and cabins were used only for heating. The cooking was done in the galley house on deck, placed, usually, in the sheltered part of the schooner just abaft the foremast. It was a low hutch with sliding doors on each side so that it could always be entered from the lee side. The galley was not a proper deck house but was a separate box secured to the deck with iron straps and bolts so that it could be unshipped and carried on top of a deck cargo. On board some schooners it was secured under the top crosspiece of a dolly winch. In the middle of the last century the galley was often an open fire on deck, which sometimes could not be lit for days on end. Later a stove was used on deck.

When a schooner was laden with coal, fuel for all the fires was invariably drawn (illegitimately) from the cargo. When it was discharged a little was retained for the next voyage. This bunker coal was kept in the forepeak under the forecastle floor. Sometimes a little was sold, hence the saying, 'Where did you get that new hat?'—'Out of the hatchway!' The system on which the food cooked by the fuel was supplied varied from port to port. In most deep-water ships, victualling was the master's responsibility. In the home trade, the crew sometimes found their own supplies and sometimes the owners victualled the ship. Frequently, however, it was still the master's job on short voyages. Because of the informality of his contact with his men he could not supply bad food. Besides groceries for a passage of average length, a ½ cwt of salt beef and some tinned beef were carried against emergencies. On long passages in the home trade the store could always be replenished by putting a boat ashore from some roadstead where the schooner was sheltering. The food was kept in a zinc-lined cupboard in the cabin aft. Water was carried in barrels of galvanised tanks on deck. Salt water was used for washing the dishes. Douglas Bennet has written an account of the way meals were conducted in the home trade :

The skipper sat on the starboard side at the foreward end of the U-shaped table, next to him was the mate, then the A.B.s in order of age, and finally the combined cook and ordinary seaman, usually the youngest on board, officiated on the port side, forward, i.e. at the foot of the stairs. At sea, of course, the helmsman was left to get on with his steering. The roasting tin containing dry hash, wet hash, schooner on the rocks or the pan of salt horse or whatever the *pièce de résistance* was, was handed to the skipper, who took what he wanted. Thereafter it veered round the table in a clockwise direction looking down, until it came to the cook, who, of course, had to leave some for the man at the wheel, his whack being put back in the galley to keep warm. Those coming on watch usually helped to carry the food aft from the galley. Next the pan of spuds was put into circulation, followed by whatever vegetable was available, bread was hacked off as requested, by the skipper, as long as it lasted, gravy went the rounds, and all hands fell to with a will.

Afterwards pint pots were filled up with tea for all hands and this was the signal at sea for dispersal, those on watch to relieve the wheel, the helmsman to come below and the cook to start clearing up. In port, depending on the skipper, all hands might linger on Sunday for a yarn, but usually it was a case of back to work. . . . The whole ceremony was thoroughly democratic and much better as far as one can make out than the goings-on in British deep-watermen, but of course in small towns where they had all grown up together and knew each other's families, nothing much different could possibly have been evolved.

The cook was sometimes a boy and, on long voyages, sometimes a special member of the crew with no other responsibilities. Usually, however, he was an ordinary member of the crew to whom the duty was given. Captain Robinson of Newhaven wrote of these part-time cooks :

> In some ships the owner paid for the food but in others he allowed the master a certain amount per day, perhaps one shilling and threepence for each man. We always found one man on board ready to do the cooking and he received five shillings a month or voyage extra for doing it. At sea he kept his regular watch, but did not do any deck work either at sea or in harbour as he looked after the cabin as well, and he trimmed and cleaned the lamps, but when discharging cargo he kept his turn on the jump or down the hold the same as the others, breaking off now and again to see to his cooking.

On the whole, the standard of feeding was high for the times, and certainly the food was adequate and usually of much better quality than that supplied on the large sailing ships of the period. But there were always hard ships. On long passages in the Newfoundland trade, the use of salt cod from the cargo brought out boils all over the bodies of the crews. In some ships in the home trade, sheep's heads were a staple diet; parsimonious Portmadoc masters were accused of stealing them from the dogs behind the butchers' shops in Milford Haven. One seaman wrote of a bad schooner in which he served as a boy :

In one schooner, on a trip to Norway, we saw nothing but salt herring for breakfast, dinner and supper. The crew lived forward, but we had our meals in the cabin. The captain and mate had milk in their tea, but the others did not. The mate buttered the hard biscuits for all, but he made sure there was most butter on his and the captain's. When in port the captain and mate had bread, but the crew still had hard biscuits.

Gastric troubles were the occupational disease of the schooner crews. These developed because of the irregularity of their meals and the hurried way in which they had to be eaten, and also because there was an over-emphasis on fried food, and perhaps most of all because of the ceaseless, violent motion. Even today little is known of the effects on health for the average man of such continuous buffeting.

Just as his sleeping accommodation and the way his food was provided depended on the port of origin of the schooner in which he served, so the way the schooner hand was paid also varied. Rivers as close to one another as the Parret and the Taw and the Torridge provided quite different conditions of service, and even within the Port of Bridgwater the custom varied between different types of ship. Schooners and ketches working in the home trade and sailing west of the port took on their crews for long periods and paid them by the month; at sea food was provided, in port a victualling allowance was paid. The master drew 10d or 1s a day for feeding each man. If he got as much as 1s 2d, as he sometimes did, then he considered himself in clover and able to make enough for his own beer. In the early years of this century the mate of a Bridgwater ketch could earn £7 a month, an able seaman perhaps £5. In contrast, in Portmadoc ships on ocean passages in the 1890s a master received £6, £7 or £8 a month and many perquisites, the mate £4 or £5, the able seaman £3 10s, the ordinary seaman from £1 10s to £2 10s, according to his experience. For those wages the crews contracted to work all cargo.

The second group of ships sailing from Bridgwater were the trows, large, shallow-draught smacks and ketches which usually worked east of the Parret, and very rarely sailed out of the Bristol Channel. The trows took their hands by the voyage, though frequently the same men would stay in the ship for a long time. The crew of two or three were paid perhaps 2s each on the pound of freight money earned by the ship. A trowman on board the *Eliza* of Bridgwater in June 1915, when she carried 130 tons of gypsum from Bristol to Penarth at a rate of 2s per ton, thus earned about 26s for the day's work. Out of this he had to buy his own food; there was no cook and each member of a trow's crew prepared his own meals.

If Appledore ships took and paid their men by the voyage, the ship found provisions as long as she was outside Appledore bar. Before sailing, and once inside the bar, the crew, if they were Appledore men, had to look after their own food, or, as expressed locally, they 'went cold kettle in over bar'. As a result of this tradition, no Appledore vessel was caught lying for long outside the bar if she could help it, it was cheaper to sail to Appledore and lie there where the crew had not to be fed. Each coastal voyage had its own price, and the lump sum increased sharply for voyages outside the Bristol Channel.

Schooners' hands used to wear the same clothes wherever they were. On the Labrador coast in winter, in the rivers of South America, in the East, the coloured flannel shirt, blue jersey, heavy cloth trousers, tweed cap or woollen stocking served equally. An extra jersey was put on in the North Atlantic, and most clothes were removed in the tropics. In eastern seas there was almost complete neglect of all but the most elementary attention to health. Appledore seamen were known all over Europe for their 'frocks', as the loose-knitted blue jerseys they used to wear were called. These frocks were worn outside the trousers and a man with one was always assured of a job aboard any English or Welsh schooner.

SEAMANSHIP

Each member of the small crew of a schooner had to be able to do all the jobs of seafaring in a sailing vessel. In many ways the work was lighter than that on board big sailing ships, in others much more exacting. There was less work aloft, but it was made more difficult by the simple rigging which, relatively bare of hand holds, did not give the feeling of security the complex and numerous lines of yard-rigged masts give to these accustomed to them. The violent motion made the work much harder again, and in bad weather in some very small ships it was difficult to go aloft at all.

Douglas Bennet has recorded the process of going about in an under-manned schooner :

At a pinch two men could put a schooner about, whether she was a two- or three-master did not matter, the limit being whether they could start the yards swinging, together. One man went forward, while the mate or skip put the helm down and shouted 'lee oh', to indicate that it had actually been done—not so obvious right away on a black windy night. As soon as she was up in the wind, the bloke forward had to let go his three jib sheets, nip across and haul the jibs over the stays, taking care to swig them in as tight as possible, as once off on the new tack in any sort of breeze it would take a handy billy to flatten them. By this time the ship would have the way off her, the topsails would be aback and the fore and afters thumping about from side to side. As the bloke forward cast off the staysail bowline, the man at the wheel ran forward to the braces and let them go, both reached the lee braces at the same time, and grabbing all three gave one tremendous heave to get the yards started. Once the yards were on the move it was hard to get the slack of the braces in fast enough, as they came round with a rattle (provided it had been timed right), all three were swigged up on two pins, after which the helmsman galloped aft to the wheel, while his mate went forward to pass the staysail bowline and afterwards coil down the braces. I suppose something on the same lines must be used on the braces of big square-riggers—in schooners, the braces were belayed on their own pins unless the vessel was on a bowline, in which case they were all made fast on two pins so that they could all be let go at once. Once the yards were round, each brace was swigged up individually starting from the fore brace and working up, but all on the same pins, and the coiling down was done all together so that they were free to run. The ends of the weather braces were permanently half-hitched to the pins to give the right checking in of the yards, the lower topsail a bit more than the fore yard, the upper topsail a bit more still. This caper was possible for two men, and was done on the odd occasion in the *Alert*, I should think a couple of good blokes could have done it in the *Banks*, but not with the standing topgallant as well; it would have taken three then as she had the longest and heaviest yards on the coast, bar of course the *Waterwitch*, which was a bigger vessel.

With both watches on deck, of course, things were a bit less hectic, the two-men routine was easier with the flying jib stowed, and I have not included the main topmast staysail which had disappeared before I arrived on the scene.

The only other events of interest, apart from when something blew or carried away, was hauling in the sheets of the fore and afters. In anything like a strong breeze it took all hands and a handy billy to shift them, especially a two-master's mainsheet. The skipper usually took the wheel and luffed her up a bit while the crew waited till the end of a roll to leeward and gave one tremendous heave, then hung on and heaved again next time. All hands had cocoa or some other form of corpse reviver at eight bells midnight, after which those coming on deck had to pump her out. It never transpired that there was no water in her.

Sailing evolutions were carried out to a routine which varied with ships and ports. When going about in a brigantine from Kent or Sussex in bad weather, all hands were called and the master took the wheel and began the manœuvre by shouting, 'Stand By!' When the crew were all at their stations he put the helm down and called 'Lee, Ho!' The man forward would ease the jib sheets and, on a vessel fitted with a Bentinck boom, on the order 'Forebowline!' would let go the forebowline. At the same time the mate and a man would let go the braces and tend staysail sheets, and then all hands would tail on to the braces.

In moderate weather, the master or mate would put the helm down and secure the wheel with a becket. He would then go forward and join the hands at work there. With a practised crew the whole evolution was carried out without a word except for these three orders.

The Bentinck boom, with which most brigantines were fitted

on the square foresail, was much handier than the conventional tacks and sheets of large sailing ships. It consisted of a light strong spar to which the foot of the foresail was secured at the clews by means of a chain at either end and amidships. The three formed a bridle with the single chain to which they were all attached and this was led through an eyebolt on deck and secured to a spider band on the foremast. At each end of the Bentinck boom there was a heavy, two-fathom steadying line, but the main control of the sail was the forebowline. One of these was attached to each leech of the foresail, led forward to the bowline block, and secured at the foot of the forestay or at the weather end of the downhaul rail.

The mainsheet, even in a ketch, was a strong, heavy rope; it had to hold the biggest spar and the biggest sail, and was the heaviest piece of running rigging in the ship. The mainboom was a large spar and the sheet had a threefold block on the boom and a twofold block on the stern bulwarks. When close-hauled in smooth water no other tackle was used, but in a brigantine in rough water and in light airs the boom worked with the ship and so the mainboom-guy tackle was secured to a samson post on deck, just abaft the main rigging, and hauled tight. This tackle pulled against the mainsheet and held the spar in one position. When running, the same tackle was used hooked on to a wire pennant that led along to the fore rigging. This was found to be an effective device against jibing.

A brigantine in a nice sailing breeze blowing on the quarter would have everything set except the staysail. As the wind increased, her crew would take in the flying jib, the topmast staysail, the gaff topsail and the topgallant sail. If the wind still rose, they would next take in the foretopmast staysail and the foresail, take a reef in the mainsail and set the staysail. If a gale developed, the middle staysail on the main, the jib and the upper topsail would come in and another reef would be taken in the main. In really bad weather, the area of the main could be still further reduced by tricing up the tack. Experienced masters in the home trade have said that they never saw weather in which a brigantine could not carry the remaining canvas, double-reefed mainsail, main staysail, lower topsail, and staysail.

Captain J. H. Waters of Faversham was at sea in small sailing ships for fifty-seven years, and for forty-five years he was a master mariner. At the request of H. Oliver Hill he wrote an account of the handling of ketches and small schooners, from which I quote as follows :

In a ketch turning to windward with all sail set and the wind increasing, take in the outer jib and then reef the mainsail and the mizzen. If the weather becomes worse, take in the main gaff topsail and put a second reef in the mizzen. Next, take in the boom jib, reef the forestaysail, and if there is more wind double-reef the mainsail. If the weather becomes worse, put the vessel on the tack most favourable according to the circumstances, take in forestaysail, and get standing jib sheeted tight to windward, watch how she bows to the sea and make the helm fast about amidships, or sometimes slightly alee, about three degrees. I have passed through many gales under this canvas in a vessel from one hundred and sixty to two hundred and sixty tons capacity.

In a two-masted schooner, as wind freshens take in main gaff topsail, maintopmast staysail next, flying or outer jib next. After that, take in upper square topsail, single or double-reef mainsail, and then take in boom jib and put one reef in the foresail. Remember that the foresail is in the main body of the vessel and has the main steadying of the vessel. Next, clew up lower topsail and stow everything as secure as possible. After that, if the weather gets worse, put the third reef in the mainsail. Reef forestaysail and then stow it. The helm should be about amidships. If the vessel is inclined to come too close to the wind, haul the sheet of the remaining jib to windward; the schooner should lay to like this.

Captain W. J. Slade has recorded :

The ketches were easier to handle than schooners, because once they gained speed enough to steer they never lost it completely even in stays. When about to get under way the anchor was hove short, mainsail, mizzen and gaff topsails set properly. The headsails, including staysail, standing jib and boom jib, were then set. If the ship had to be canted first on the port tack, the staysail and jibs were pulled over the port or weather side. The order would then be given to break out the anchor. As soon as it was off the ground the ship would pay off, filling the mainsail, mizzen and gaff topsails with wind. When sufficiently off, the jibs would be hauled in to leeward and the staysail bowline let go so that the ship would start reaching ahead. The anchor would then be hove right up to the pipe and later catted. To get a schooner under way was very much on the same lines, but, having square canvas aloft bent to yards, she had to be canted with her yards aback, and often after lifting the anchor she took sternboard until off from the wind far enough to fill all fore and aft sails and it became a matter of judgment for the master to give the order to haul around the yards. To beat out of a harbour, a ketch was faster mainly because she never completely lost her way, while a schooner came to a dead stop when her yards became aback in stays. On the other hand, I personally found the schooners with a small exception more dependable in stays than a ketch, especially in a sea way, mainly because once the yards became aback she had to come round.

We often had to get under way in a tidal river such as the Mersey with a strong flood tide and with the wind aft. To leave the anchorage for sea under these conditions no sail could be set until anchor was hove short. Then the square topsails would be loosed ready to set and the headsails put ready to set. The boom jib and standing jib would be hoisted and the lower topsail sheeted home with the yards kept square. A glance at the anchor chain would be given to see if the ship was forging ahead. If not, the upper topsail would be set and the foresail. If the ship then started ahead against the tide, the anchor was hove up to the hawse pipe. When under way, all sail was set as soon as possible and the anchor catted as convenient.

Again, to get a ketch under way in these conditions, a somewhat different style was used because, of course, there were no square topsails. The anchor was hove short and a couple of headsails set. Then the mainsail set with the sheet pulled in. When the ship started ahead, the anchor was hove up to the pipe. If she didn't start ahead against the tide, the mainsheet was veered out. All going well, up came the anchor and all sail set as soon as possible.

All this was a matter of judgment and the master always worked by his plan of campaign from the word 'go'. In putting out of a harbour every tack had to be planned out in the master's mind and a slight error in judgment could throw the whole plan out of gear—sometimes with dire consequences.

All topsail schooners, no matter how small, would keep the square canvas on for running before the wind. On bigger schooners the lower topsails carried almost always to the last, no matter whether facing the wind or running before it. It was made of heavy No 1 extra quality canvas to stand the hard weather.

IN HARBOUR

Methods of loading and discharge varied with the nature of the cargo, the size of the ship, and the customs of the port and of the ship's port of origin. Most ketches and smacks, and even large schooners, had on each side of the bulwarks amidships a section which could be lifted out to allow access to the deck for cargo work. Until motor winches came into use just before the first world war, all cargo worked by the ship was moved by hand. The two main methods of discharge were the dolly winch and the jump.

The dolly winch comprised a simple iron geared winch with wooden drums (Plate 14, Volume 2) from which a line was led aloft and over a block on a swinging gaff and down into the hold. It was worked by two men. In small ships, and in most west coast harbours for most cargoes, the dolly winch was always used. After the first world war it was usually driven by a chain from a small petrol or paraffin motor housed in a box on deck (Plate 37, Volume 2), but as late as 1947 I saw a sloop, the *Anna Bhan*, discharging sand on to a beach of Tobermory Bay with a dolly winch worked by two men, a shovel crew in the hold and a basket on the swinging gaff.

The jump has now completely disappeared, though it was almost universally used on the south-east coasts for coal cargoes and seems to have been used regularly at Exeter, on the Truro river and at Cardiff. It took many forms and lent itself to use in most of the circumstances a small vessel was likely to meet with. But it required more men to work it than the dolly winch, and so, in general, its use tended to be confined to the larger vessels, three-masted schooners and brigantines, while small schooners and ketches with only three or four men used the dolly winch, unless they could employ an extra hand or two from shore to help with discharging. Such extra hands were called 'hufflers' on the Sussex coast, 'hobblers' at Appledore and at the end of the last century might be paid 1½d for every ton taken out of the vessel. Of the employment of extra men for jumping, Captain J. R. Robinson of Newhaven wrote : 'It seems impossible to me now, but I had three men that lived in Brighton and who used to go home for the night and had to get up at three a m and walk to Newhaven to be in time to start work at six a m and then work out eighty tons and over during the day, but they didn't do it every day.'

A simple type of jump was worked as follows. A portable trestle about twelve feet long and seven feet wide, rather like a gigantic stepladder, which was always carried on board the collier, was set up over the hatchway which was being worked. It consisted of two pairs of beams set up as triangles joined at the top by a main timber and down one of the sides by rough 'steps' of unfinished scaffold poles with their ends squared. Sometimes these steps were made up of sweeps and odd spars. Aloft, a swinging gaff was used, the fall of the line from the block aloft being split with a spreader into three soft manilla lines. At the other end was a basket. The basket was filled by the shovel gang in the hold and then the three men working the jump went up to the third of the four steps. If the basket was to go only as high as the ship's side, they would give one long pull, lifting their hands as high as they could on the rope and then, after the pull, lifting their hands as high as they could again and then jumping off on to the deck, so that they brought the basket about two feet above the hatch coaming. The mate would then swing the gaff and tip the basket into the scales or over the side into the waiting lighter, or into a cart at a quay, or to a stacking gang if the coal was being piled on shore. If the basket had to be raised higher, the men might take two pulls before they jumped or perhaps jump from the fourth step. In extreme cases—when discharging at low water on to a wharf above the ship's side they might also take a further pull after they had jumped. However far the basket had to go, by the time it was swung empty on board again the three men were back on the jump and ready to lower away for another pull. At the basket end of the line there was a special hook with a flat inside edge to reduce the risk of damaged fingers, a danger because of the speed with which the jump was worked.

Collier brigs in the lower Thames regularly discharged their cargoes into barges in this way, and in the Kentish and Sussex ports the coal was jumped straight on to dry land. At Whitstable, a two-stage jump was sometimes used, one on board the ship, the other on the quayside. The jump itself and the attendant gear were essentially portable and were usually carried in the schooner. There were great local variations in the method of its use. At some ports the jump itself was set up on shore; some regular coal wharves in early days had fixed jumps built up on the quay— this may have been the case at Exeter and at some Suffolk ports.

The system depended upon speed of working. If there was only one pull and a jump to do, eighty tons could be lifted in a working day of six to four-thirty; two pulls slowed down the whole process. The three men on the jump changed places with the shovel crew in the hold every three hours, the mate at scales and runners worked at his job all day, the master took no part in discharging except to surpervise. The advantage of the jump lay in its speed; the same number of men could move only fifty or sixty tons in a day with a dolly winch, and it is said that the work was harder.

In the coal ports of the north of England and at Lydney in Gloucestershire (Plate 45) schooners were loaded at shoots, a railway wagon load at a time tipped into the hold. Some of these shoots were hand-operated, and the wagon was carefully balanced so that one man could tip it. While they waited in tiers to go under the shoots, the crews of the schooners exchanged visits and gossip. Whenever ships were brought together waiting in harbour, all the news of the coast was exchanged between their crews.

Schooners in the home trade often carried one anchor chain fleeted along the deck and made fast to ringbolts, in case it was wanted in a hurry. The other anchor might have fifteen fathoms of chain on deck and the rest below. The anchors on a brigantine or a three-masted schooner would be twelve or fifteen hundred-weight with seven-eights inch chain cable. The chain locker on small ships was right forward, sometimes it was under the fore-castle floor, and sometimes in a compartment around the main-mast, the after part of which was used as the pump well. A spare large anchor was usually carried lashed on deck, and perhaps two kedges. Small ships carried about ninety fathoms of cable on the best bower and seventy-five fathoms on the working anchor.

In Newhaven brigantines anchored in heavy weather, and in many other ships as well, the weight of the ship was taken not on the windlass but on the samson post near the mainmast aft to which the mainboom guy tackle was attached when the ship was under sail. The cable was brought inboard in the usual way, but just forward of the windlass a spring was made fast. This was led under the windlass and aft and passed round the sam-son post. The spring was then doubled and frapped.

In ships which sheltered so frequently, and which worked tides and in restricted waters, the windlass was an important part of the lives of the crews. In its original form, it consisted of a horizontal octagonal oak drum on an axle between two uprights, the windlass bitts. The end of the axle outside the bitts carried two small wooden drums and these were pierced with square holes for handspikes, as the central drum itself had been in big ships in the eighteenth century. A central pawl working on a ratchet wheel at the middle of the barrel prevented the drum from reversing. Originally the windlass lacked even this refine-ment; that on the trow *William* built in 1809 and lost 130 years later, was just a straight drum without any means of preventing its turning in the wrong direction.

The handspikes, stowed somewhere forward when not in use, were three or four feet long, squared off at one end. To work the windlass two men inserted a spike each, parallel with one another, putting them in holes projecting in the near vertical (Plate 16, Volume 2). Heaving together, they then pulled the spikes round until they were parallel with the deck. They were then withdrawn and the process repeated. Such windlasses were fitted in all sloops and West Country sailing barges and in many small ketches. They were used a great deal in large ships in the early nineteenth century. But small crews needed some other device to give more power for breaking out and the pump-handled windlass was introduced very early in the nineteenth century and came into general use in most craft of over fifty tons or so about fifty years later. Known as 'Armstrong's Patent', in common with every other labour-saving device, the pump-handle windlass remained the standard equipment of merchant schooners and was still being built into new Danish schooners after the second world war.

The windlass took many forms but basically it consisted, as did its predecessor, of an oak drum, mounted horizontally between two greenheart uprights which were stayed against forward stresses by means of timber baulks let into the deck beams. The drum was reinforced by steel plates on alternate faces and by steel strips screwed on at the juncture of the faces. Outside the windlass bitts were two smaller drums, like those on the old hand-spike windlass, but these were mere survivals, used as mooring bitts. These drums were still fitted with square holes in case the pump handle gear should break down. As on the earlier windlasses, the centre of the drum had a set of very coarse teeth, perhaps as much as six inches broad, and against those teeth worked several pawls loosely pivoted on the after side of a third upright, the pawl bitt, which was of immense strength and rooted deep in the deadwood about the keelson.

On either side of the coarse central teeth were gear wheels, cut with much finer cogs and fitted with rims outside the teeth. Fitted loosely over these rims and pivoted at the other ends to rods from a rocker at the head of the pawl bitt were the pawl plates. There were two of these flanged triangular plates to each wheel, bolted together to enclose the rims and fitted with loose pawls which engaged with the teeth of the wheel on the upward movement of the rod and so turned the windlass drum through a few degrees. The pawl plates were about equal in length to the radius of the wheel on which they worked, so that they gave the greatest mechanical advantage to the men working the rocker arms (Plates 17 and 18, Volume 2).

The rocker arm at the head of the pawl bitt had sockets in its two ends for the insertion of the pump handles. These were usually five or six feet long and had oak staffs scored transversely at their ends to act as handles. The windlass was worked by pushing down and heaving up on each side in turn. The barrel was turned by the wheel on the side where the rocker arm was moving upwards, that is to say, on the downstroke of the pump handle on the opposite side.

Acknowledgment of Quotations

The extract from *The Mirror of the Sea* by Joseph Conrad which prefixes the text is reproduced by kind permission of Messrs J. M. Dent & Sons, Ltd.

The various extracts from *The Last of the Windjammers* by Basil Lubbock are reproduced through the courtesy of Messrs Brown Son & Ferguson of Glasgow.

The quotation from *The History of American Sailing Ships* is made by kind permission of W. W. Norton & Company, New York and Putnam & Company, London and New York.

The quotations from *Immortal Sails* by Henry Hughes are made by kind permission of Robert Ross & Co. Ltd., Southampton and London.

Acknowledgment of Illustrations

Plates, 1, Crispin Gill; 2, 4, 6, 13, 25, 38, 40, 42, 44, National Maritime Museum; 3, 5, 17, 19, 23, 33, 34, 36, 43, H. Oliver Hill; 7, 12, 15, 20, 21, 22, 26, 27, 28, 29, 30, 31, 39, 45, Basil Greenhill; 8, 11, 18, 46, Bristol Museum; 9, Giles M. Tod; 10, 16, W. J. Lewis Parker; 24, Percy Harris; 32, 41, Gillis Collection; 14, 37, Graham Gullick; 35, Captain William Lamey.
Drawings, 1, 2, 3, 11, 12, David R. MacGregor; 4, National Maritime Museum; 5, 9, Richard Ashburner; 6, 7, 14, 15, 16, 17, 18, 19, 20, Douglas Bennet; 8, Roger Finch after a drawing by Gordon Harris; 10, 22, Roger Finch; 13, Roger Finch in collaboration with Captain R. Arthur Jones; 21, Ann Giffard after a drawing by W. J. Slade.

The decorative sketch on the title page is by J. C. Burnie. It shows a standing topgallant schooner of about 1900 under all sail.

Appendix One

ACCOUNT BOOK of the schooner *Thetis* of Fowey, May 1873—February 1876.
Thetis 63972, Two-mast schooner, wood, felted and yellow metalled, built at Fowey and launched in March 1873, 180 tons gross, 103·9 ft. x 23·6 ft. x 12·6 ft. registered at Fowey as owned by Pearce and Company.

CHINESE COPY OF THE ACCOUNTS BOOK OF THE 'THETIS'

NAMES OF THE OWNERS OF THE SCHOONER 'THETIS'

No.	Name	No. of Shares
1	Mr. KNIGHT	7
2	„ SOBEY, Collon, St. Veep	2
3	„ COLLINS, Draper, Lostwithiel	4
4	„ REED, Rg., Lostwithiel	1
5	„ OLFORD, Jno.	1
6	„ LUKE	8
7	„ BEALE, Capt.	7
8	„ STOCKER	4
9	„ PEARCE	8
10	„ HITCHENS, Ths.	3
11	„ BARRATT	3
12	„ HITCHINS, Jno., St. Agnes	1
13	„ OLLIVER	2
14	„ HAYE	2
15	„ Dr. TREFFRY	2
16	„ HICKS, Bodithiel, St. Pinnock, Liskeard	2
17	„ PARKYN	3
18	„ HENWOOD, Miss M. A. MEADOW	1
19	„ BARTLETT, Revd. Jno.	2
20	„ THOMAS, Miss	1
		64

THE OWNERS OF THE SCHOONER "THETIS"

1873

Receipts	£	s.	d.
Mr. Knight 15 @ £57 17 9 per share	868	6	3
,, Luke 8 ,, ,,	463	2	—
Capt. Beale 7 ,, ,,	405	4	3
Mr. Stocker 4 ,, ,,	231	11	—
,, Pearce 8 ,, ,,	463	2	—
,, Hitchens, T. 3 ,, ,,	173	13	3
,, Barratt 4 ,, ,,	231	11	0
,, Olliver 2 ,, ,,	115	15	6
,, Haye 2 ,, ,,	115	15	6
Dr. Treffry 2 ,, ,,	115	15	6
Mr. Hicks 2 ,, ,,	115	15	6
,, Parkin 3 ,, ,,	173	13	3
Revd. I. Bartlett 2 ,, ,,	115	15	6
Miss Thomas 1 ,, ,,	57	17	9
Mr. I. Hitchens 1 ,, ,,	57	17	9
	3704	16	0
	£3704	16	—

IN ACCOUNT WITH T. PEARCE

1873

Date	Disbursements	£	s.	d.	£	s.	d.
Mar. 15	Mr. Nurse, as per bill				2	3	—
,, ,,	Launching, 24 Men @ 1/- each				1	4	—
,, 21	Harvey & Co. Screw	10	—	—			
	Discount 2¼%		5	—	9	15	—
,, 27	Gill & Roberts, Metal, Felt & Nails	189	11	2			
	Discount 3½%	6	13	—	182	18	2
Apl. 21	Mountford Homer & Mountford, Anchors, Cables & Chains	229	1	4			
	Discount 2¼%	5	15	11	223	5	5
May 2	Giles Ship's Book					5	6
,, 13	Lacey Blockmaker	48	0	2			
	Discount 2¼%	1	4	—	46	16	2
,, ,,	Knight, as per bill	37	13	4			
,, ,,	Lovering ,, Discount		19	—	36	14	4
,, ,,	Hawken Smith	43	4	10			
	Discount	2	6	—	40	18	10
,, ,,	Luke & Co.						
	Discount				100	13	2
,, ,,	Capt. Beale, as per sheet				94	12	3
,, ,,	,, ,, Fitting out as per sheet				33	19	6
,, ,,	Butson building 250 Tons @ £9 15 0	2437	10	—			
,, ,,	,, ,, metaling	16	13	—			
,, ,,	,, ,, building house	8	9	1	2462	12	1
,, ,,	Chrometer				25	—	—
,, ,,	Barratt, Sailmaker	265	2	6			
	Discount	2	5	6	262	17	—
,, ,,	W. H. Luke				156	—	—
,, ,,	Agency Registering etc.				9	—	—
					£3704	17	2

THE OWNERS OF THE SCHOONER "THETIS"

1873	Receipts	£ s. d.	£ s. d.
May	1st CARGOE Fowey to New York Clay in Casks 277 tons 5 cwts. @ 20/6d.		284 3 7
July	2nd CARGOE New York to Solonica Petroleum Oil in cases 6369 @ 45 cents per case & 5%	626 18 10	
	Lump sum for taking Cargoe of Oil from Solonica to Volo	40 — —	666 18 10
			951 2 5

IN ACCOUNT WITH T. PEARCE

1873	Disbursement		£ s. d.	£ s. d.
	Master May 15/73 to Nov. 20/73	WAGES mth dys		
	Master	6 6 @ £6 per month	37 4	
	Mate	6 6 @ £5 5	32 11	
	B.S.N.	6 6 @ £3 15	23 5	
	Cook	6 6 @ £3 15	23 5	
	A.B.	6 6 @ £3 10	21 14	
	A.B.	6 6 @ £3 10	21 14	
	O.S.	6 6 @ £2 10	15 10	
	O.S.	6 6 @ £2 10	15 10	190 13 —
	Master May 15/73 to Nov. 20/73	VICTUALLING dys 190 @ 1/1 per day		
	Master		10 5 10	
	Mate		10 5 10	
	B.S.N.		10 5 10	
	Cook		10 5 10	
	A.B.		10 5 10	
	A.B.		10 5 10	
	O.S.		10 5 10	
	O.S.		10 5 10	82 6 8
				272 19 8

At a Meeting of the Owners of the Schooner "THETIS" held at Mr. Nurse's at The Ship Inn, Fowey, this day May 13th, 1873. It is resolved that Capt. W. Beale be appointed the Master at a salary of £6 per month, Gratuities, and 10% on the profits and that he is to have thirteen pence per day per man, for Victualling the ship, and it is likeways resolved that Mr. Thomas Pearce be appointed the Agent of the Vessel at five pounds per year,

Wm. H. V. Luke
T. H. Knight
J. Olford
Wm. Collins
Chs. Hicks
Rich'd. Reed
John Olliver
Richard Barratt
Miss M. A.
W. R. Sobry

THE OWNERS OF THE SCHOONER " THETIS "

1873	Receipts	£	s.	d.
	Brot. forward	951	2	5
Novr.	3rd CARGOE			
	Volo to Dundalk (Ireland)			
	Barley 1550 grs. @ 5/6 per qr.	426	5	—
Novr.	Dundalk to St. Michael's			
	in Ballast			
1874 Jany.	4th CARGOE			
	St. Michael's to London			
	900 boxes Oranges 45 tons @ £6 10 per ton	292	10	—
	393 ,, 13 cwt. @ £3 5 ,,	63	17	3
	Sundries	1	10	—
		357	17	3
	Carrd. forward	1735	4	8

IN ACCOUNT WITH T. PEARCE

1873	Disbursements	£	s.	d.
	Brot. forward	272	19	8

WAGES

	m	dys		£	s.	d.
Master Nov. 20/73 to Jan. 29/74	2	9	@ £6 per month	13	16	—
Mate	2	9	" £5 10	12	13	—
B.S.N.	2	9	" £4 0	9	4	—
A.B.	2	9	" £3 15	8	12	6
A.B.	2	9	" £3 15	8	12	6
A.B.	2	9	" £2 15	6	6	6
O.S.	2	9	" £3	6	18	6
Cook						
				74	15	—
	Deduct shipping fees				15	—
				74	—	—

VICTUALLING

	days		£	s.	d.
Master Nov. 20/73 to Jan. 29/74	70	@ 1/1 per day	3	15	10
Mate	"		3	15	10
B.S.N.	"		3	15	10
A.B.	"		3	15	10
A.B.	"		3	15	10
O.S.	"		3	15	10
Cook	"		3	15	10
			30	6	8
	Carrd. forward	377	6	4

THE OWNERS OF THE SCHOONER "THETIS"

IN ACCOUNT WITH T. PEARCE

1873	Receipts	£	s.	d.
	Brot. forward	1735	4	8
		1735	**4**	**8**

1873	Disbursements	£	s.	d.	£	s.	d.
	Brot. forward				377	6	4
	PORT CHARGES						
May	Fowey as per Capt. List	40	16	7			
July	New York	145	17	9			
Aug.	Solonica	48	19	10			
Sept.	Volo	8	10	10			
"	Almero	1	—	10			
Nov.	Fowey	2	4	5			
"	Kingston	1	1	6			
Dec.	Dundalk	37	—	4			
"	Fowey	2	18	4			
1874							
Jan.	St. Michaels	65	12	8			
"	London	46	—	2	400	2	1
	BILLS						
	Mrs. Nurse	5	—	3			
	Mr. Lovering	1	8	10			
	" Butson, Shipbuilder	3	4	11			
	" Barratt, Sailmaker	1	18	2			
	Agency	5	—	—	16	12	7
					794	—	7
	Master's primage on £941 4 1d. @ 10%				94	2	—
					888	2	8
	Stamps for Foreign bills, Postage, etc.				—	7	9
					888	11	4
	Profit				846	13	4
					1735	**4**	**8**

235

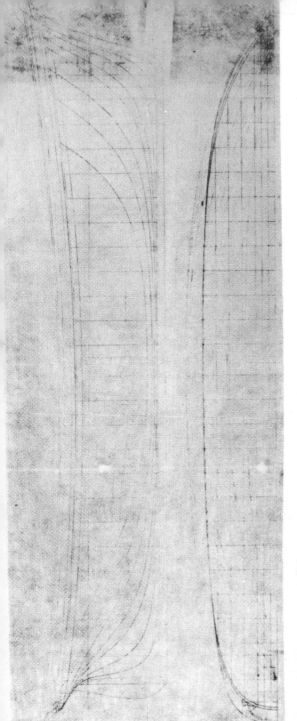

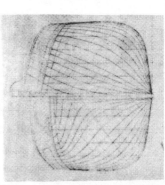

Builder's draft of an Ashburner built schooner; probably " William Ashburner."

Profit

£ s. d.
846 13 4

At a meeting of the Owners of the Schooner " THETIS " held at Mrs. Nurse's Ship Inn, Fowey, on Feby. 17/74, the foregoing accounts were audited and passed (from May 15/73 to Jany. 29/74)

Signed by the Owners present

Wm. Phillips
J. Bauden
W. W. Beale
D. Sargent
Wm. Collins
Mary Ann Kenwood
John Olford
Alfred Leeke
T. H. Knight
John Thomas
A. Barrett
Frank Paskyn, Rev.
Wm. R. Sobey

£846 13 4

LIST OF SHAREHOLDERS

#	Name	Shares	@ £13 4 7d.	£	s.	d.
1	Mr. Pearce	8	@ £13 4 7d.	105	16	8
2	Captn. Blake	7	W. W. Beale	92	12	1
3	Mr. Collins	4	Wm. Collins	52	18	4
4	" Stocker	4		52	18	4
5	" Hitchens, Thos.	4		52	18	9
6	" Barratt	3	R. Barratt	39	13	2
7	" Parkyn	3	N. B. Parkyn	39	13	2
8	Dr. Jeffry	2	H. N. Purcell	26	9	2
9	Mr. Haye	2		26	9	2
10	" Oliver	2	John Olliver	26	9	2
11	" Hicks	2	D. Sargent	26	9	2
12	" Bartlett, Revd.	2		26	9	2
13	" Sobey	2	W. A. Parkyn	26	9	7
14	" Reed	1	R. Reed	13	4	7
15	" Olford	1	John Olford	13	4	7
16	" Luke	4	Alfred Luke	52	18	7
17	" Hitchens, J.	1		13	4	7
18	Miss Henwood	1	H. Henwood	13	4	7
19	Miss Hill	1		13	4	7
20	Mr. Bawden	1	J. Bawden	13	4	7
21	" Philips	1	W. Philips	13	4	7
22	" Sargant, D. Toeburgay, Mr. Liskeard	2	D. Sargant	26	9	2
23	Mrs. Furniss	3		39	13	9
24	Mr. Knight	1	T. H. Knight	13	4	7
25	" Thomas	2	R. Pearn	26	9	2

£846 13 4

THE OWNERS OF THE SCHOONER "THETIS"

IN ACCOUNT WITH THOS. PEARCE

Receipts

1874		£	s.	d.
Jan.	From London to Cardiff in Ballast			
Feb.	1st CARGO			
	from Cardiff to Madeira			
	Coals 296 tons @ 13/- per to	192	8	0
	from Madeira to Farpam Bay			
	in Ballast			
	Carrd. forward	192	8	0

Disbursements

PORT CHARGES

1874		£	s.	d.
Feb.	Fowey	1	3	7
	Cardiff	56	11	8
Mar.	Fowey	1	7	7
Mar.	Madeira	30	18	6
Apl.	Tarpam Bay	21	6	7
June	London	54	5	7
July	Fowey	40	2	2
Aug.	Cetto	19	3	10
Sept.	Smyrna	44	15	3
Oct.	Coom Kale	7	1	7
Nov.	Fowey	1	19	6
Dec.	Ostend	33	4	8
	Fowey	2	11	
1875				
Jan.	Porthcawl	48	17	3
Mar.	Naples	29	19	0
Apl.	Palerma	50	13	2
June	New York	122	1	0
July	Fowey	1	3	7
Aug.	Invergorden	18	6	2
		585	13	3

BILLS

1874		£	s.	d.
Feb. 17	Mrs. Nurse's Bill	5	2	8
Nov. 30	Messrs. Fox & Co., Telegram	2	2	0
Dec. 22	Mr. Dingle	18	9	0
Dec. 30	Mr. Lovering	6	13	4
1875				
Feb. 8	Property Tax	3	19	4
	Mr. Butson	22	7	8
	Agency	5	0	0
		61	7	3
	Carrd. forward	647	7	3

Receipts—Contd.

Brot. forward

Disbursements—Contd.

Carrd. forward

		£	s.	d.
	Brot. forward	192	8	0
Apl. 2	2nd CARGO			
	from Tarbam Bay to London			
	Pineapples, lump sum	450	0	0
	from London to Fowey			
	in Ballast			
July	3rd CARGO			
	from Fowey to Cetto			
	China Clay 304 tons @ 19 francs per ton			
	5776 frcs. Exchange 25 frcs. 15 cents.	229	13	2
	less carriage Clay to Fowey			
	304 tons @ 1/-	15	4	0
		214	9	2
	Carrd. forward	**826**	**17**	**2**

				£	s.	d.
	Carrd. forward			647	7	3
WAGES		m	dys			
Master Jan. 30/74 to June 15/74	@ £6 per month	4	17	27	8	0
Mate	@ £5 10	4	17	20	2	4
Boatswain	@ £4	4	17	18	5	4
Cook	@ £4	4	17	18	5	4
A.B.	" £3 15	4	17	17	2	6
O.S.	" £3 10	4	17	15	19	8
O.S.	" £3	4	17	13	14	0
O.S.	" £2 15	4	17	12	11	2
				148	8	4
Less advanced at Cardiff £2 15 0						
Discharging fee 15 0				3	10	0
				144	18	4
VICTUALLING			dys			
Master Jan. 30/74 to June 15/74	@ 1/1 per day		137	7	7	8
Mate			137	7	7	8
Boatswain			137	7	7	8
Cook			137	7	7	8
A.B.			137	7	7	8
O.S.			137	7	7	8
O.S.			137	7	7	8
O.S.			137	7	7	8
				59	7	4
	Carrd. forward			**851**	**12**	**11**

Receipts—Contd.

1874   Brot. forward

	£ s. d.	£ s. d.
Brot. forward		826 17 2
Aug.		
4th CARGO		
from Cetto to Smyrna		
Patent Food 300½ tons @ 5 francs per ton		
+5% 157990		62 14 9
from Smyrna to Coom Kale		
in Ballast		
Dec.		
from Coom Kale to Ostend		
Barley 1550 grs. @ 5/- per gr.	387 13 4	
10% Extra for Continent	38 15 4	
Demurrage 4 days @ £4	16 0 0	442 8 8
Carrd. forward		**1332 0 9**

Disbursements—Contd.

1874   Carrd. forward

	£ s. d.	£ s. d.
Carrd. forward		851 12 11

WAGES

	m dys		£ s. d.	£ s. d.
Master June 16/74 to Dec. 18/74	6 3	@ £6 per month	36 12 0	
Mate	6 3	@ £5 10 :	33 11 0	
Boatswain	6 3	@ £3 15 :	22 17 6	
Cook	6 3	@ £3 15 :	22 17 0	
A.S.	6 3	@ £3 10 :	21 7 0	
O.S.	6 3	@ £3 :	18 6 0	
O.S.	6 3	@ £2 10 :	15 5 0	192 3 0

VICTUALLING

	days		£ s. d.	£ s. d.
Master June 16/74 to Dec. 18/74	186	@ 1/1 per day	10 1 6	
Mate	186 :		10 1 6	
Boatswain	186 :		10 1 6	
Cook	186 :		10 1 6	
A.S.	186 :		10 1 6	
A.S.	186 :		10 1 6	
O.S.	186 :		10 1 6	
O.S.	186 :		10 1 6	80 12 0
Carrd. forward				**1124 7 11**

Receipts—Contd.
Brot. forward — 1332 0 7

	£ s. d.	£ s. d.
from Ostend to Porthcawl in Ballast		
Mar. 6th CARGO from Porthcawl to Naples Iron 302 tons 4.3.2. @ 10/6d. per ton		294 13 8
from Naples to Palermo in Ballast		
Apl. 7th CARGO from Palermo to New York Fruit 3990 Boxes @ 49 cents per box		381 18 8
Aug. 8th CARGO from New York to Invergordon Oil Cake 280 tons 13 cwts. @ 15/- per ton	350 16 3	
5% on Freight	17 10 9	368 7 0
		2376 19 11

Carrd. forward

Disbursements—Contd.
Brot. forward — 1124 7 11

WAGES

Master Dec. 19/74 to Aug. 5/75	m days		£ s. d.	£ s. d.
Master	7 18	@ £6 per month	45 12 0	
Mate	7 18	@ £5 5	39 18 0	
Boatswain	7 18	@ £3 17 6	29 9 0	
Cook	7 18	@ £3 17 6	29 9 0	
A.S.	7 18	@ £3 12 6	27 11 0	
O.S.	7 18	@ £3 5	24 14 0	
O.S.	7 18	@ £3 5	24 14 0	
O.S.	7 18	@ £2 5	17 2 0	238 9 0

VICTUALLING

Master Dec. 19/74 to Aug. 5/75	days		£ s. d.	£ s. d.
Master	230	@ 1/1 per day	12 9 2	
Mate	230		12 9 2	
Boatswain	230		12 9 2	
Cook	230		12 9 2	
A.S.	230		12 9 2	
O.S.	230		12 9 2	
O.S.	230		12 9 2	99 13 4
				1462 10 3

Carrd. forward

1875

Receipts—Contd.
Brot. forward

£	s.	d.	£	s.	d.
			2376	19	11

			2376	19	11

			2376	19	11

1875

Disbursements—Contd.
Brot. forward

	£	s.	d.	£	s.	d.
Mr. Butson's bill				1462	10	3
Mr. Hawken				24	1	10
				10	4	5
				1496	16	6
				88	0	0
Master's Premium on £880. 3. 5d. @ 10%						
				1584	16	6
				791	14	8
Postages, etc.						
Profit						

			2376	19	11

		£ s. d.
Aug. 19	Profit	791 14 8

At a meeting of the owners of the Schooner " THETIS "
held at Mrs. Nurse's Ship Inn, Fowey, on Augst. 10,
1875, the foregoing accounts were audited and passed
from Jany. 29/74 to Augst. 5/1875

Signed by the owners present.

Wm. Collins
John Olliver
Charles Hicks
H. Hill
S. Sargant
I. Hitchins
For Thos. Hitchins, J. Hitchins
John Olford
Rev. Barrett
W. Phillips
Rd. Reed
Alfred Luke
James Haye
J. Bawden
T. H. Knight
Edwd. Stocker Jn.

	£ s. d.
	791 14 8

LIST OF SHAREHOLDERS

1875 Aug. 19		Shares		£ s. d.
1	Pearce	8	« £12 7 5d.	98 19 4
2	Capt. Beale	7	W. N. Beale	86 11 11
3	Mr. Collins	4	Wm. Collins	49 9 8
4	" Stocker	4	E. Stocker, Jnr.	49 9 8
5	" Hitchens, Thos.	4	For Thos. Hitchins, J. Hitchins	49 9 8
6	" Barrett	3	Revd. Barrett	37 2 3
7	" Parkyn	3	Paid	37 2 3
8	Dr. Treffry	2	Paid	24 14 10
9	Mr. Hay	2	James Haye	24 14 10
10	" Olliver	2	John Olliver	24 14 10
11	" Hicks	2	Charles Hicks	24 14 10
12	" Bartlett, Revd.	2	Paid	24 14 10
13	" Sobey	2	Paid	24 14 10
14	" Reed	1	Rd. Reed	12 7 5
15	" Olford	1	John Olford	12 7 5
16	" Luke	4	Alfred Luke	49 9 8
17	" Hitchens	1	J. Hitchin	12 7 5
18	Miss Henwood	1	Paid	12 7 5
19	Mr. Hill	1	H. Hill	12 7 5
20	" Bawden	1	J. Bawden	12 7 5
21	" Phillips	1	Wm. Phillips	12 7 5
22	" Sargant	1	Sargant	12 7 5
23	Miss Furniss	3	Paid	37 2 3
24	Mr. Knight	2	T. H. Knight	24 14 10
25	" Thomas	2	Capt. Hackin	24 14 10
		64		791 14 8

THE OWNERS OF THE SCHOONER "THETIS"

IN ACCOUNT WITH THOS. PEARCE

Receipts

1875		£	s.	d.	£	s.	d.
Aug.	1st CARGOE Invergordon to Shields in ballast						
Aug.	1st CARGOE Shields to Piraesis Coals 14½ Keel @ £14 10 0d. per keel				204	16	3
Oct.	Piraeus to Lixuri and Argostole in ballast						
Nov.	2nd CARGOE Lixuri and Argostle to Hamburg Currants 479451 tons @ 35/- per 2240 lbs.				374	11	5
					579	7	9
						over	

Disbursements

1875	PORT CHARGES	£	s.	d.	£	s.	d.
Aug.	Shields	50	18	6			
Sept.	Fowey	1	13	1			
Oct.	Piraeus	18	11	1			
Nov.	Cephelonia	56	16	0			
Dec.	Fowey	1	17	7			
1876							
Jan.	Hamburg	55	4	0			
Feb.	Hamburg out	31	14	9			
Mar.	Fowey	4	1	4			
June	Buenos Ayres	108	1	2			
Aug.	Paysandu	51	17	11			
Oct.	Fowey	1	3	7			
Nov.	Bristol	63	4	4			
					445	4	0

BILLS	£	s.	d.	£	s.	d.
Mrs. Nurse's	4	6	11			
Mr. Lacey	1	10	0			
,, Dingle	6	13	10			
,, Hocken	3	4	6			
,, Lobb	1	15	7			
,, Lovering	3	15	11			
Property Tax	6	3	4			
Mr. Hawken	86	17	6			
,, Barrett	3	1	0			
,, Dingle	2	12	6			
,, Brokenshaw	3	4	2			
Mrs. Slade and Sons	3	11	0			
Mr. Wine coals	10	0	6			
,, Button						
		over		133	13	6
				445	4	0
					over	

THE OWNERS OF THE SCHOONER "THETIS"
IN ACCOUNT WITH THOS. PEARCE

Receipts

1876		£	s.	d.
	Brot. forward	579	7	8
Feb.	3rd CARGOE			
	Hamburg to Buenos Ayres			
	Lump Sum	450	0	0
June	Buenos Ayres to Paysande			
	in ballast			
Aug.	4th CARGOE			
	Paysander to Bristol			
	Hides 260 tons 8 cwt. 3 qr. 27 lbs. @ 47/6d.	618	11	4
	Primage @ 5%	30	11	4
	Bones 12 tons 7 cwt. 1 qr. 0 lbs. @ 25/-	15	19	1
	Primage @ 5%	15	0	6
	Demurrage	30	0	0
		695	14	5
	Carrd. forward	**£1725**	**2**	**1**

Disbursements

1876		£	s.	d.	£	s.	d.
	Brot. fqrward	133	13	3	445	11	0
	BILLS						
	Mr. Lobb	8	11	8			
	,, Thomas	13	12	5			
	,, Lovering	4	1	6			
	,, Lacey	2	0	8			
	Dover Signal Station	1	0	0			
	Telegram		1	0			
	Bill Stamp		3	0			
	Postage, etc.		9	0			
	Agency	5	0	0			
					167	13	6

WAGES

	m	dys					£	s.	d.
Master Aug. 6/75 to Jan. 11/76	5	6	@	£6	0	0 per month	31	4	0
Mate ,,	5	6	@	£5	5	0 ,,	27	6	0
Boatswain ,,	5	6	@	£4	0	0 ,,	20	16	0
Cook ,,	5	6	@	£4	0	6 ,,	20	16	0
A.B. ,,	5	6	@	£3	12	0 ,,	18	17	0
O.S. ,,	5	6	@	£3	10	0 ,,	13	0	0
O.S. ,,	2	5	@	£3	5	0 ,,	16	18	0
A.B. Aug. 6/75 to Oct. 30/75	2	25	@	£3	15	0 ,,	10	12	0
A.B. Dec. 27/75 to Jan. 11/76		16	@	£3	12	6 ,,	1	18	8
							161	8	2
Less discharging fees								13	0
							160	15	2
							£773	**12**	**8**

THE OWNERS OF THE SCHOONER "THETIS"

IN ACCOUNT WITH THOS. PEARCE

1876

	£	s.	d.
Brt. forward	1725	2	1
	1725	**2**	**1**

1876

Brt. forward   £773 12 ...   £ s. d.   £ s.

Disbursements

VICTUALLING

	dys		£	s.	d.
Master Aug. 6/75 to Jan. 11/76	159	@ 1/2 per day	9	5	6
Mate " "	159	"	9	5	6
Boatswain " "	159	"	9	5	6
Cook " "	159	"	9	5	6
A.B. " "	159	"	9	5	6
O.S. " "	159	"	9	5	6
A.B. Aug. 6/75 to Oct. 30/75	86	"	5	0	4
A.B. Dec. 27/75 to Jan. 11/76	16	"		18	8
			70	**17**	**6**

WAGES

	m	dys			£	s.	d.
Master Jan. 12/76 to Nov. 9/76	9	29	@ £6 0 0	per month	59	16	0
Mate " Oct. 28/76	9	17	@ £5 5 0	"	52	6	6
Boatswain "	9	17	@ £4 0 0	"	38	5	4
Cook "	9	17	@ £3 12 6	"	38	5	4
A.B. "	9	17	@ £3 12 6	"	34	13	7
A.B. "	9	17	@ £2 10 0	"	23	18	4
O.S. " Nov. 9/76	9	29	@ £2 0 0	"	19	18	8
					301	17	4
Less discharging fees paid by crew						15	0
					301	2	4
Less advanced crew					2	3	0
					298	19	4
					293	19	4

    1143 9 6

over

THE OWNERS OF THE SCHOONER "THETIS"
IN ACCOUNT WITH THOS. PEARCE

1876	Receipts	£	s.	d.
	Brot. forward	1725	2	1
		£1725	**2**	**1**

1876	Disbursements		dys		£	s.	d.
	Brot. forward				1143	9	6
	VICTUALLING						
	Master Jan. 12/76 to Nov. 9/76	303	@ 1/2 per day		17	13	6
	Mate " Oct. 28/76	303	:		17	13	6
	Boatswain " "	291	:		16	19	6
	Cook " "	291	:		16	19	6
	A.B. " "	291	:		16	19	6
	A.B. " "	291	:		16	19	6
	O.S. " "	291	:		16	19	6
	O.S. " Nov. 9/76	303	:		17	13	6
					137	18	0
					1281	7	6
	Master's Primage on £443. 14. 7d. at 10%				44	7	5
					1325	14	11
	Profit				399	7	2
					£1725	**2**	**1**

THE OWNERS OF THE SCHOONER "THETIS"

	Receipts	£	s.	d.
Profit		399	7	2

At a meeting of the Owners of the Schooner "THETIS"
held at Mrs. Nurse's Ship Inn, Fowey, on Novr. 13th,
1876, the foregoing accounts were audited and passed
from August 6th, 1875 to Novr. 9th, 1876.

Signed by the owners present.

Arch. Barrett
Alfred Luke
Chas. Olliver
Daniel Sargant
Hicks
G. S. Treffry
John Olford
James Haye
Rd. Reed
T. H. Knight

£	s.	d.
399	7	2

IN ACCOUNT WITH THOS. PEARCE

No.	Name	Shares		£	s.	d.
1	Mr. T. Pearce	8	@ £6 4 6d. pd.	49	16	6
2	Capt. Beale	7		43	11	6
3	Mr. Collins Rose Hill	4	T. Knight for Mr. Collins	24	18	0
4	Mr. Stocker	4	pd.	24	18	0
5	Thos. Hitchens	4	pd.	24	18	6
6	,, Barrett	3	Revd. T. Barrett	18	13	6
7	,, Parkym	3	pd.	18	13	0
8	Dr. Treffry	2	G. S. Treffry	12	9	0
9	Mr. Haye	2	James Haye	12	9	0
10	,, Olliver	2	Chas. Olliver	12	9	0
11	,, Hicks	2	Hicks	12	9	0
12	Rev. J. Bartlett		pd.			
13	Mr. W. Sobey {Mr. S. Sobey Penzepple / Liskeard}	2		12	9	0
14	,, Reed	1	Rd. Reed	6	4	6
15	,, Olford	1	John Olford	6	4	6
16	,, Luke	4	Alfred Luke	24	18	0
17	,, Hitchens	1	pd.	6	4	6
18	Mrs. W. C. Seabrook	1	pd.	6	4	6
19	Mr. Hile	1	pd.	6	4	6
20	,, Bawden	1	pd.	6	4	6
21	,, Phillips	1	pd.	6	4	6
22	,, Sargant—Treburguy nr. Liskeard	2	Danield Sargant	12	9	0
23	Miss Furniss	3	T. H. Knight pd.	18	13	6
24	Mr. Knight	1		6	4	0
25	Rev. Thomas	2	pd.	12	9	0
		64		398	8	0
	Balance carrd. forward			19	2	
				399	7	2

THE OWNERS OF THE SCHOONER "THETIS"

Receipts

1876		£	s.	d.
Nov. 13	Balance brot. forward		19	2
Nov.	1st CARGOE Bristol to Barcelona Lump Sum	270	0	0

1877		frcs.	c.	£	s.	d.
Feb. 14	Barcelona on shore at Aquebella					
Apr. 3	Wreck sold as follows					
	Medicine Chest	40	50			
	Carpenters tools	27				
Apr. 11	Sale of ship	2500				
	" rigging, sails, boats and stores	6550				
	" Chronometer and Barometer	580				
	Exchange 28.15	9697	50	344	9	1

carrd. forward   615 8 3

IN ACCOUNT WITH THOS. PEARCE

Disbursements

PORT CHARGES

1876		£	s.	d.	£	s.	d.
Nov.	Bristol	56	2	8			
Dec.	Fowey	2	8	9			
1877							
Feb.	Barcelona	73	17	5			
Apr.	Cagliare	86	8	11	218	17	9

WAGES

		m	dys				£	s.	d.	£	s.	d.
Master	Nov. 10 76 to Apr. 23.77	5	14	@ £6	0	0 per mth.	32	16	0			
Mate	" Mar. 1.77	3	20	@ £5	0	0	19	5	0			
Boatswain	" Feb. 22.77	3	19	@ £3	15	0	13	12	6			
Cook	15.76 to Mar. 1.77	3	15	@ £3	10	0	12	5	0			
A.B.	8.76	3	22	@ £3	12	0	13	10	8			
A.B.	28.76	3	2	@ £3	10	0	10	14	8			
O.S.	20.76	3	1	@ £2	15	0	8	6	10			
O.S.	10.76	3	20	@ £2	10	0	9	3	4	119	14	0
	Less discharging fees paid by Crew							12	0	119	2	0

VICTUALLING

		dys			£	s.	d.	£	s.	d.
Master	Nov. 10.76 to Mar. 1.77	112	@ 1/2 per day		6	10	8			
Mate		112			6	10	8			
Boatswain	4.76 to Feb. 22.77	111			6	9	6			
Cook	15.76 to Mar. 1.77	107			6	4	10			
A.B.	8.76	114			6	13	0			
A.B.	28.76	94			5	9	8			
O.S.	29.76	93			5	8	6			
O.S.	10.76	112			6	10	8	49	17	6

carrd. forward   387 17 3

THE OWNERS OF THE SCHOONER "THETIS"

IN ACCOUNT WITH THOS. PEARCE

1877	Receipts	£	s.	d.	1877	Disbursements	£	s.	d.
	Brot. forward	615	8	3		Brot. forward	38?	17	3
						BILLS			
						Mr. Butson	3	17	9
						" Lobb	1	15	0
						" Lacey		12	9
						" Hawken	1	11	6
						" Dingle	2	6	8
						" Lovering	1	19	2
						" Barratt	41	18	7
						Mrs. Nurse	3	18	4
						Property Tax	5	13	3
						Postages, etc.	5	12	0
						Agency	4	0	0
						Balance	68	5	0
							456	2	8
							159	8	3
		£615	8	3			615	8	3
							159	8	3
						Balance from above			
						Less Mr. Morecomc's Bill			
						Balance to divide	159	17	6

THE OWNERS OF THE SCHOONER "THETIS"

		Shares		£	s.	d.
1	Mr. T. Pearce	8	£2 9 7¾	19	17	2
2	Capt. Beale Pd.	7	W. M. Beale	17	7	6¼
3	Mrs. Collins Pd. sent	4	Cheque	9	18	7
4	Mr. Stocker Pd.	4		9	18	7
5	,, Thos. Hitchens Pd.	4		9	18	7
6	,, Barratt Pd.	3	Revd. Barratt	7	8	11
7	,, Parkyn Pd. sent	3	Cheque	7	8	11
8	Dr. Treffry Pd. sent	2	Cheque	4	19	3½
9	Mr. Haye	2	Cheque	4	19	3½
10	,, Olliver Pd.	2	John Olliver	4	19	3½
11	,, Hicks Pd.	2	C. Hicks	4	19	3½
12	Bartlett, Revd. Pd. sent	2	Cheque	4	19	3½
13	Mr. Sobey Pd. sent	2	Cheque	4	19	3½
14	,, Reed Pd. sent	1	Cheque	2	9	7¾
15	,, Olford Pd. sent	1	Cheque	2	9	7¾
16	,, Luke Pd.	4	Paid	9	18	7
17	,, Hitchin	1	Cheque	2	9	7¾
18	Mrs. W. C. Seabrooke Pd. sent	1	Cheque	2	9	7¾
19	Mr. Hile	1	Cheque	2	9	7¾
20	,, Bawden Pd.	1	Wm. Phillips	2	9	7¾
21	,, Phillips Pd.	1	Wm. Phillips	2	9	7¾
22	,, Sargent Pd.	2	C. Sargent	4	19	3½
23	Miss Furniss Pd. sent	3	Cheque	8	8	11¼
24	Mr. Knight sent	1	Cheque	2	9	7¾
25	,, Thomas, Revd.	2		4	19	3½
		64		158	17	4

IN ACCOUNT WITH T. PEARSE

1877		£	s.	d.
	Balance to divide	158	17	6
		£158	17	6

At a meeting of the Owners of the Schooner "THETIS" held at Mr. Morcom's Royal Hotel Par Station on May 26th/77 the foregoing accounts were audited and passed leaving a Balance of £158 17 6d. to be at once divided between the Owners as a final settlement.

Signed by Owners present.

Revd. Barrett
John Olliver
Alfred Luke
C. Hicks
Wm. Phillips

Appendix Two

Cargo Book of the ketch *Alford* of Bideford, February 1895—February 1896.

Alford, 79357, ketch, wood, built by H. M. Restarick at Bideford and launched in June 1885, 77 tons gross, 66 net, 76 under deck, 77·5 ft. x 19·7 ft. x 7·8 ft., registered at Bideford as owned by John W. Banbury of Bude.

I am indebted to the late Mr Philip Kershaw for permission to reproduce this document.

CARGO BOOK OF THE "ALFORD" OF BIDEFORD, 65·78 TONS, LIVERPOOL, 23rd OCTOBER, 1895
MASTER : J. B COOK

1895. Jan. 8th : Sailed from Bude to Briton Ferry Light, arrived 10th.

Date Left	Port Left	Date Arrived	Port Arrived	Cargo
Feb. 27th	London	Mar. 4th	Bude	Manure
Apl. 1st	Bude	Apl. 2nd	Saundersfoot	Light
Apl. 5th	Saundersfoot	Apl. 10th	Ipswich	Coal
Apl. 19th	Ipswich	Apl. 23rd	Haverfordwest	Manure
May 10th	Haverfordwest	May 9th	Saundersfoot	Light
May 23rd	Ipswich	May 20th	Haverfordwest	Manure
June 8th	Haverfordwest	June 9th	Saundersfoot	Light
June 14th	Saundersfoot	June 16th	Bardon	Coal
June 27th	Bardon	June 30th	Exeter	Oats
July 9th	Exeter	July 10th	Plymouth	Light
July 18th	Plymouth	July 20th	Bude	Wood, Goods and General
July 30th	Bude	Aug. 2nd	Garston	Light
Aug. 8th	Garston	Aug. 13th	Bude	Coal
Aug. 23rd	Bude	Aug. 26th	Newport	Light
Aug. 27th	Newport	Sept. 2nd	Clonakilty	Coal
Sept. 7th	Clonakilty	Sept. 10th	Garston	Light
Sept. 14th	Garston	Sept. 17th	Bude	Coal
Sept. 24th	Bude	Sept. 26th	Newport	Light
Sept. 28th	Newport	Oct. 2nd	Truro	Coal
Oct. 10th	Truro	Oct. 10th	Penteen	Light
Oct. 14th	Pentewer	Oct. 19th	Garston	Clay
Oct. 30th	Garston	Nov. 2nd	Bude	Coal

MASTER : J. E. HANBURY

Date Left	Port Left	Date Arrived	Port Arrived	Cargo
Dec. 10th	Bude	Dec. 22nd	Newport	Light
Dec. 25th	Newport	Dec. 28th		Coal
1896				
Jan. 10th	Cork	Jan. 12th	Bude	Grain and Manure
Jan. 20th	Bude	Jan. 22nd	Newport	Light
Jan. 25th	Newport	Feb. 1st	Plymouth	Coal
Feb. 13th	Plymouth	Feb. 17th	Bude	Wood, Gravel and General

Appendix Three

Note by Captain W. J. Slade on the Setting of Gaff Topsails in Schooners and Ketches

In writing about gaff topsails and the methods of setting them, there appear to be different ideas in different circumstances. Most deep-water, foreign-going schooners, and I believe American fore-and-aft schooners, carried jib-headed sails stowed aloft. They were bent to hoops on the topmast so that the jackstay could be dispensed with. The drawback in this method was that the weather of the sail when set on the lee side blew away from the masthead. In order to make it stand to its work, the tack of the sail had to be shifted to the weather side of the gaff between the peak halyards of the mainsail or foresail, as the case may be and the gaff (Plate 10). If the ship had to go about in stays, a sailor had to go aloft to shift over the tack from one side to the other. This was all very well where there was plenty of room to sail, but to use this method on the coast in small schooners and ketches would be a nuisance to the master and the crew, especially as with small crews of from three to five men all told none could be spared aloft for this purpose. In beating out over Liverpool Bar or any other river or harbour, all hands were needed on deck to swing the yards from side to side. There were also the four headsails to handle every tack.

I spent over forty years in coastal schooners and ketches. In some of the bigger ketches a square-headed topsail was carried and, when taken in, it was stowed aloft in the rigging, which was not an easy job when there was often a yard twenty feet long attached to 120 yards of canvas. The sail was sometimes carried above a reefed mainsail and, when orders came to take it in and stow it, one man did the job alone. If it happened to be the lee side, the sailor went aloft by the weather rigging, crossing over when the masthead was reached, and getting on top of it to ride it down with arms and legs around it like a cowboy with a bucking bronco, and at the same time passing the gasket round it. Once a turn round the eyes of the rigging was attained, the rest was easier. The main thing was to tackle the job with no fear. This was, in my opinion, the hardest job of all on board coasters. If the sail had to be taken in on the weather side, it was generally difficult to get the yard to come over clear of the peak

253

halyards. If the ship was sailing by the wind, the master at the wheel would often bring her up nearly head to wind, and the down-haul on the head of the yard would bring it over easily, but this had to be understood and done quickly. It was much more difficult running before a strong wind, when a sailor often had to go aloft to get the yard over to the weather side. This manœuvre of bringing a ketch up in the wind could not be done in a topsail schooner because she would be caught aback. Whether in a ketch or schooner, the squareheaded topsail was a hard sail to handle. The only difference was that a schooner did not carry it set as long as a ketch, which made it easier with conditions not so bad.

To describe the West Country method of setting this sail is very simple. It was hoisted by halyards leading down to the deck from the topmast head. The end of the halyards was connected to the yard about one-third from the forward end so that, when set properly, the big bulk of the sail is aftside of the topmast and it can easily be seen that only a small portion of the luff is foreside of the topmast, similar to the set of the standing lug in a boat. Where the luff of the sail crosses the topmast about three feet above the cap of the mainmast, a grummet strop is worked around the topmast. This is connected to the eyelet hole provided in the weather of the sail. This keeps the sail to the mast in its proper place when set, and when taken in and stowed the grummet strop keeps the sail hanging direct from the cap of the mainmast head. In order to make it stand properly when set, a wire jackstay is fixed. One end (the upper end) is shackled to the cap and the lower end seized to the after shroud of the standing rigging. Two sliding thimbles travel up and down over the jackstay, secured to the luff of the sail. This makes the sail stand to its work on either tack without the necessity of dipping the tack as previously described. I ought to mention that in order to keep the yard to the mast a traveller is fitted to run up and down the topmast. The halyards are rove through the eye of the traveller before connecting them to the yard. The halyards from the yard up through the cheave in the topmast are of chain as this will stand any possible chafing.

A jib-headed gaff topsail, if set from aloft, has hoops round the topmast and the usual traveller. It has a wire jackstay from the mast-head cap to the after shroud, similar to the squareheaded sail. To set either of these sails, the halyards are pulled up, the sheet is now pulled out to the gaff end and set tight with the hand winch. The tack is now set down to the heel of the mast by a tackle as tight as possible.

Setting Gaff Topsails from the Deck

This was not the usual way of setting these sails when I was a boy, except perhaps in the small smacks and ketches where two men all told sailed them. The old Appledore skippers would try anything to get a little extra speed and often scoffed at the idea of setting gaff topsails from the deck. They knew, of course, there were men who could go aloft in all conditions and think nothing of it. These men were called to the colours in the 1914-18 war. The ships had to be sailed just the same, but it soon became a question of who can we get to go aloft to furl a gaff topsail? It must be admitted that a gaff topsail set from aloft would stand to its work and give greater efficiency, but the old men who were left could not be expected to go aloft as they did years before when they were young. It therefore became a necessity to set gaff topsails flying from the deck in big or small ships. These sails were set on a jackstay leading from a point about five or six feet above the cap on the topmast to the deck. A traveller on the upper part of the topmast with the halyards running through could still be used. Whether square-headed or jib-headed, they were set in the same way. The upper part of the jackstay was generally of chain for about one and a half fathoms. The same applied to the part on deck if one wanted greater efficiency. The sail was hoisted up after reeving the jackstay through thimbles seized to the weather of the sail. The clew was hove out to the gaff end. The lower end of the jackstay was then put through an eyebolt in the deck. The tack tackle was hooked in the end, thus setting up tack and jackstay simultaneously. I must say this was my way of setting it and I have no knowledge of how others did it. They probably had their own way which was just as good. It all amounted to the same thing. Halyards first, sheet out to gaff end and jackstay and tack last. These methods differ with different men.

You will notice that I have not referred to the jackyard topsail as this is in fact a topsail with a jackyard on the head, similar to a square-headed one, and in many places the square-header is referred to as a jackyard topsail. I cannot see the difference. The jackyard topsail on racing yachts generally had a yard on the foot to give a greater spread of canvas. The head yard was the jack and the one on the foot was the jenny. They were also used in the oyster dredgers in Falmouth Harbour years ago.

Well, I can't think of any more to write on gaff topsails, so I'll close with one of Uncle George Quance's yarns, well-known in Appledore.

It was the rule in the 1890s for an Appledore boy to get half wages when he could furl the topsail at sea in all weathers. Uncle George was on his way home to lunch one day when he was stopped by the mother of the boy who sailed with him in the *Nouvelle Marie*. She said, 'My boy Sammy is a big boy now and should have half wages.' 'Well,' said Uncle George, 'the rule is, as you know, the gaff topsail has to be taken in.' 'Oh,' she said, 'my Sammy has been doing that for years.' Eventually the *Nouvelle Marie* sailed, and sure enough the gaff topsail had to be furled off Hartland Point.

'Up you go, Sammy,' says Uncle George, and up Sammy went. He only got about six or seven feet up when his legs started to shake and he had to come down. Uncle George said, 'Why were your legs shaking, Sammy?' 'It wasn't my legs shaking,' said Sammy, 'it was the wind blowing up the legs of my trousers, and if the old b . . . wants half wages she can come here and let the wind blow up the legs of her trousers and see how she likes it.'

Have just thought of the mizzen gaff topsail of a ketch. This sail is set from the deck. It has a yard 18 to 20 feet long on the head. The after shroud of mizzen rigging is used as a jackstay. An ordinary hank similar to those on head stays is put on this after shroud to travel up and down. In one eye of the hank a piece of ratline line is spliced. The other end of the line is then put through the cringle in the tack and then back to the other eye in the hank. It is put through the eye and a figure-of-eight knot secures the sail from being blown overboard if taken in when the wind is fresh.

Bas 42209/1/30 1m 10/77 TPC

INDEX

Illustration pages are indicated by italics